CONDITIONAL FEES

A Survival Guide

2nd edition

Edited by

Fiona Bawdon, Michael Napier and Gordon Wignall

The Law Society

The authors have asserted the right under the
Copyright, Designs and Patents Act 1988
to be identified as authors of this work.

First published 1995
Reprinted February 1996
2nd edition 2001

Material in Appendices 1–13 is Crown copyright. Crown copyright legislation is reproduced under the terms of Crown Copyright Policy Guidance issued by HMSO. Crown copyright material is reproduced under Class Licence Nmber C01W0000461 with the permission of the Controller of HMSO and the Queen's Printer for Scotland.
Appendix 21 is reproduced with the kind of permission of the General Council of the Bar.
Appendix 22 is reproduced with the kind permission of the Association of Personal Injury Lawyers and the Personal Injuries Bar Association.
Appendix 23 is reproduced with the kind permission of the Chancery Bar Association.
Appendix 24 was compiled with the help of Emmanuel Gilbert and www.TheJudge.co.uk.

ISBN 1 85328 472 6

Published in 2001 by the Law Society
113 Chancery Lane, London WC2A 1PL

Typeset by J&L Composition Ltd, Filey, North Yorkshire
Printed and bound by Antony Rowe Ltd, Chippenham, Wilts

Contents

List of contributors

Fiona Bawdon is a freelance journalist, specialising in writing about the law. She was co-author of the first book published on conditional fees (*Conditional Fees: A Survival Guide*, Law Society 1995) and was founding editor of *Litigation Funding*, the only magazine devoted exclusively to the new funding regime.

Sallie Booth is a Partner at Irwin Mitchell Solicitors dealing mainly with multi-party and medical negligence cases on behalf of claimants. She has been involved in the implementation and administration of conditional fee cases since they were first introduced in August 1995.

Emmanuel Gilbert is Managing Director of TheJudge.co.uk Ltd, which provides information and advice on all aspects of after-the-event insurance (AEI). His company runs a website which is an online searchable database of the AEI policies and premiums that are available. He acts as a consultant to both solicitor firms and insurers and speaks regularly at seminars on AEI. He also writes for *Litigation Funding* magazine.

Mike Napier is the Senior Partner of Irwin Mitchell, President of the Law Society 2000–2001 and a member of the Civil Justice Council. He is also a Visiting Professor at Nottingham Law School, a past President of the Association of Personal Injury Lawyers and a Council member of JUSTICE. His publications include *Conditional Fees – A Survival Guide* (Law Society 1995) and *Recovering Damages for Psychiatric Injury* (Blackstone Press 1995). He is also a contributing author to *Blackstones Civil Practice 2000* and editor-in-chief of *Litigation Funding*.

Gareth Phillips is a solicitor with wide experience of both practice and research in the field of civil litigation. He has worked in private practice and in-house, representing both claimants and defendants, and was actively involved in the development of the latest version of the Law Society's model conditional fee agreement. After graduating from Southampton University, he has worked in both Swansea and London.

Gordon Wignall is a barrister in the chambers of Michael Pert QC at 36 Bedford Row. He has a special interest in issues relating to costs and funding. He has been a contributor to *Litigation Funding* since its inception, and is a former chair of the Legal Aid Practitioners Group.

Abbreviations

AEI	after-the-event legal expenses insurance
APIL	Association of Personal Injury Lawyers
AVMA	Action for the Victims of Medical Accidents
BEI	before-the-event legal expenses insurance
BMIF	Bar Mutual Indemnity Fund
ChBA	Chancery Bar Association
CFA	conditional fee agreement
CPR	Civil Procedure Rules
IT	information technology
PIBA	Personal Injuries Bar Association
RPI	Retail Prices Index

Table of cases

Table of statutes

Table of statutory instruments and European legislation

STATUTORY INSTRUMENTS

EUROPEAN LEGISLATION

Note on *Callery* v. *Gray*

PART II

Whilst it was possible to accommodate the decision of the Court of Appeal in *Callery* v. *Gray* [2001] EWCA Civ 1117 within the text of this book, the editors were not so fortunate with Part II of the judgment (*Callery* v. *Gray* [2001] EWCA Civ 1246). Part II dealt with the question whether Mr Callery's AEI premium of £350 was reasonable. This Note seeks to summarise the main conclusions of the Court of Appeal. Numbers in paragraphs refer to paragraph numbers of the judgment.

The Court decided that in determining whether a premium is reasonable and therefore recoverable by reason of s.29, Access to Justice Act 1999, a distinction should be made between the contractual benefits which the premium buys and the use to which the insurer puts the premium 11.10 (7). Satellite litigation about the premium is not to be encouraged, but an insurer must be entitled to put in evidence when necessary. At the same time, a judge need only give 'broad consideration' to that evidence since the Court is not to be expected to 'carry out an audit of an insurer's business' (12).

Four elements of premium income had been identified by Master O'Hare in a report to the Court of Appeal annexed to the judgment (although not forming part of it) (13). These were: the 'burning' cost (the cost of meeting claims under policies issued), risk/profit cost (the cost of reinsurance and the profit element), administrative costs, and distribution commission (advertising, marketing and commission payments). All of these are, in principle, proper constituents of premium income. (It should be noted that Mr Callery's premium had been individually assessed according to a premium table supplied by the insurer. A much higher premium charged under a block scheme may well have been 'hard to justify' (14).)

The primary liability covered by Mr Callery's policy was that of his opponent's costs. The circumstances in which this liability might have arisen were:

(a) following a judgment on liability;

(b) following a failure to beat a Part 36 offer;

(c) following the failure of losing an issue such as an interim hearing;

(d) any other costs order at the insurer's discretion.

The Court of Appeal held that none of these fell foul of s.29.

As to the benefits bought by an insurance premium, any collateral benefits, such as counselling or help about the home would be likely to result in a reduction in recoverable premium (20–21). This did not apply in Mr Callery's case.

The Court was asked to consider whether own costs cover could be recoverable by reason of s.29. The answer was that an indemnity in respect of such costs was within the ambit of s.29, with the consequence that a premium covering both sides insurance was also recoverable. Section 29 was to be interpreted 'so as to treat the words "insurance against the risk of incurring a costs liability' as meaning 'insurance against the risk of incurring a costs liability that cannot be passed on to the opposing party"' (30–31).

The end result was that the Court accepted that Mr Callery's premium of £350 was proportionate to the risk and recoverable in full (37). The policy was 'tailored to the risk and the cover was suitable for [his] needs'. It was attractive because it was part of a delegated authority scheme without any involvement of a claims manager until a settlement offer was received.

Two general observations of the Court of Appeal are of interest. The first is that the Court recognised claimant lawyers' practice of ring-fencing their clients' damages (31). The second is the Court of Appeal's view that a solicitor is under a duty to give reasoned advice to a client so that an insurance policy can be selected which 'caters for his needs on reasonable terms' (see 11).

Gordon Wignall
September 2001

CHAPTER 1

Conditional fees in context

Fiona Bawdon and Mike Napier

PAYMENT BY RESULTS

The background to the statutory CFA scheme

1.1 The principle of a lawyer's fee being linked to the outcome of the service he provides stretches back far further than just the six years since conditional fees were introduced. As the examples below demonstrate, the introduction of conditional fees was not such a dramatic departure as some might have thought.

1.2 In non-contentious legal business – that which does not involve court proceedings – it has long been possible for solicitors to agree with the client that the amount of payment will depend on the outcome of the work done. For example, a solicitor handling a business acquisition might agree to charge a fee only if the deal goes through, or agree to different levels of fee, depending on success or failure. In a case of debt recovery where proceedings have not been issued, a solicitor might be paid only if the money is recovered, or he might be paid on a sliding percentage scale, depending on the amount recovered. In a planning appeal, the size of payment may depend on the outcome. Examples of contentious and non-contentious business are set out at Appendix 18.

1.3 Even in contentious areas, like personal injury, a non-contentious business agreement can be used to allow payment by way of a contingency fee. In other words the solicitor can receive a direct proportion of any damages won. Non-contentious business arrangements are only appropriate in personal injury claims which are straightforward. In such cases the client signs an agreement stating that he has told the solicitor not to issue proceedings. If the case fails to settle, this document is then scrapped and a new funding arrangement entered into.

1.4 In cases before an employment tribunal and under the Criminal Injuries Compensation Scheme, both of which are deemed to be non-contentious and where there is no liability for the other side's costs,

1

solicitors (although not barristers) can already operate fully-fledged contingency arrangements, taking a proportion of damages if the case succeeds.

1.5 Before the introduction of conditional fees in 1995, solicitors in areas of law like personal injury had long operated informal speculative arrangements for impecunious clients with strong cases. This might be where liability is fairly obvious and only quantum is likely to be decided, for instance in the case of a passenger in a road accident who is bound to be able to claim damages from one source or another. In this situation, the solicitor may tell the client that, in theory, he is liable for costs and disbursements, but, in reality, the case will be won and these will be met by the other side. If such a case were unexpectedly lost, the solicitor would either charge no fee or a reduced fee. This type of arrangement was approved as lawful by *Thai Trading Co* v. *Taylor* [1998] QB 781, CA, and then disapproved by *Awwad* v. *Geraghty* [2000] 3 WLR 1041, CA. This 'less if you lose' type of arrangement has now been given statutory force by the enactment of the Access to Justice Act 1999 ('the 1999 Act'). The 1999 Act permitted considerable flexibility in conditional fee arrangements (referred to throughout this book as 'CFAs'), and these can broadly be classified into two categories: those which allow an uplift to be charged for success (the original type of conditional fee) and those which do not (the discounted fee). It is of course possible to have a mixture of the two, a standard form of arrangement which is envisaged, for instance, in the Chancery Bar Association model terms of agreement (see Appendix 23a).

1.6 In Scotland, so-called speculative fees – where the lawyer waives his bill if he loses – have been a feature for over a century. However, since the passing of legislation in August 1992, solicitors have been able to increase their charges by a success fee of up to 100 per cent in the event of speculative litigation succeeding.

1.7 In 1990, Rule 8 of the Solicitors Practice Rules was amended to allow solicitors in England and Wales to be paid on a contingency basis when they are representing clients making claims in foreign jurisdictions where 'no win no fee' arrangements are allowed, such as in the USA.

1.8 Solicitors doing civil legal aid work paid for by the Legal Services Commission (LSC) (formerly the Legal Aid Board), are already used to being paid by results. The LSC calls this 'risk sharing'. For instance, if a case in the county court is lost, the solicitor will be paid the prescribed Community Legal Service funding rate of about £66 an hour (plus any enhancement allowed under the regulations). If a case is won and the claimant recovers costs from the other side, the solicitor will be paid the full rate due between the parties, which is likely to be about £120 per hour for the highest grade fee earner. This discrepancy is particularly significant in cases like clinical negligence where the high volume of work involved means there is a large financial difference to the firm between winning and losing.

1.9   This risk sharing has been further developed by the LSC in the Community Legal Service Funding Code. The Code provides for 'investigative support' and 'litigation support' to assist with the costs of investigating and running a case until a CFA can be signed. If the case is won, then the LSC will take a share of the success fee.

1.10   Another feature of conditional fees before April 2000, the deduction of lawyers' costs from damages, was also nothing new. The LSC's statutory charge, which has been in existence since the inception of the legal aid scheme, gives the LSC first claim on any damages recovered and enables it to deduct the costs it has incurred during the case.

1.11   Firms doing work in volume for legal expenses insurers, and other major clients, such as trade unions, will also be used to working on a payment by results basis. Such clients may use their considerable buying power to make it clear that they do not expect to be sent the bill if a case loses. The firm will only be paid if it wins and recovers costs from the other side.

OTHER JURISDICTIONS

United States of America

1.12   In the USA, a fee arrangement whereby a lawyer does not get paid unless he wins the case is called a contingency fee; in the UK it has come to be called a conditional fee. However, the distinction, as far as the name is concerned, is misleading, because a conditional fee is a particular kind of contingency fee. Conditional fees have been described by critics as 'contingency fees by the back door' (and the Lord Chancellor's 1989 Green Paper talked of 'contingency fees'). What we now know as conditional fees are, like the US system, contingent upon the case being successful. However, conditional fees and the legal system in which they operate have marked differences from the contingency fee system in the USA. Indeed, since the introduction of recoverability of the success fee and insurance premium (see below), conditional fees and contingency fees have moved further apart than before. The key difference between the two now is that since 1 April 2000 the CFA scheme, as it applies by reason of the substitutions and amendments brought about by the

3

Access to Justice Act 1999, leaves the client's damages substantially intact. Before this date, a successful client could lose a substantial proportion of his damages (probably up to the Law Society's recommended maximum of 25 per cent) in his lawyers' success fees. However, the introduction of full recoverability means that the losing opponent pays the success fee and the client retains all of his damages if the case is won (although there are limited circumstances in which a lawyer may apply to the court for his client to pay any amount of a success fee which is not recovered from the losing side (see 2.72 below)). With US contingency fees, the client typically can lose up to 40 per cent of his damages in lawyers' fees.

1.13   With contingency fees, the lawyer's fee is directly dependent on the size of the award. With conditional fees, the lawyer's fee is based on his normal hourly rate, which may or may not be enhanced by an uplift set according to his assessment of the case's prospects for success.

1.14   Another fundamental difference between the two systems is the absence in the USA of the so-called English rule, known here as 'loser pays'. This rule means that losing conditional fee clients have to pay the other side's costs, either out of their own resources, or by taking out insurance (see Chapter 7) to cover this eventuality. The provision in the Access to Justice Act 1999 and subordinate legislation which make the success fee and insurance premium recoverable from the losing party is an extension of the 'loser pays' principle.

1.15   Recoverability of the success fee and insurance premium is also likely to put paid to any fears that conditional fees would lead to a ratcheting-up of damages (as in the USA) to compensate for the fact that part of the award will be lost in lawyers' fees. Under the new system, these extra costs are intended to be paid by the losing party. This, together with the fact that in England and Wales damages are not set by juries but by judges following established guidelines, suggests that conditional fees will have little impact on the level of awards.

Australia

1.16   Although we hear little about the Australian system of conditional fees, the detailed workings of which vary from state to state, a closer parallel to the UK is provided by this jurisdiction rather than by the USA.

1.17   In a legal profession split into solicitors and barristers (but where firms practise as both), and where there is a 'loser pays' rule but no readily available after-the-event insurance to protect against paying the other side's costs, conditional fees have become an established part of the

Australian legal system. In South Australia, the maximum success fee allowed is 100 per cent (as it is in this country), while in New South Wales the success fee is limited to 25 per cent.

Canada

1.18   Canada has a system of contingency fees similar to that operating in the USA. However, it also has a 'loser pays' rule, which is credited as one reason why contingency fees are not widely used.

THE PATH TO CONDITIONAL FEES

1.19   Until recently there was a three-pronged bar on the use of contingency fee arrangements for contentious business. They were prohibited:

(a) as a matter of public policy under common law since they were regarded as champertous and therefore a species of unlawful maintenance (that is to say that the lawyer is deemed to be improperly funding the action in order to profit by taking his usual fees as a slice of the damages);

(b) by Solicitors Act 1974, s.59 (contentious business arrangements), echoing the public policy bar;

(c) by Rule 8 of the Solicitors Practice Rules (see Appendix 14), in turn echoing the 1974 Act.

1.20   In 1979, the Royal Commission on Legal Services rejected contingency fees on the basis that any change in the law which gave lawyers a direct financial interest in their cases would endanger the profession's independence. This remained the prevailing view until 1988, when both the Civil Justice Review and the Marre Committee (set up jointly by the Law Society and Bar Council to look into the future of the legal profession) recommended that contingency fee arrangements should be looked at again.

1.21   In 1989, the Lord Chancellor's Department's Green Paper *Contingency Fees* formally mooted for the first time proposals for a system of payment by results via contingency fees. The proposals were in tune with the government's stated policy of deregulation where possible, and encouraging competition and consumer choice. They also reflected wider calls for a re-examination of the issue of 'no win, no fee' arrangements, where lawyers get paid by results.

1.22   Responses to the Green Paper were largely in favour of allowing a restricted 'no win, no fee' regime. The ensuing Courts and Legal Services Act 1990 (which came into force on 1 October 1993 (see Appendix 1a) paved the way for our existing CFA system. The Act did not itself introduce CFAs, but gave the Lord Chancellor powers to develop regulations under which the scheme would operate when it was introduced at a later stage. Section 58 gave him powers to specify what types of cases could and could not be run on a CFA basis and also the maximum percentage success fee which could be charged.

1.23   The Act removed the public policy and statutory bars against the use of contingency fees in contentious business agreements but restricted this concession to CFAs. Under these changes, a contingency arrangement was allowed only where a CFA was used in accordance with the Order and Regulations approved by Parliament in June 1995 which introduced conditional fees for personal injury, insolvency and human rights claims with effect from July 1995. Practice Rule 8 was amended to reflect this (see Appendix 14).

1.24   Personal injury was the obvious area of private client work in which to pilot CFAs. The Law Society and claimants' solicitors' groups had long called for this method of funding to be made available to client who could not obtain access to justice. With shrinking legal aid eligibility, more and more middle income personal injury victims were unable to claim damages for their injuries because they were unable to meet the cost of bringing a case. Conditional fees were widely seen as an effective way of filling this funding gap.

1.25   Conditional fees were also to be piloted in the commercial field by being allowed for insolvency work. As with personal injury law, the new funding method was seen as a way of increasing access to justice by overcoming the problem of insolvent businesses and those acting on their behalf, who were otherwise unable to pursue worthwhile litigation because of a lack of funds. The anecdotal evidence is that few insolvency cases have been brought on CFAs.

1.26   Human rights cases, then a relatively small but crucial area of law, constituted perhaps an unlikely candidate for inclusion among the first phase of CFAs, and was included thanks largely to the influence of Liberal peer and QC Lord Lester of Herne Hill. Anecdotally, again, only a few ECHR cases have been taken to Strasbourg so far using conditional fees. However, with the coming into force of the Human Rights Act 1998, this will become a much larger area of civil law where proceedings can be brought using a CFA.

1.27 In 1997, the Lord Chancellor announced CFAs would be extended to virtually all areas of civil litigation. This was followed in July 1998 by the Conditional Fee Agreements Order 1998, SI 1998/1860, which extended conditional fees to all civil proceedings (see Appendix 5).

1.28 Substitutions and amendments to the Courts and Legal Services Act 1990 (the original enabling legislation) have been made by Part II of the Access to Justice Act 1999, the main effects of which are:

(a) to legitimise two principal types of payment-by-results fee arrangements (both, confusingly, called 'conditional fees'), being CFAs where the lawyer can charge an uplift of up to 100 per cent on his normal fee if he wins; and CFAs (previously known as 'speccing' or '*Thai Trading*-type arrangements') where the lawyer charges his usual fee if he wins, and either no fee or a discounted fee if he loses; a mixture of the two is also possible whereby a lawyer charges an uplift on his normal fee if he wins and a discounted rate if he loses;

(b) the general availability of conditional fees for all kinds of 'proceedings', apart from crime and family; 'Proceedings' were defined as 'any sort of proceedings for resolving disputes (and not just proceedings in a court)' (1990 Act, s.58A(4));

(c) the recoverability of the success fee (1990 Act, s.58A(6)) and insurance premium (s.29) from the losing party.

FRIVOLOUS LITIGATION?

1.29 Critics of conditional fees claimed that they would lead to an explosion of frivolous claims, and pointed to the USA as a warning of what might be to come. As we have shown, there are significant differences between the situation here and in the USA. In any event, the characterisation of US contingency fees as a model of excess, where out of control juries set astronomical damages from which lawyers make a killing is, in reality, a gross distortion. As Barry Nace, former President of the Association of Trial Lawyers of America says in the introduction to the book, *Keys to the Courthouse* (ATLA), this type of criticism invariably comes from the defendants, not the claimants:

> seldom is heard a discouraging word from the thousands of victims who were able to retain, on a contingency basis, quality lawyers who proved a match and more for corporate counsel.

In the main, and for all its bad press, the US system works well. Nace describes it as 'this great equalizer in our justice system'. It is the extreme case which grabs headlines, but the median award by a US jury in the mid-1990s was $62,000. Juries may sometimes set dazzlingly high damages, but invariably these are later reduced by a judge. Moreover, punitive awards, such as the notorious McDonald's coffee spill case, are invariably misreported and misunderstood. In this particular case, what was not widely reported was the fact that the claimant, a pensioner, was hospitalised for over a week with third-degree burns, and left with permanent scars and hospital bills of about $10,000 after the spill. Nor is it widely known that, despite over 700 complaints about coffee burns in 10 years, McDonald's continued to insist its coffee was served at 180–190°F – up to 55° hotter than coffee served at home. Further, the jury's award of $2.7m punitive damages was subsequently reduced to $480,000.

Lawyers' liability for wasted costs as a check on frivolous litigation

1.30 The USA does not have a 'loser pays' rule and the claimant's lawyers in the McDonald's case could not have been held personally liable if the case had lost. There is, however, no watertight guarantee of the same protection for lawyers operating under our system. The solicitor who brings and loses a frivolous case could be pursued by the successful defendant for wasted costs.

1.31 Such cases are rare, but they are possible. A ruling was made on this issue in the claims brought by British smokers against Imperial Tobacco (*Hodgson and others* v. *Imperial Tobacco Ltd and others* [1998] 1 WLR 1056, CA). The claimants' lawyers were acting under CFA terms and wanted to establish that, if they lost, they would not be vulnerable to wasted costs orders or allegations of maintenance and champerty. (The claimants did not have insurance to cover the other side's costs if they lost.)

1.32 The Court of Appeal decided that a solicitor who loses a CFA case which complies with the CFA Regulations has a high degree of protection from being personally liable for costs. The same protection applies against wasted costs orders, so long as the history of the case shows they have acted reasonably.

1.33 Giving judgment in the *Imperial Tobacco* case, Lord Woolf MR said:

> There is no reason why the circumstances in which a lawyer, acting under a CFA, can be made personally liable for the costs of a party other than

his client should differ from those in which a lawyer who is not acting under a CFA would be so liable . . . The existence of a CFA should make a legal adviser's position as a matter of law no worse, so far as being ordered to pay costs is concerned, than it would be if there was no CFA. This is unless, of course, the CFA is outside the statutory protection.

The plaintiffs' lawyers are in no different position because they are acting under a CFA than they would be acting for a legally aided client with a nil contribution . . .

The parties now agree that the court has a limited additional jurisdiction to make an order for costs against legal advisers personally in circumstances in which it would not be possible to make a wasted costs order. This limited jurisdiction is only going to be relevant in a very small minority of cases.

1.34　Since the *Imperial Tobacco* case, the debate about the liability of lawyers for maintenance and champerty has continued, fuelled by a series of decisions by the courts. While *Awwad* v. *Geraghty* (see para.1.5 above) is the most recent and most important decision on the legality and enforceability of speculative funding arrangements, the 1999 Act provides certainty of immunity from personal claims for costs against solicitors who lose a case funded by a CFA, provided the agreement falls within the framework of the Act and subordinate legislation.

Financial risks as a check on frivolous litigation

1.35　The financial risk to a firm of bringing frivolous conditional fee cases is graphically illustrated by the figures in the table set out in Appendix 19. This shows the level of success fee that would be needed, calculated on an actuarial basis, to reflect the level of risk inherent in a case. According to this table, a case which has a 50 per cent chance of success merits a 100 per cent uplift, the maximum allowable. If a firm were to take on a case which was more risky, say with only a 40 per cent chance of success, the full level of risk could not be reflected in the success fee – a strong financial disincentive against taking it on.

1.36　Significantly, six years since conditional fees were first introduced, there is no evidence that they have led to a spate of unmeritorious claims.

CONFLICT OF INTEREST

1.37　Critics of conditional fees remain concerned about the potential they bring for conflict of interest between client and lawyer. The Bar Council, for example, has asserted that CFAs give the lawyer 'too great a financial interest in the outcome of the case'.

1.38   This does not seem to be a concern shared by clients. A study carried out for the Law Society (*Personal Injury Litigation* (1993)) before CFAs were introduced, found that a substantial proportion of potential clients saw the assimilation of interest between solicitor and client as a benefit. Conditional fees were seen as demonstrating the solicitor's confidence in the case and as acting as an incentive for him to work harder. 'The great thing about that idea [no win, no fee] is that you'd know your solicitor was very confident about the case. He's putting his money where his mouth is,' was one comment in the survey.

1.39   This attitude is backed up by anecdotal evidence of lawyers doing CFA work. In the personal injury field, where the bulk of conditional fee cases have been brought, claimant lawyers report that CFAs are popular with clients. They say their clients like the idea of their lawyer having a stake in the outcome of their case, and not having to worry about paying the fees of two sets of lawyers if they lose.

1.40   However, research into clients' experiences of CFAs (Yarrow and Abrams *Nothing to Lose?* (University of Westminster, 1999)) suggests some CFA clients may not even realise that their lawyer does not get paid if the case loses.

Under-settling

1.41   One of the main concerns about CFAs expressed by critics is that they will lead to under-settling. It is feared that lawyers will be tempted to take low settlements in order to trigger their success fees, rather than going to court and risking not getting paid anything if the case loses. While this is a legitimate concern, and something which lawyers must be careful to police, no evidence has yet emerged that this is happening. To date, no complaints about CFAs have been made to the Office for Supervision of Solicitors. Moreover, the researchers in the *Nothing to Lose?* study, alert to the dangers of under-settling, were no doubt looking for evidence of it in their interviews with clients. Not only did they fail to find any firm examples of CFAs leading to under-settling, but, if anything, they found that the reverse might be the case. They conclude:

> There was very little evidence of solicitors putting pressure on clients to settle . . . Only one client (on a speculative fee) believed that he might have undersettled due to the solicitor's financial interest . . . The reverse situation could apply: one client accepted a payment into court although the solicitor wanted to carry on. One client who switched from paying privately to a CFA said that he might have settled for less, if he had been paying himself to avoid financial risk. CFAs may, therefore, prevent clients settling for low amounts, as long as the solicitor and after the event insurer are willing to continue backing the case.

This conclusion should, however, be read with the caveat that the study was very small (40 clients were interviewed and there was no control group of non-CFA clients against which to make comparisons), and, as the researchers emphasise, under-settling would in any event be very difficult for clients themselves to detect.

1.42 Perhaps the most significant indicator that firms doing CFAs are not routinely playing it safe and under-settling, is the level of after-the-event insurance (AEI) claims. Although insurers will not reveal their claims record for commercial reasons, we know CFA cases are being lost. AEI providers complain privately that they are losing more cases than expected, and several have tightened their criteria to try to reduce losses.

Judicial views

1.43 While the potential for conflict of interest needs to be taken seriously, some of our senior judges see it more as a convergence of interest. In a speech in March 1994, the then Master of the Rolls, Sir Thomas Bingham (as he then was), described the assimilation of interests between solicitor and client as one of the advantages of conditional fees:

> Suppose, in litigation conducted under a contingency fee regime a substantial offer is made at an early stage; the offer is rejected; the case goes to trial years later; and the client loses. In the United States, both client and lawyer are better off if the offer is accepted; so would the client be in England; but the lawyer is much better off in England if the offer is rejected [because he will be paid for the extra work win or lose].

Lord Bingham's view of the merits of contingency arrangements is echoed by legal observers in other jurisdictions. In Australia, a 1994 report by the Sackville Committee to the Attorney-General on access to justice concluded:

> It may be said that clients would prefer their lawyers to be interested in the outcome of litigation since the lawyer is likely to display greater diligence and commitment to the case. Where the lawyer is sure of payment, whatever the outcome, he or she may have less incentive to pursue a matter diligently or expeditiously. Indeed, there may be an incentive for the lawyer to proceed to trial unnecessarily ... to gain higher fees than would be gained by settling at an earlier stage.

The committee recommended that those Australian states which did not permit contingency arrangements should provide for a success fee above the lawyer's normal rates.

The lawyer's approach to potential conflicts

1.44 It is important, however, not to down-play the risks of conflict of interest that do exist. The potential for conflict between the financial interests of the lawyer and those of the client is a live professional issue for all lawyers every day. Those being paid by the hour, theoretically at least, have an interest in stringing out the amount of time a piece of work takes to complete; those paid a fixed fee, have a theoretical interest in rushing through it, cutting corners as they go. In recognition of this, a fundamental part of lawyers' training is learning to reconcile these conflicting impulses. For example, in personal injury cases, every time an offer to settle is made by the defendant or a payment made into court, the lawyer faces a potential conflict of interest: whether to snap up an offer, conclude the case and get paid, or to push it on to get more for the client.

1.45 However, if all legal work, especially litigation, carries conflict problems, conditional fees are at the extreme end of what can be thought of as a conflict of interest continuum. In a conditional fee case, the potential for conflict of interest is greater because the lawyer risks not just getting paid *less* if the case is unsuccessful, but getting *nothing at all*. A lawyer acting under a CFA, therefore, might feel tempted to look more favourably on a low offer to settle than he would if he were assured of payment whatever the outcome, since if he were to take a case to trial under a CFA he might risking getting paid nothing.

1.46 The Part 36 claimant's offer to settle introduced under the Civil Procedure Rules (CPR) creates a new element in the conflict continuum. By virtue of this change to the procedural rules, the claimant can now make the first move and suggest a figure which he is prepared to accept. He no longer has to wait for the defendant to make an offer which he either accepts or rejects. A lawyer acting on a CFA, with one eye on his firm's bank balance, would, therefore have the perfect mechanism for accelerating a case to a 'successful' conclusion.

1.47 Accordingly, lawyers should not be complacent. Solicitors and barristers need to be constantly alert to their motives in taking decisions relating to cases, and to police their own behaviour. They should also be careful not to over-stretch themselves financially in the numbers of CFAs they take on. The shakier their financial position, the more likely they are to be tempted to under-settle.

SO FAR, SO GOOD?

1.48   Conditional fees have, so far as anyone can judge at this still early stage, been a success in personal injury cases, the main area of law where they have been used.

1.49   However, this does not necessarily mean that they will be equally successful in the other areas of law where they can now be used. Their success in the personal injury arena has been based largely on a combination of two factors. The first is high success rates, some 95 per cent of personal injury cases resulting in a successful outcome. The second is high volume. These two factors have made personal injury cases attractive to AEI providers, so that insurance has been readily available.

1.50   The experience with clinical negligence cases shows what might happen in other areas where there are fewer cases and lower success rates. Although CFAs were allowed for clinical negligence at the same time as they were introduced for personal injury actions generally, relatively few clinical negligence cases have been brought using this method of funding. They present a far higher risk to AEI insurers (which is reflected in higher premiums, sometimes running to several thousands of pounds), and a much heavier financial burden to clients and firms.

1.51   As a result, although some clinical negligence victims have undoubtedly benefited from the introduction of conditional fees, their numbers are small. In the main, the greater uncertainty over prospects for success and the high costs of insurance have tended to deter clinical negligence firms and their potential clients from using conditional fees. Indeed, the government has recognised the inherent difficulties with clinical negligence and CFAs by retaining legal aid for these cases after it has been withdrawn for other personal injury work in April 2000.

CONCLUSION

1.52   Conditional fees have not been as radical a departure as some have suggested. Most firms across a wide variety of areas of law will already be used to operating on some form of payment-by-results basis. Conditional fees for litigation are a new area where lawyers can now be paid according to the outcome.

1.53   Conditional or contingency fees are a well established feature in many foreign jurisdictions, not just the USA. The picture painted in the media of the supposed excesses of US contingency fees are often wildly inaccurate. In any event they could not be replicated here because of inherent differences in the two systems.

1.54 There is no evidence so far of conditional fees being abused. The dire predictions of the prophets of doom have not been realised. Pre-existing sanctions to deter spurious claims, such as wasted cost orders, still provide the necessary deterrent. Moreover, the right of the losing party to challenge the successful party's level of success fee and insurance premium will introduce some additional control.

1.55 Conditional fees do, however, bring with them greater potential scope for conflict of interest. Lawyers should be constantly alert to the danger of putting the financial interests of their firm above those of their client (as they must be in any event, whatever the funding method). So far, however, there is no evidence of clients' interests being compromised.

1.56 Conditional fees are working well in personal injury cases. However, whether this success is replicated in other areas of law (as the government hopes) will depend on a number of related issues, the main one being the availability of affordable and accessible after-the-event insurance.

1.57 All the evidence is that clients like conditional fees. They are also confused by them. Research shows that clients may fail fully to grasp the complexities of the agreements to which they are being asked to sign up. This problem is compounded if they are required to sign not just the CFA, but also an after-the-event insurance contract and possibly a disbursement funding agreement as well. Lawyers must be aware of the potential for confusion and make sure they take all reasonable steps to keep clients well informed.

CHAPTER 2

The regulatory framework

Gareth Phillips and Gordon Wignall

INTRODUCTION

Statutory enforceability of contingent arrangements

2.1   As explained in Chapter 1 a conditional fee arrangement ('CFA') is a form of contingent fee which judges refused to enforce at common law as a matter of public policy (see *Giles* v. *Thompson* [1994] 1 AC 142, HL and *Awwad* v. *Geraghty* [2000] 3 WLR 1041, CA for a discussion of the relevant public policy issues). Other restrictions existed in statutory form and as rules of professional practice. The path to Parliamentary approval of CFAs is described in more detail at 1.19ff above.

2.2   CFAs were first rendered potentially enforceable by reason of the Courts and Legal Services Act 1990, s.58, which came into force on 1 October 1993 (see Appendix 1a). By this Act legitimacy was conferred on agreements between lawyers and their clients, even though their fees and expenses were expressed to be payable only 'in specified circumstances' (s.58(1)(b),(3)). Part II of the Access to Justice Act 1999 substituted a new s.58 in the 1990 Act, supplemented by a new s.58A (see Appendix 1b). These provisions retain the key characteristics of the old s.58 format, rendering it impossible for the judges to declare such agreements unenforceable in certain categories of proceedings. Part II of the 1999 Act also made it possible for the success fee and for insurance premiums to be recovered from the losing party. Sections 28 ('litigation funding agreements') and 31 ('rules as to costs') are not yet in force, whilst the remainder of Part II came into force on 1 April 2000. The effect of ss.58, 58A is that there must be strict compliance with both the Act and the relevant regulations for a CFA to be enforceable. It will otherwise be unenforceable as a matter of public policy because of the survival of the rule against champerty, and a quantum meruit payment is unlikely to be recoverable (see *Awwad* v. *Geraghty* [2000] 3 WLR 1041).

Function of this chapter

2.3   This chapter will seek, first, to provide a working account of the structure of the Courts and Legal Services Act 1990, s.58, in its original format. Secondly, it will examine the new statutory basis by which CFAs are permitted by reason of Part II of the Access to Justice Act 1999. Thirdly, it will look at the effects of the Civil Procedure Rules (CPR) and the Costs Practice Direction. Finally, it will look to the rules of professional practice laid down by the Law Society. (The rules relevant to CFA practice at the Bar are considered separately in Chapter 6.) The profession's response to the old CFA scheme as set out in the 1990 Act was to recommend a voluntary cap on the amount of damages which could be used to fund the lawyers' success fee, a cap which was universally applied. Since the new scheme permits the success fee to be recovered from the losing party, the cap is no longer seen as a necessary control. CFAs entered into before 1 April 2000 are not treated as funding arrangements for the purposes of CPR Rule 43.2 (see Costs Practice Direction, para.57.8(2)).

COURTS AND LEGAL SERVICES ACT 1990

Conditions of enforceability set out in the 1990 Act: criminal and family proceedings excluded

2.4   The Courts and Legal Services Act 1990, s.58, (see Appendix 1a) conferred statutory protection on written agreements whereby advocates and litigators provided that fees and expenses should be paid 'only in specified circumstances' (s.58(1)(b), (3)). In order to be enforceable these agreements had to comply with such requirements as were prescribed by the Lord Chancellor (s.58(1)(c)). Further, they were restricted to classes of proceedings to be specified by the Lord Chancellor (s.58(1)(a), (4), (10)) making it impossible for the Lord Chancellor to make an Order permitting CFAs to be entered into in respect of criminal proceedings and many family law proceedings (the list set out in s.58(10) was subsequently revised by the Family Law Act 1996, Sched. 8 para. 61, Sched. 10).

Subordinate legislation introducing CFAs: 1995 and 1998

2.5   In 1995, the Lord Chancellor brought forward two Statutory Instruments which introduced CFAs and governed their use, the

Conditional Fee Agreements Order 1995, SI 1995/1674 (see Appendix 4) and the Conditional Fee Agreements Regulations 1995, SI 1995/1675 (see Appendix 6). In 1998 the types of proceedings which could be covered by CFAs were extended by the Conditional Fee Agreements Order 1998, SI 1998/1860 (see Appendix 5). The contents of these Statutory Instruments are discussed in the following paragraphs.

CONDITIONAL FEE AGREEMENTS ORDER 1995, SI 1995/1674; CONDITIONAL FEE AGREEMENTS ORDER 1998, SI 1998/1860

2.6   The 1995 Order (see Appendix 4) came into force on 25 July 1995 and set out the types of proceedings which at that time could be covered by a CFA: personal injury, insolvency, and those being brought before the European Commission of Human Rights and the European Court of Human Rights. The definition of personal injury adopted in the Order was the same as set out in the Rules of the Supreme Court (Ord.1, r.4(1)) and did not extend to professional negligence actions (*Hopkins* v. *Mackenzie* [1995] 6 Med LR 26). This meant that CFAs were not restricted to the prosecution of actions, but were also open to defendants.

2.7   The 1995 Order was subsequently revoked by the 1998 Order which came into force on 30 July 1998 (see Appendix 5). The 1998 Order declared 'all proceedings' (whether or not 'concluded without the commencement of court proceedings') to be specified for the purposes of s.58(3) of the 1990 Act. This meant that as long as they were not prohibited from being enforceable because they were criminal or family proceedings as listed in s.58(10), then it was possible to enter into CFAs in respect of them.

CONDITIONAL FEE AGREEMENTS REGULATIONS 1995, SI 1995/1675

Requirements of CFAs

2.8   The Conditional Fee Agreements Regulations 1995, SI 1995/1675 (see Appendix 6) came into force on 25 July 1995 and set out four key elements which had to be included in a CFA in order for it to be enforceable. These were set out in reg.3 which required that a CFA must state:

(a) the particular proceedings or parts of them to which it relates (including counterclaims, appeals and enforcement proceedings) (reg.3(a));

(b) the circumstances in which the legal representative's fees and disbursements are payable (reg.3(b));

(c) what payment is due in the event of partial failure, if the specified circumstances do not occur, and on termination of the CFA (reg.3(c));

(d) the amounts payable, or the methods used to calculate the amounts payable, in respect of the (b) and (c) above, and whether those amounts are limited by reference to the damages recovered (reg.3(d)).

The requirement that provision had to be made specifying what payments fell due under the circumstances set out in reg.3(c) meant that account also had to be given of any disbursements which became payable. Regulation 3(d) meant that it was necessary to specify whether a cap existed under the agreement.

Additional requirements

2.9   Regulation 4 also required the CFA to confirm that the solicitor had discussed specified points with the client before signing. These were:

(a) whether the client might be entitled to legal aid in respect of the proceedings (reg.4(2)(a));

(b) the circumstances in which the client might be liable to pay the legal representative's fees and expenses under the agreement (reg.4(2)(b));

(c) the circumstance in which the client may be liable to pay the costs of any other side (reg.4(2)(c));

(d) the circumstances in which the client may seek [a court assessment] of the fees and expenses of the legal representative and the procedure for so doing (reg.4(2)(d)).

Form of agreement and amendments to agreements

2.10   By reg.6 a CFA had to be in writing and signed, and by reg.7, any extension of a CFA to cover further proceedings (or part of them) meant that all the provisions of regs.3 to 6 applied to the extended agreement.

2.11   In the case of CFAs between one legal representative and another, the requirements of reg.4 did not apply, and the agreement did not have to be signed.

Success fee not recoverable

2.12   Consequently, as a result of the Courts and Legal Services Act 1990, s.58, and subsequent Statutory Instruments, solicitors were able to enter CFAs in respect of many types of contentious proceedings. The scope of the type of proceedings in which such arrangements could be entered was initially limited but then extended to all civil proceedings (but not family or crime) by the 1998 Order.

2.13   It should be remembered, however, that under this form of agreement the success fee which was charged when a solicitor successfully concluded a case was payable by the client out of his winnings (subject to the caps voluntarily imposed by the professions). Similarly, the cost of any after-the-event insurance policy to protect against an award of legal costs to the other side was also payable by the client. CFAs were accordingly not as popular as they might have been, as they almost inevitably involved the client in deductions from their full entitlement to damages. It is important to remember that under the Costs Practice Direction, no CFA entered into before 1 April 2000 is a 'funding arrangement' as defined by CPR Rule 43.2 (see Costs Practice Direction, para.57.8.

ACCESS TO JUSTICE ACT 1999 AND THE NEW CFA SCHEME

Introduction: CPR and the removal of legal aid

2.14   The late 1990s saw the government undertake a fundamental review of both the civil justice system and the means by which legal services could be provided and financed. The civil justice reforms, which became synonymous with Lord Justice Woolf, sought radically to alter the administration of civil justice with a view to bringing about a more efficient and cost-effective system. The so-called Woolf reforms resulting in the new Civil Procedure Rules are the subject of many detailed analytical works and are largely outside the scope of this book. However, they were part of an overall package which sought radically to change the manner in which civil claims could be processed.

2.15   The CPR were followed by the Access to Justice Act 1999. Many of the wider changes introduced by the Access to Justice Act, such as the extensive changes to the system of public funding of cases, are also outside the scope of this book. One change envisaged by the new legislation is central to our subject, however, and that is the virtual withdrawal of legal aid from personal injury claims, since it was envisaged that CFAs would fill the gap. However, there was concern that CFAs in their original form would not be viewed as sufficiently advantageous when compared with legal aid. Whilst a party with the benefit of a legal aid certificate would not expect to see any deductions from the compensation which he had won (save for the effect of the statutory charge), the compensation of a party whose claim was funded by a CFA would be reduced by the success fee and the cost of the after-the-event insurance premium. As a result, the government embarked on a consultation exercise with a view to establishing a workable but more attractive version of the 1995 scheme. The practical effect has been a huge potential expansion of the use of CFAs.

Enforceability and the basic criteria under the new CFA regime

2.16 By the Access to Justice Act 1999, s.27, the Courts and Legal Services Act 1990, s.58 as originally enacted was replaced by a new series of provisions contained in a substituted s.58 and a new s.58A which came into force on 1 April 2000 (see Appendix 1b). As with the original s.58, a CFA must meet the conditions laid down by these sections (as well as by those set out in the relevant Statutory Instrument (see 2.28 below)) to be enforceable. Section 58(1) (as substituted) expressly states that:

> A conditional fee agreement which satisfies all of the conditions applicable to it by virtue of this section shall not be unenforceable by reason only of its being a conditional fee agreement; but ... any other conditional fee agreement shall be unenforceable

The basic statutory conditions of enforceability are as follows (all references provided hereafter being references to the new ss.58 and 58A). They resemble the underlying framework of the original Act:

(a) the agreement must be in writing (s.58(3)(a));

(b) it must not relate to proceedings in which conditional fee arrangements are prohibited (s.58(3)(b));

(c) it must comply with requirements laid down by the Lord Chancellor (s.58(3)(c)).

If the CFA provides for a success fee, then:

(a) it must relate to proceedings allowed by the Lord Chancellor (s.58(4)(a));

(b) it must state the percentage increase (s.58(4)(b));

(c) it must not exceed the allowed maximum percentage increase (s.58(4)(c)).

2.17 Conditional fee agreements in non-contentious business are expressly allowed (s.58(5)).

2.18 It is important to remember that by the Access to Justice Act 1999, s.27, a CFA is defined to include *any* arrangement where fees are payable 'only in specified circumstances'. Any arrangement of this nature which fails to comply with the regulations is therefore unenforceable. So-called '*Thai Trading*' arrangements (see para.1.5 above), whether the lawyer agrees to act speculatively without a success fee or at a discounted rate, are caught by the statutory definition of CFA, and must comply with the regulations.

Environmental Protection Act 1990, s.82

2.19 As with the Act in its original form, CFAs cannot be employed in criminal or family proceedings (s.58A(1)). The exclusion in respect of criminal proceedings was originally applied to proceedings under the Environmental Protection Act 1990, s.82. The position was later changed so as to allow CFAs in such proceedings, save that no success fee can be claimed (the Conditional Fee Agreements Order 2000, para. 3). 'Family proceedings' is defined to form the same list as that contained in s.58(10) of the original Act (s.58A(2)).

Subordinate legislation

2.20 The requirements which the Lord Chancellor may lay down under s.58(3)(c) in order for a CFA to be enforceable include the provision of prescribed information which has to be given to the client before a CFA is made (s.58A(3)(a)). Section 58A(3)(a) therefore paves the way for subsequent regulations (see the Conditional Fee Agreements Regulations 2000, SI 2000/692, below at 2.28ff below). This format again replicates the format of the original Act. Provision is also made, however, for costs orders to include payment of success fees – in other words, for the first time, success fees are potentially payable by a losing opponent (s.58(A)(6)). The costs orders which can be made in respect of success fees are set out at 2.58–2.60 below and the rules governing their recoverability are considered at 2.61–2.70 below.

Access to Justice Act 1999, s.28: 'litigation funding agreements'

2.21   Section 28 of the 1999 Act (which is not yet in force) introduces a new s.58B into the 1990 Act (app.2). Section 58B allows for the provision of 'litigation funding agreements' whereby a funder agrees to fund another person's litigation in return for the litigant's agreement to pay a sum to the funder in specified circumstances (s.58B(2)). Section 28 was introduced as an amendment to the Access to Justice Bill in response to suggestions that it might be possible to establish a form of contingent legal aid which would be run independently of the state. As enacted, s.58B(2)(b) will allow a funder to enforce an agreement under the terms of which a client agrees to pay part of his damages, or part of a sum recovered from the losing side, back into the fund. The original advocates of such schemes were the Bar Council (in favour of a 'CLAF' (contingent legal aid fund)) and the Law Society (in favour of a 'CoLAF' (conditional legal aid fund)).

2.22   Litigation funding agreements will constitute another express exemption to the principle of unlawful maintenance. Their enforceability will be subject to the following:

(a) the funder must be a person, or a person of a description, prescribed by the Lord Chancellor (s.58B(3)(a));

(b) the agreement must be in writing (s.58B(3)(b));

(c) the agreement must not relate to proceedings to which a CFA cannot apply (s.58B(3)(c));

(d) the agreement must comply with prescribed requirements (s.58B(3)(d));

(e) the sum to be paid by the litigant must consist of any costs payable to him in respect of the proceedings to which the agreement relates, together with an amount related to the funder's expenditure in funding such services (s.58B(3)(e));

(f) the amount related to the funder's expenditure in funding the services must not exceed such percentage of that anticipated expenditure as may be prescribed by the Lord Chancellor in relation to proceedings of the description to which the agreement relates (s.58B(3)(f)).

2.23   The Lord Chancellor also has power to require funders to provide prescribed information to the litigant before the agreement is made (s.58B(5)(a)). Further, provision is made for a costs order to include payment of an amount due under a litigation funding arrangement (s.58(B)(8)).

Access to Justice Act 1999, s.29: recoverability of insurance premiums

2.24   The Access to Justice Act 1999, s.29, makes specific provision for the recovery of insurance premiums paid in respect of the risk of incurring a liability for costs in court proceedings (see Appendix 3). The relevant principles which are applicable for the purposes of determining whether a claim to the recovery of an insurance premium is reasonable are set out at 2.71 below. An insurance premium is recoverable in costs-only proceedings (*Callery* v. *Gray* [2001] EWCA Civ 1117) (see 2.75–2.76 below).

Access to Justice Act 1999, s.30: recoverability by membership organisation of additional amounts

2.25   The Access to Justice Act 1999, s.30, goes on to make provision for prescribed membership organisations to recover in costs an additional amount in respect of any provision made by the organisation in connection with the risk of having to meet a costs liability on behalf of a member (app.3). (See also the Access to Justice (Membership Organisation) Regulations 2000, SI 2000/693 at 2.40ff below.)

Access to Justice Act 1999, s.31: indemnity principle

2.26   Although not yet in force, the rather obliquely worded Access to Justice Act 1999, s.31 (see Appendix 3) gives rise to a power either to vary, or even wholly dispose of the indemnity principle. The proposal to abrogate the effect of the indemnity principle is of particular interest. Whilst the principle seems unlikely to be abolished altogether, new rules proposed to modify its effect will need to be considered carefully, as they may have implications which go beyond the immediate aim, which was to make an exception to the principle in the case of collective CFAs.

Summary of the substituted statutory framework

2.27   Consequently, the Access to Justice Act 1999 provides the means for a root and branch re-shaping of CFAs. Success fees are now recoverable as costs from the other party. Similarly, insurance premiums or equivalent amounts are also recoverable by membership organisations such as trade unions. The scope for a client to make full recovery of compensation is thus broadened radically. The 1999 Act allows for the grand scheme of such changes. The practical details are set out in the regulations which the Act empowers the Lord Chancellor to make, and amendments to the appropriate Civil Procedure Rules and attendant Practice Direction.

CONDITIONAL FEE AGREEMENTS REGULATIONS 2000, SI 2000/692

Introductions: definitions

2.28 The main requirements for an enforceable CFA under the new regime are set out in the Conditional Fee Agreements Regulations 2000, SI 2000/692 ('the CFA Regulations 2000') (see Appendix 8), reg.1 of which sets out the definitions of various terms used throughout the Regulations. The definition of 'client' in reg.1 may arguably include both a lay client and a funder, but in our view the client is certainly more obviously intended to be the recipient of the information.

General requirements

2.29 The new legislation goes on at reg.2 effectively to repeat the requirements of reg.3 of the 1995 Regulations when setting out what must be stated as to the proceedings covered by a CFA, the circumstances in which payment is due, and the methods by which payment is to be calculated (see 2.8 above).

Requirements for contents of CFAs providing for success fees

2.30 The main changes to the earlier scheme are set out at regs.3 and 4, reg. 3 prescribing new requirements for CFAs in cases where a success fee is claimed.

Reasons for setting the success fee at a particular level: financing element not recoverable

2.31 Regulation 3(1)(a) provides that the CFA must specify the reasons why the success fee is set at the stated level. It will also be necessary by reason of reg.3(1)(b) to identify how much of the percentage uplift relates to the postponement of payment – the financing element. Such an element is not recoverable against the other party under the CPR (see 2.61 below).

Limited waiver of client confidentiality

2.32 Further, reg.3(2)(a) requires a CFA to provide that on an assessment of any fees which are subject to a percentage uplift, then the legal representative or client may disclose to the court or any other person as required the reasons for setting the percentage uplift at the level stated in the agreement.

Recovery of 'unreasonable' fees from a client

2.33 Importantly, reg.3(2)(b) restricts the amount of the success fee payable under the CFA by the client (even though it is potentially recoverable against the other party) to that allowed by the court on an assessment if part is disallowed on the ground that it was unreasonable 'in view of facts which were or should have been known' when the CFA was made (reg.3(2)(b)) (see also 2.68–2.70 below). The level of success fee payable by the client is similarly restricted to that agreed between the parties if the issue of costs is settled by negotiation (reg.3(2)(c)). In either case the shortfall between the success fee as assessed or agreed and the amount originally agreed will not fall to be paid by the client unless the court is satisfied that the full amount should be payable. It is because the court can order a client to pay an amount which it does not compel the losing side to pay that the term 'no win no fee' is, strictly speaking, inappropriate. The procedure by which a legal representative can apply for payment of a disallowed percentage uplift is considered at 2.72–2.74 below, and some guidance as to the practical steps to be followed in order to ensure maximum recoverability of the percentage uplift is to be found in the section on calculating the success fee at 4.19ff below.

2.34 The situations in which courts will make orders that fees should continue to be payable are likely to be rare if they have been disallowed on an assessment between the parties on the basis that they are unreasonable. One can possibly envisage a situation where a client has been particularly difficult or misleading, and has hindered a proper and accurate risk assessment. In such circumstances it is arguably appropriate to seek the court's approval of the shortfall being payable by the client. Otherwise, matters such as excessive time being demanded by the client would be dealt with in the normal way as basic costs, and the shortfall should be payable by the client without having to seek a specific order. Presumably the situation in which an experienced commercial client knowingly agrees to an excessive rate of success fee due to the case's importance to him or his organisation will be a further situation where the court might allow such fees as against the client. The provision does throw up a potentially awkward problem where a client instructs a solicitor to accept an offer of settlement which includes a reduced level of success fee. Generally the solicitor would be under a duty to follow his client's instructions and accept the offer. The model agreement (see Appendix 20) seeks to guard against this problem by making specific provision whereby the client agrees not to give such instructions if those circumstances arose.

2.35 It should be noted that whilst reg.3(2)(b) restricts the amount of a success fee which can be recovered from the client, no such limitation exists in respect of base fees. Control mechanisms here are the professional requirements that a solicitor gives his client proper costs information at the commencement of an agreement, and the power of the court to assess the client's costs. The added protection contained in the Law Society model CFA should also be noted at 5.81 below.

Information to be given before a CFA is made

2.36 Regulation 4 makes considerable changes to the requirements for information to be given to clients. The core matters about which the client must be provided with information prior to the making of a CFA are set out in reg.4(2). They are:

(a) the circumstances in which the client may be liable to pay the costs of the legal representative (reg.4(2)(a));

(b) the circumstances in which the client may seek an assessment of the legal representative's fees and expenses and the procedure for so doing (reg.4(2)(b));

(c) whether the legal representative considers that the client's potential liability for costs is insured under an existing contract of insurance (reg.4(2)(c));

(d) what other methods of financing the costs are available (reg.4(2)(d));

(e) what method of financing the costs the legal representative considers may be appropriate, his reasons for the recommendation and whether he has an interest in making the recommendation (reg.4(2)(e)).

If the client requires 'any further explanation, advice or other information' about these matters prior to the making of the agreement, then reg. 4(1)(b) obliges the legal representative to provide such further material as the client may 'reasonably require'. In addition, prior to the making of the agreement the legal representative must 'explain its effect' to the client. All of the core matters referred to above and the general effect of the CFA must be given orally to the client, whilst para.(e) of the core matters and the general effect must also be explained in writing (reg.4(5)). Regulation 2(2) requires that if the CFA is one to which reg.4 applies then it must contain a statement that the requirements of reg.4 have been complied with.

Signature

2.37 Regulation 5 states that a CFA must be signed by both the client and the legal representative.

CFAs between more than one legal representative

2.38 As to agreements between legal representative and additional legal representative (normally barristers), the information required to be given by a legal representative to a client does not need to be given (reg.4(6)), and there is no requirement for the CFA to be signed by either party (reg.5(2)). Chapter 6 considers the barrister–solicitor relationship in more detail.

Amendments to CFAs

2.39 Regulation 6 provides for amendments to be made to CFAs to cover further proceedings, specifying which of the previous regulations about client information apply to the amended agreement.

ACCESS TO JUSTICE (MEMBERSHIP ORGANISATION) REGULATIONS 2000, SI 2000/693

2.40 For the purposes of the recovery of costs liabilities under s.30 of the 1999 Act, trade unions and other prescribed organisations need to be able to satisfy the provisions of the above Access to Justice (Membership Organisation) Regulations 2000, SI 2000/693, which also came into effect on 1 April 2000. Such organisations will then be able to recover in successful cases an additional amount to cover the self-insurance element. Limitations on the amount which a prescribed organisation may recover under the CPR are considered at 2.62 below.

2.41 The only organisations which are able to take advantage of these provisions are those prescribed by the Lord Chancellor (reg.2). No detailed criteria are available setting out the grounds on which an entity may expect to achieve prescribed status, but the Lord Chancellor's department has indicated that it will consider applications from a wide variety of organisations (details are available from the Lord Chancellor's department website under 'Prescription Applications' (dated 2 April 2001)).

2.42 In order to recover the self-insurance element the agreement must:

(a) be in writing (reg.3(2));

(b) contain a statement specifying:

    (i) the circumstances in which the member or other party may be liable to pay costs of proceedings (reg.3(3)(a));

    (ii) whether such liability arises if the circumstances partly occur, or irrespective of whether they occur, or on termination of the agreement for any reason (reg.3(3)(b));

    (iii) the basis on which any liability is calculated (reg.3(3)(c));

    (iv) the procedure for seeking assessment of such costs (reg.3(3)(d)).

A written copy of the agreement containing these matters must be given to the member or other party to proceedings whose liabilities the organisation is undertaking to meet (reg.3(4)). The sum to be claimed should not exceed the likely cost of an equivalent insurance premium against the risk of meeting a cost liability in such proceedings (reg.4).

COLLECTIVE CONDITIONAL FEE AGREEMENTS REGULATIONS 2000, SI 2000/2988

2.43 Conditional fee style arrangements are likely to be attractive to bulk purchasers of legal services such as trade unions, insurers or other large organisations who deal regularly with large quantities of litigation. The legislative requirement for each separate action to have a separate CFA does not sit easily with commercial reality. It creates an administrative burden which is unwieldy and unnecessary in the case of experienced, sophisticated organisations who are well versed in the litigation process. Consequently, the government consulted with a wide variety of bodies with a view to producing regulations to cover collective CFAs. The Collective Conditional Fee Agreements Regulations 2000, SI 2000/2988 will be found at Appendix 10.

2.44 By reg.3, a 'collective conditional fee agreement' ('CCFA') is defined as a CFA which does not refer to specific proceedings but which provides for fees to be payable on a common basis in relation to each class of proceedings to which it refers. The 'client' under a CCFA is the person who will receive the advocacy or litigation services to which the agreement relates (reg.1).

2.45 The collective elements of the CCFA are to be set out in a distinct document signed by both the legal representatives and the funder (reg.6(1)), save that this requirement does not apply where the parties to the CCFA are legal representative and additional legal representative (reg.6(2)).

2.46 The CCFA must provide that when accepting instructions in relation to specific proceedings the legal representative must inform the client as to the circumstances in which he may be liable to pay the legal representative's costs (reg.4(2)(a)) and provide any further explanation, advice or other information about this as the client may reasonably require (reg.4(2)(b)). Regulation 4(2) again does not apply where the parties are a legal representative and an additional legal representative. It must also provide that after accepting individual instructions the legal representative must confirm his acceptance of instructions in writing to the client (reg.4(3)).

2.47 Where a CCFA provides for a success fee, the agreement must provide that the legal representative will prepare and retain a separate risk assessment in respect of any specific proceedings (reg.5). As with reg.3 of the CFA Regulations 2000, initial restrictions are placed on the extent to which a legal representative is entitled to recover that amount of a success fee which the court does not consider reasonable given the facts which were known, or which ought to have been known, by the legal representative when the percentage uplift was set.

2.48 It should be noted that there is no restriction on who may use collective CFAs, and the fact that a case is funded by means of a collective CFA will not affect the duty of care owed by the legal representative to the client.

CPR PARTS 43–48 AND THE COSTS PRACTICE DIRECTION

2.49 Taking effect at the same time as the amendments to the Civil Procedure Rules (see Appendix 11) was the new Practice Direction (see Appendix 12) relating to costs which supplements CPR Parts 43 and 48 (referred to in this work as the 'Costs Practice Direction' or 'Costs PD'). This integrated Practice Direction, which replaces the previous individual Practice Directions for those Parts, contains material crucial to the manner in which the courts will enforce the amended rules. The Civil

Procedure (Amendment No. 3) Rules 2000, SI 2000/1317 came into effect on 3 July 2000 and contain a number of important amendments to the previous CPR Parts 43–48 and also to the Costs Practice Direction. These amendments are designed specifically to deal with the new position on CFAs. Specific rules as to notification cover CFAs entered into before 3 July 2000 where a party intends to recover an additional liability (see 2.55 below).

2.50   The Costs Practice Direction is divided into separate sections, each of which provides guidance on the application of different rules contained in CPR Parts 43–48. Each section, however, is itself divided into paragraphs, and, save where some other reference is expressly used below, it is the paragraph numbers which are provided as references below.

Definitions: the courts' approach to the recoverability of additional liabilities

2.51   CPR Rule 43.2 includes a number of definitions relevant to CFAs. Where a CFA claims a success fee, or insurance premium or membership organisation equivalent, it is known as a 'funding arrangement' (CPR Rule 43.2(1)(k)) and the amount of each is an 'additional liability' (CPR Rule 43.2(1)(o)). A definition is given of 'insurance premium' which appears broad enough to cover a variety of after-the-event insurance products, whether taken out to cover the risks of having to meet both sides', or just the opponent's, costs. 'Insurance premium' is defined as 'a sum of money paid or payable for insurance against the risk of incurring a cost liability in proceedings taken out after the event that is the subject matter of the claim' (CPR Rule 43.2(1)(m)). It will be for the courts to determine whether premiums including high market costs or substantive commissions will be recoverable in full, although the Costs Practice Direction gives some guidance (see 2.71 below).

General provisions in the Costs Practice Direction: form and content of bills of costs

2.52   The Costs Practice Direction contains a number of provisions in its initial six sections relating to the scope and manner of claiming costs which are relevant to CFAs. Section 4 deals with the form and contents of bills of costs, as well as dealing with a number of specific items which might be included in a claim. Under para.4.17 it should be noted that the percentage increase of the success fee will need to be shown separately from base costs in the bill (para.4.17(1)).

Estimates of costs

2.53   Section 6 of the Costs Practice Direction defines the 'estimates of costs' which are sought to be recovered from the other party as required to be produced from time to time under the rules (for example, when completing the allocation questionnaire). By para.6.2(1) an estimate of costs is an estimate of base costs (including disbursements) already incurred and to be incurred. Additional liabilities need not be revealed in the estimate (para.6.2(2)). It was feared by many claimant practitioners that if costs estimates were to be global and include the amount of additional liabilities, experienced and sophisticated representatives for the opponent would be able to estimate with reasonable accuracy the level of success fee, thus gaining an indication of how the claimant viewed the strength of his case. The earlier drafts of the Costs Practice Direction had followed this course, but the final version ensured that the confidentiality of the level of success fee is preserved during proceedings.

Providing information about funding arrangements: notification

2.54   Possibly the most important provision in the costs rules in practical terms is the duty of notification of the existence of the CFA where additional liabilities are claimed from the other side. The amended CPR Rule 44.15 sets out the basic requirement to notify both the court and other parties (CPR Rule 44.15(1)). This must be done in respect of both the original funding arrangement and any changes, notification after any changes being required within seven days (CPR Rule 44.15(2)). (The relevant CPR rules and Costs Practice Direction provisions are considered in more detail below.)

Time for notification: CFAs entered into between 1 April and 2 July 2000

2.55   Section 19 of the Costs Practice Direction confirms the general obligation to inform any other party about a funding arrangement if a party is to recover an additional liability in respect of a CFA (para.19.1(1)), although there is no obligation to specify the amount or basis of calculation until assessment. Generally, notice must be given to the court and other parties, either on the commencement of proceedings (para.19.2(2)), filing of first document (such as a defence) (para.19.2(3)), or within seven days of the funding arrangement being entered into if later (para.19.2(4)). Supplementary rules as to notification of changes are contained in para.19.3, changes being required where the information previously provided is 'no longer accurate' (para.19.3(1)). Attention is drawn to by para.19.1(3) to para.57.9 of the Costs Practice Direction. Paragraph 57.9(3) required a party which had entered into a CFA between 1 April 2000 and 2 July 2000 and which intended to recover additional liabilities to notify the opposing party by 31 July 2000.

Extent of information to be provided: notification prior to proceedings

2.56   The extent of the information to be provided is set out at para.19.4. The Costs Practice Direction does not deal specifically with notification before the start of proceedings but merely recommends a change in the protocol. This omission is unfortunate, as the recoverability of success fees in cases which settle without proceedings is likely to be a contentious issue and will probably arise regularly in practice. The Protocols Practice Direction does, however, make a brief reference to the desirability of giving notice (para.4A.1). It is arguable that the timelines with which a notice was given after signing a CFA or taking out a policy will be a factor to be taken into account in determining its recoverability. Good practice will surely be to give notice sooner rather than later.

Recovery of additional liability restricted if notification is not given

2.57   Where a party fails to provide notification about a funding arrangement, he may find that the additional liability for the period during which information was not provided is not recoverable from the paying party (see 2.63 below and the provisions relating to relief from sanction at 2.65ff below).

Costs orders relating to funding arrangements

2.58   CPR Rule 44.3 sets out the normal rule governing the court's discretion and the circumstances to be taken into account when exercising its discretion as to costs. CPR Rule 44.3A inserts a provision that the court will not assess success fees and insurance premiums until 'the conclusion of proceedings, or the part of the proceedings, to which the funding arrangement relates' (CPR Rule 44.3A(1)). Thus the rules ensure that the level of success fee being charged does not become apparent to the other party before resolution. The provision extends to interim hearings where there would be a clear risk of giving an indication to an opponent how strong or otherwise a party's case was felt to be.

Summary and detailed assessments

2.59   The Costs Practice Direction, para. 3.1 (supplementing the definition of 'summary assessment' at CPR Rule 43.3) makes it clear that when carrying out a summary assessment where there is an additional liability, the court can either assess base costs alone or both base costs and additional liability. This is subject, however, to the general rule postponing the assessment of the additional liability. Section 14 sets out the provisions of the Costs Practice Direction governing summary assessments where the costs claimed include an additional liability, being divided into orders made before the conclusion of the proceedings (paras.14.1–14.4) and orders made at the conclusion of proceedings (paras.14.5–14.9). When carrying out a detailed assessment of costs where there is an additional liability, the courts can assess both base costs and additional liability, or where base costs have already been assessed, additional liability alone (Costs PD, para.3.4 supplementing the definition of 'detailed assessment' at CPR Rule 43.4). Again, the court should not embark on an assessment of the additional liability until the conclusion of the proceedings (CPR Rule 44.3A(1) and Costs PD, para.13.12(1)). The procedure for a detailed assessment of costs is set out at CPR Part 47 supplemented by sections 28–49 of the Costs Practice Direction. Particularly important provisions are those dealing with the details of any additional liability which must be provided (see Costs PD, paras.32.4, 32.5, and 32.7). Where the receiving party claims an additional liability, a party who serves points of dispute may include a request for information about other forms of financing costs which were available to the receiving party (Costs PD, para.35.7). The paying party may obtain a wide variety of material by virtue of paras.40.2(i) and 40.14 (see also *Bailey* v. *IBC Vehicles* [1998] 3 All ER 570), and also by way of CPR Part 18.

2.60   CPR Rule 44.3A(2) goes on to say that at the conclusion of proceedings, the court may make a summary assessment of all the costs (CPR Rule 44.3A(2)(a)), or a summary assessment of all but the additional liabilities, the additional liabilities being assessed at a detailed hearing (CPR Rule 44.3A(2)(b)), or for all matters to be referred to a detailed assessment (CPR Rule 44.3A(2)(c)). In other words, the court may may not summarily assess the success fee or other additional liabilities whilst ordering the base costs to be assessed at a detailed assessment.

Limits on recovery under funding arrangements

2.61   CPR Rule 44.3B limits the recovery of the additional liability in a number of situations. The main one is the part of the success fee which relates to the lawyer's cost of funding the action through postponement of fees (CPR Rule 44.3B(1)(a)) (this is that part of the uplift percentage which is required to be separately stated in the CFA by the CFA Regulations 2000, reg.3(1)(b) (see 2.31 above)).

2.62 Secondly, a membership organisation may not recover any provision in respect of the arrangements it makes to meet costs liabilities permitted by the Access to Justice Act 1999, s.30(1) and the Access to Justice (Membership Organisations) Regulations 2000, SI 2000/693, if any part of that sum 'exceeds the likely cost to that party of the premium of an insurance policy' which the organisation could otherwise take out in respect of those risks (CPR Rule 44.3B(1)(b) amplified at Costs PD, para.11.11, which refers in turn to para.11.10 (see 2.71 below)). (The requirements of the Access to Justice (Membership Organisation) Regulations 2000 are considered at 2.40 above.)

2.63 Thirdly, failure to comply with the duty to provide information about an additional liability means that a party may not recover the additional liability (CPR Rule 44.3B(1)(c)), save that the party is permitted to apply to the court for relief from this sanction (see 2.65ff below). (See 2.54–2.57 above where the provisions relevant to notification are set out.)

2.64 Fourthly, CPR Rule 44.3B(1)(d) provides that a party is not permitted to recover any percentage increase if he has failed to comply with an order for the disclosure in assessment proceedings of the reasons for setting the percentage increase at the level stated (CPR Rule 44.3B(1)(d)). It is possible to apply for relief from this sanction (see below).

Relief from sanction

2.65 The Costs Practice Direction provides at section 10 that a party in default may apply for relief from the sanctions imposed by CPR Rule 44.3B(1)(c) or (d) (i.e. where there have been failures either to provide information about additional liabilities or to make disclosure in the assessment proceedings).

2.66 The precise detail of the information to be provided is set out in the Practice Direction. Paragraph 10.1 necessitates an application being made as quickly as possible after the default has been realised to a costs judge or a district judge under CPR Part 23. Notice of any such application will need to be served on counsel if he is likely to be affected (para.10.2).

Factors to be taken into account in deciding whether a percentage uplift is reasonable

2.67 CPR Rule 44.5 is the general rule which sets out the factors to be taken into account in deciding the amount of costs. On the standard basis the key factor is whether the costs were 'proportionately and reasonably incurred' (CPR Rule 44.5(1)(a)(i)). Section 11 of the Costs Practice Direction states that whilst proportionality is applicable to base costs as one of the factors to be taken into account under CPR Rule 44.5, it is not applicable to additional liabilities (which includes the success fee) (see, for example, paras.11.5, 11.6 and 11.9).

2.68 When assessing the additional liability the court 'will have regard to the facts and circumstances as they reasonably appeared to the solicitor or barrister when the funding arrangement was entered into and at the time of any variation' (Costs PD, para.11.7). Again, this was an area of controversy at the time of consultation over the content of the Costs Practice Direction, since it was originally proposed that proportionality should be one of the factors in assessing the reasonableness of the success fee. The level of success fee can be seen as a pure issue of risk management, to which proportionality is irrelevant. Conceptually the success fee is derived from an assessment of risk, wholly independent of the value of the case or how much work will be involved. A straightforward claim for a modest sum which does not justify a great deal of time being spent on it may nonetheless be a high risk. For example, it may turn on the evidence of the only witness. The solicitor may have justifiable reservations about the quality of this evidence, and, having carried out his risk assessment, can strongly argue for a 100 per cent success fee. If proportionality were to be applied to the success fee there is a high probability that it would have to be cut down. This would be a blow to the whole concept of risk taking and assessment. Happily, the Costs Practice Direction does not apply proportionality to the additional liabilities, and para.11.9 expressly states that a success fee should not be reduced simply because the total amount of costs may appear disproportionate. In *Callery* v. *Gray* the Court of Appeal has stated that although it is appropriate for an insurance premium and success fee to be determined at the earliest possible stage in the case of a straightforward personal injury action where there is 'no special feature which raises apprehension', a success fee in excess of 20 per cent will not be justified (see para.104). The Court of Appeal made it clear that its decision on the appropriate limits of success fees was restricted to personal injury actions which have 'sufficient common characteristics to justify a standard approach to determining uplift'. The 20 per cent limit does not apply where an individual assessment of the risks of a particular case is required, for instance where the case does not fall within a generic class with which the solicitor is familiar.

2.69 Having made it clear that the court will have regard to the facts and circumstances as they appeared to the legal representative at the time at which the CFA was entered into, section 11 goes on to set out the factors which will be taken into account in determining whether the levels of additional liability are reasonable. In respect of the success fee, relevant factors include the risks of failure (para.11.8(1)(a)), the legal representative's liability for any disbursements (para.11.8(1)(b)) and the availability of other methods of funding (para.11.8(1)(c)).

2.70 It is important however not to overlook para.11.8(2), which states:

> The Court has then power, when considering whether a percentage increase is reasonable, to allow different percentages for different items of costs or for different periods during which costs were incurred.

This paragraph has led to uncertainty as to how it will be applied in practice and the extent to which the courts will be willing to disagree with the percentage uplifts assessed by legal representatives. An attempt to step into the shoes of the lawyer at the time at which a CFA was made is fraught with difficulties. Whatever test the courts finally choose to adopt, it is important that this does not bring in by the back door a test which suggests that the level of the percentage uplift is in some sense disproportionate to the costs overall. Further, it is difficult to see how the courts can legitimately use this section to readjust a percentage uplift just because the course of the litigation has resulted in a set of factual circumstances which, if known to the lawyer at the time of the CFA, would have resulted in a different assessment of risk. The courts will not increase the levels of success fee, so why should they adjust them down? One of the attractions of CFAs in the minds of some commentators was that lawyers would have to share the risk. This means that lawyers must be able to take the advantage of those cases where a high measure of risk in one case turned out to be to the advantage of the lawyer. Although some cases will turn out to be easier to bring to a successful conclusion, others will turn out to be certain losers. If the courts were to reduce the percentage uplifts in some cases, with the result that the percentage uplift can be reduced but never increased, this would mean that the lawyers will not properly be able to share the risks overall. Fewer lawyers will be able to take on CFA work and the market-place will become restricted.

Factors to be taken into account in deciding whether the cost of insurance is reasonable

2.71 Factors to be taken into account for the purposes of CPR Rule 44.5 when determining whether the cost of an insurance premium is reasonable, include the cost when compared with the likely cost of a CFA with success fee and supporting insurance policy (Costs PD, para.11.10(1)), the level and extent of the cover provided (para.11.10(2)), the availability of pre-existing insurance cover (para.11.10(3)), whether there would be a rebate on any part of the premium in the event of an early settlement (para.11.10(4)), and the extent to which commission is payable to the receiving party, his lawyers or agents (para.11.10(5)). Thus it is possible that a claimant who has taken proceedings under a CFA will not be able to recover some or all of his insurance premium if, for instance, he ignored a pre-existing insurance policy. The additional amount is, in theory, recoverable from the client. Also note that the fact that the amount of commission payable to solicitors is to be taken into account raises the contentious question whether excessive amounts of commission might be disallowed as against the other side. At the time of writing the Court of Appeal in *Callery* v. *Gray* [2001] EWCA Civ 1117 has yet to give its judgment on the recoverability of insurance premiums.

Disallowed fees

2.72 CPR Rule 44.16 covers the situation where the court has disallowed part of the success fee, but the legal representative applies for an order that the disallowed amount should continue to be payable by the client. The court is given power to adjourn the proceedings to allow the client to be notified. (The CFA Regulations 2000, reg.3(2)(b) requires a CFA which provides for a success fee to state that any part of the percentage uplift which has been disallowed on assessment should cease to be payable unless the court considers otherwise (see 2.33 above)).

2.73 Section 20 of the Costs Practice Direction deals with the detailed procedure where a practitioner wishes to recover from the client a success fee percentage disallowed on assessment. In the case of a summary assessment, the court must give directions to enable the legal representative to apply for the disallowed percentage to be payable by the client (para.20.3(1)), although in some circumstances the court has power to determine the matter then and there (para.20.3(2)).

2.74 In the case of detailed assessment proceedings, various procedural steps are set out according to a strict timetable, which should be noted throughout. The receiving solicitor is required to notify counsel if counsel is affected (para.20.4(1)), and he must respond within 10 days or be deemed to have accepted the reduction (para.20.4(2),(3)). The receiving solicitors must also notify the client and provide a written explanation of the points of dispute within 14 days of service (para.20.5). If he intends to make an application that the client must continue to pay an amount of the percentage uplift which has been disallowed, then the receiving party's solicitor must file a certificate stating the amount of the percentage increase in dispute (para.20.6(1)), whether an application will be made that the disputed amount should continue to be paid by the client (para.20.6(2)), that a written explanation to the client has been provided (para.20.6(3)) and whether the client wishes to attend the hearing (para.20.6(4)). The client and counsel (as appropriate) must be notified of the date of the hearing (para.20.7(1)), counsel being permitted to make written or oral submissions (para.20.7(2)). As with a summary assessment, the court has power in certain circumstances to determine whether a disallowed amount can be payable without an adjournment (para.20.8(2)).

Costs-only proceedings

2.75   CPR Rule 44.12A makes provision for a new procedure for costs to be assessed where the parties have settled the substantive dispute without proceedings but are unable to agree costs. The claim is to be brought under CPR Part 8, but the court must dismiss the claim if it is opposed, and can effectively only act as arbiter if both sides agree. This means that a lawyer will need to secure the opponent's consent to this procedure before concluding the settlement of the substantive claim.

2.76   Section 17 of the Costs Practice Direction sets out the details of the costs-only procedure under CPR Rule 44.12A. Under CPR Rule 44.12A(4), the court can only deal with a costs-only claim if the parties agree. A claim will be treated as opposed if the defendant indicates in the acknowledgement of service to the CPR Part 8 proceedings that he intends to contest it, and if this is the case, the court has no discretion and must automatically dismiss the claim (Costs PD, para.17.9 and CPR Rule 44.12A(4)(b)). If an additional liability is claimed where no substantive proceedings have been issued the court is to have regard to the circumstances of settlement as to whether it is appropriate, for example, the stage at which settlement was reached and at what level (Costs PD, para.17.8(2)). An insurance premium can be recovered in costs-only proceedings (*Callery* v. *Gray* [2001] EWCA Civ 1117).

THE LAW SOCIETY POSITION

2.77 The history of the Law Society's response to the validity of contingency fees is set out in Chapter 1. Rule 8 of the Solicitors' Practice Rules has been the main focus of the Law Society's response to such arrangements, and permits a solicitor to undertake any CFA which is lawful under the statutory framework of the Courts and Legal Services Act 1990, whether under the scheme valid prior to the Access to Justice Act 1999 or afterwards.

2.78 There is to be no additional Practice Rule to govern the working of conditional fees. However, practitioners should not interpret this as a free-for-all. In addition to the rules and regulations set out earlier in this chapter, many of the Law Society's rules and regulations will have a bearing on conditional fees. Practitioners should be careful to take these into account at every stage of a CFA in the same way as they would with any other type of work. In particular, Rules 1 and 15 of the Practice Rules contain material which is relevant to CFAs, whilst *The Guide to the Professional Conduct of Solicitors 1999* (published by the Law Society) also contains relevant guidelines which may be of relevance (see 2.99 below).

SOLICITORS' PRACTICE RULES, RULE 1

2.79 Practice Rule 1 sums up the basic principles of conduct governing the way solicitors behave toward their clients, requiring a solicitor (a) to act in his client's best interest and (b) to do nothing to bring himself or his profession into disrepute.

2.80 These two provisions can be read together. The 'best interests' provision should be kept in mind when considering the detail of the CFA, even if the Law Society model agreement is being used, and the arrangement as a whole. The individual agreement clauses may seem fair, but when they are taken in combination, they must still be in the client's best interests. The Law Society's model agreement takes into account the provisions of the Unfair Terms in Consumer Contracts Regulations 1994, SI 1994/3159 (implementing Council Directive 93/13/EEC). Any solicitor drafting his own agreement will need to make sure it complies with these terms.

2.81 One obvious danger area where a solicitor must be careful to act in his client's best interests is in the calculation of the success fee. Notwithstanding the change in that the success fee is now payable by the opponent rather than the client there may still be a problem if a solicitor's insistence on claiming a high success fee in an inappropriate case leads to difficulties in settling. The problem is also likely to arise where a solicitor decides to employ the CPR rule 44.16 procedure to claim a shortfall in success fee from the client, it having been disallowed against the other side. There is a clear conflict of interests in this situation, and the sum of money involved may be substantial. It is questionable whether a client should be properly advised to take independent advice in such a scenario.

2.82 Other danger areas where accusations of unfairness could apply include allegations of under-settling, whereby it is said that a legal representative encourages a settlement at an undervalue in order to secure the payment of his costs. This is a fear which has been widely expressed by opponents of conditional fees, but there is no evidence of this as an area of abuse (see 1.41–1.42 above).

2.83 Further, a solicitor must preserve his independence and integrity since conditional fees do give solicitors a financial stake in the outcome of the case. They must ensure that this is not allowed to skew their judgement or influence their handling of proceedings.

2.84 Clients must be free to instruct the solicitor of their choice. This general principle holds good with conditional fees as it does with other types of case. However, it is likely that only firms who are members of various insurers' panels will be able to handle cases which those insurers cover. This does not constitute a breach of Rule 1 of the Practice Rules. Various forms of after-the-event and other policies will be offered by a variety of insurers, and a broad spread of firms is likely to be covered overall. In any event the right is not absolute, and is likely to be judged on its overall context.

2.85 A solicitor must not compromise his duty to the court. With a conditional fee arrangement, where the solicitor has a financial interest in the result, the temptation to mislead the court in order to improve the case may be greater than with traditional fee arrangements. It must, however, be strongly resisted. Any breach of this requirement would have serious implications for the solicitor.

2.86 The duty of the solicitor to notify the court of the existence of the CFA only exists where he is claiming an additional liability. The relevant rules and are set out in CPR Rule Part 44.15 and section 19 of the Costs Practice Direction (see 2.54 above).

SOLICITORS' PRACTICE RULES, RULE 15: SOLICITORS' COSTS INFORMATION AND CLIENT CARE CODE 1999

2.87   The Solicitors' Costs Information and Client Care Code 1999 made under Practice Rule 15 ('the 1999 Code') sets out the Law Society's written professional standards on costs information for clients. The current rule was introduced on 3 September 1999 and states that solicitors shall give information about costs and other matters and operate a complaints handling procedure in accordance with the requirements laid down by the Law Society. A breach could lead to a fine of up to £1,000, and the costs in the particular case being disallowed.

2.88   When a solicitor operates under a CFA, all the usual costs and client care provisions apply, plus the additional requirements as set out in the relevant regulations and Civil Procedure Rules. The 1999 Code applies specifically to CFAs. Many of the provisions in the 1999 Code are very similar to the statutory requirements for CFAs. However, a solicitor should ensure that he complies with both. Whether use is made of the Law Society model agreement or an individualised agreement is developed, the information to be given to the client is governed by Practice Rule 15 and the 1999 Code.

2.89   The requirements under Practice Rule 15 are divided broadly into (a) the information to be given at the outset of a matter and (b) updating that information. In both instances the information to be given should not be inaccurate or misleading. It should be confirmed in writing as soon as possible. Thus the duty under Practice Rule 15 appears to go beyond that which is required in respect of most of the information required by the CFA Regulations 2000, reg.4(2).

Information at the outset

2.90   The information required by the 1999 Code should be set out in a client care letter. This should give a clear explanation of the issues in the case. This explanation is likely to be very similar to the matters which the solicitor will set out in the risk assessment in a CFA. The name and status of the person with day-to-day care of the case, and of the person with overall responsibility, must be set out. The name of a contact will also need to be given in case of any problems. The solicitors' practice should have a written complaints procedure which must be made available to the client on request.

2.91   The information required in respect of costs must also be set out. Practitioners are under a duty to give the client the best possible information about likely overall costs, including a breakdown as to fees, VAT and disbursements. Even though the client may have been told that the solicitor is acting on a 'no win no fee' basis, he will still need to be presented with a cost estimate. Whilst on the face of it the client has no responsibility to pay the solicitor's costs if the client loses, the solicitor may well seek to recover disbursements and basic fees not recovered from the losing party. The solicitor needs to ensure that the client is fully informed as to the likely level of this potential liability.

2.92 If the solicitor is operating on a 'no win reduced fee' basis, the client must be informed of the likely level of fees at this reduced rate. If the client wins, his costs will normally be met by the other side. However, the solicitor must explain that the amount recovered inter partes from the losing side may not be enough to cover these in full. For example, the basic charging rate to the client in the CFA may be higher than can be recovered inter partes. The solicitor will probably seek to recover the shortfall from the client's damages. Again, there may be a shortfall if part of the work done for the client, or some of the disbursements incurred are held to have been unreasonable. This potential liability must be made clear to the client. Alternatively, if part of the success fee is disallowed against the other party, there is the possibility that the legal representative may apply for an order under CPR Rule 44.16 to enable recovery against the client. If the client is paying for disbursements as they go along, the solicitor will need to make clear the times when such payments will be due.

2.93 The costs breakdown must be based on realistic estimates or ranges of figures. A client can ask that an upper limit of costs is set which should not be exceeded without agreement. If the estimate is not fixed, this should be made clear. The basis upon which charges are calculated needs to be explained, and if on the basis of an hourly rate, this should be made clear. This costs estimate will also prove useful for the firm, as it will enable the solicitor to take a view as to the commitment being entered into by the practice, and what will be forgone in the event that the case is unsuccessful. The solicitor should also state the reasons for setting the percentage uplift of the success fee. As indicated above, the solicitor will have to indicate the issues in the case in any event, and showing the success fee calculation is really only an extension of this.

2.94 Under the 1999 Code the solicitor is also under a duty to explore and explain other funding options such as Community Legal Service Funding, insurance or trade union funding. The duties in this respect are similar to those in the CFA Regulations 2000, reg.4(2)(d),(e), save that under the Regulations all the information needs to be confirmed in writing. The solicitor must consider whether the client's liability for his own costs could be met by insurance. This would include considering legal expenses, motor, household and other standard types of cover. Similarly, the solicitor must consider whether an existing insurance policy would cover the potential liability for opponents' costs. Further, the solicitor should consider whether an after-the-event insurance policy is appropriate if it is intended to act under a CFA. As discussed in Chapter 5 (see note 20 to the model agreement), the solicitor is not expected to act as broker when advising on these insurance products, but he should be able to give general advice on the type of products available. If insurance cover is available, whether pre-existing or after the event, the solicitor should explain the options even if the firm is unable to provide that cover. It is clearly in the client's best interest to know that he may be able to protect himself from the risk of having to pay the other side's costs, albeit by using another solicitor.

2.95 The solicitor will need to go through the client's potential eligibility for public funding of his case. However, in the context of personal injury matters, legal aid was to all intents and purposes removed as of 1 April 2000, which should be explained. The availability of funding from the Legal Services Commission in other types of case should be investigated and the outcome relayed to the client.

2.96 The solicitor is required to engage in a cost-benefit and risk analysis of the client's case, including the possibility of having to bear the opponent's costs. If it is proposed to use a CFA without the benefit of after-the-event insurance the solicitor must give a strong, unequivocal warning about the client's liability to bear the other side's costs if the case is lost. This is particularly important where CFAs are talked of loosely as 'no win no fee' arrangements. The onus is on the individual lawyer to be sure that his client fully understands that although his own firm's fees will be waived, he may still be lumbered with a huge bill from the other side. The ability of the opponent to meet the client's bill if the client is unsuccessful also needs to be considered.

2.97 A solicitor must bring to the client's attention the costs implications of terminating the agreement. This is an area which is full of potential conflict. Although the conditions of the model agreement set out these consequences, it is probably not enough merely to ask the client to read those conditions. Further detailed exposition is needed if the duties to explain costs under the 1999 Code are to be met. No client, however unreasonable, should ever suddenly find himself having to meet an unexpectedly huge bill on termination of the agreement.

Updating the information

2.98 A solicitor should provide his client with regular updates as to progress, costs and other issues at regular intervals, and at not less than six-monthly intervals. The cost-benefit and risk analysis should be updated and any changes communicated to the client. You should inform the client if any previous cost estimates are likely to be exceeded.

THE GUIDE TO THE PROFESSIONAL CONDUCT OF SOLICITORS 1999: GUIDING PRINCIPLES

2.99 A number of the Law Society's guiding principles as set out in *The Guide to the Professional Conduct of Solicitors 1999* are relevant to CFAs.

Principle 11.01 impartial advice

2.100 A solicitor must give the client 'frank and impartial' advice. In the context of conditional fees, a solicitor must not allow his judgement to be influenced by his financial interest in a case.

Principle 12.09 unfair advantage

2.101 A solicitor should not abuse the relationship with the client by taking advantage of the client's age, inexperience, ill-health, want of education or business experience or emotional or other vulnerability. This may well be relevant in the context of personal injury matters where clients have suffered an injury and many of them may be in poor health. Further, CFAs are a complex addition to the lawyer's armoury. They are frequently presented simplistically in the media as 'no win no fee' arrangements. Many clients, including those who are reasonably experienced and educated, may struggle to grasp the implications of the deal unless they have had a full and careful explanation from their solicitor. Solicitors should not assume that an otherwise sophisticated client needs only a perfunctory outline.

Principle 5.01 availability of public funding

2.102 Whilst the scope of public funding is much reduced, particularly with regard to personal injury matters, the solicitor remains under a duty to consider the possibility where appropriate. Even if it is available, a client may still prefer to enter into a CFA, but the decision needs careful consideration. This duty is effectively duplicated by the CFA Regulations 2000, reg.4(2)(d) and by Practice Rule 15 (above).

Principle 14.12 overcharging

2.103 A solicitor must not take advantage of a client by overcharging for work done. CFAs are necessarily speculative ventures. Sometimes all the risks and issues in a case cannot be anticipated. Whilst the client has a measure of statutory protection from a solicitor who charges an excessive success fee which cannot be recovered from the other side, there might still be an issue if the rate charged for basic charges cannot be sustained against the losing party and the solicitor seeks to recover the shortfall. The client has the potential protection of assessment.

Principle 15.04 conflicts of interest

2.104 A solicitor must not act where his interests conflict with the interests of a client. One of the major areas of concern among commentators is the danger of a conflict of interest between the solicitor and his client. Potentially, the solicitor's interests under a CFA may be in almost constant conflict with those of the client. In theory it may be in a solicitor's interests to under-settle a case so that the solicitor is guaranteed his fee. Alternatively, it may suit him to drag out the case so that the costs (including the success fee) are increased. In essence, the potential for conflict is always present. Whilst Principle 15.05 has been understood not to be interpreted to include costs in the context of conventional costs, with CFAs the amount a solicitor is paid is directly related to what happens in the case. To avoid any risk of breaching this principle the solicitor should follow the same rule of thumb throughout a CFA: put the client's interests first.

SOLICITORS' PUBLICITY CODE 1990

2.105 Whilst an in-depth analysis of the 1990 Code is outside the scope of this chapter, the solicitor should beware of offending against it in any publicity material which the firm employs. In particular, the solicitor should beware of anything that gives misleading price indications, particularly relevant when the public perception of what have become known as 'no win no fee' agreements may be somewhat simplistic.

The indemnity principle

2.106 Whilst the power to remove or abrogate the indemnity principle is contained in s.31 of the 1999 Act, at the time of writing it is still with us. Whilst there are proposals expressly to abrogate it in respect of collective CFAs, the extent of such abrogation and its possible application to other CFAs is not yet clear. It can only therefore be re-emphasised that care must be taken by a solicitor not to breach the principle, particularly when agreeing terms which appear attractive to the client who is expecting a 'no win no fee' arrangement.

CHAPTER 3

Running a litigation practice on conditional fees

Fiona Bawdon and Mike Napier

INTRODUCTION

3.1 To date, there are no reports of firms which have operated conditional fees getting into difficulties financially. However, all firms need to be cautious. Even firms whose personal injury departments have found conditional fee work profitable should not assume that this success will automatically transfer to all other areas of work. Not all types of litigation have such a high success rate as personal injury; and firms should tread especially carefully in areas where they do not already have considerable expertise and experience together with a strong record of winning.

3.2 Effective risk management is the key to making conditional fees work. To do this, a firm will need to develop clear internal protocols to be followed by all litigators. Some elements of risk management will be standard across all litigation departments, but individual areas of law will also need their own special considerations and safeguards.

3.3 Practitioners will also need to be familiar with the law and practice governing the operation of conditional fees: the statutory framework, regulations, rules and Practice Directions (see Chapter 2).

ASSESSING AND MANAGING RISK

How much risk are you prepared (and financially able) to bear?

3.4 Solicitors will need to have a clear picture of the approach that is right for their particular firm. It will be easier to assess the strengths and weaknesses of a new case if a firm has already developed a policy about how much risk it is willing to bear in each 'key area' (see 3.7ff below). It may not be necessary to develop hard and fast rules, but a broad framework against which potential cases can be measured will be useful. It must be remembered that the general principles of insurance law can be said to apply to risk management where CFA work is undertaken. This means that solicitors will need to be able to spread the risk within different classes of cases where possible. Moreover, as the Court of Appeal pointed out in *Callery* v. *Gray* [2001] EWCA Civ 1117, detailed individual assessments of the peculiar features of cases will not be so important in straightforward matters where a solicitor knows from experience that the only real likelihood of failure will be as a result of some unforeseen circumstance (see para.84). This chapter (and Chapter 4) must be read in the light of that observation.

Who is responsible for your internal risk management procedures?

3.5   It is unlikely that a partnership will want to give a free hand to every fee earner to decide for himself which cases to take on under a CFA. It may be prudent to consider appointing one or more partners in each relevant field of law with overall risk management responsibility to whom all potential CFAs are referred for approval. Cases which look particularly difficult or are over a certain size may need to be referred upwards to the firm's managing partner or the managing board. The aim should be to ensure that the criteria for assessing the critical areas listed below are applied consistently throughout the firm and regularly reviewed.

3.6   It is important to remember that one firm's minor case will be a major commitment for another. Where a firm decides to draw the line, whether as a general policy, or on a case by case basis, needs to be decided long before a commitment is made to a particular CFA.

THE KEY AREAS

Identifying core issues

3.7   Successful risk management is almost entirely dependent on identifying at the outset, so far as possible, the core issues which will determine the outcome of the case: facts, evidence, law (see screening at 4.4ff below).

The length of time before getting paid

3.8   Consideration must be given to the consequences of delay in payment. What delay can a particular firm tolerate before being paid? Are there some types of case which will take longer to conclude than the firm is prepared to fund? Would this rule out those cases which are likely to last two, three or four years? The length of litigation is notoriously difficult to predict, but lawyers will need to err on the side of pessimism in their predictions. If the case reaches an early conclusion it will be a nice surprise, but if it takes as long as was feared, then at least the firm will have been prepared.

Complexity

3.9 There must be some examination of the complexity of cases. Are some types of case inherently too risky for CFAs? In personal injury, for example, a practice must decide whether to restrict itself to doing, say, road accident cases until it has developed the confidence in its procedures to tackle, for instance, asbestos litigation. In contract disputes, should a firm restrict itself to cases involving defective goods rather than professional negligence? If a case falls into the broad category which a firm is prepared to consider for CFAs, then as thorough an assessment of liability as possible needs to be undertaken on the evidence available. Experienced litigators often have an instinctive gut reaction as to whether a case is a good one or not, based on what they see as its nub. With conditional fees, those gut feelings will need to be tested against the essential criteria: what is the central point of the case? Is the evidence on the client's side?

Contributory negligence

3.10 Even if a firm is prepared to take on a case because liability seems likely to be determined in the client's favour, the value of the case will be reduced if the claimant is found partly to blame. If there is a risk of contributory negligence, this needs to be taken into account in the overall assessment of the case.

Counterclaim

3.11 As with contributory negligence, however good the nub of the client's case, the picture can be dramatically changed if the defendant mounts a successful counterclaim, a frequent factor in commercial litigation. Where a counterclaim is a possibility, then the likelihood of this happening and the impact on the calculations of success needs to be considered very carefully.

More than one defendant

3.12   Cases with more than one defendant are inherently riskier because there is more that can go wrong and they are more expensive to run. They are harder to predict because of the possibility of winning against one and losing against another. After-the-event insurers are particularly wary of multiple defendant cases, as are barristers.

Split trials

3.13   Trying liability first may be a great money-saver if the case loses at the first hurdle, and a great boost to the continuing prospects and conduct of the case if it succeeds. It is important to remember that if a client wins at a split trial, the success fee does not have to change to cover the rest of the case. It is based on the original risk assessment, as recorded in the CFA. Where it is possible or essential to try a preliminary issue, or to try liability ahead of damages (especially where considerable work on quantum may be required), a sensible policy is to think of staging a case to minimise the amount of unpaid work.

Causation

3.14   If an assessment of the evidence and of the law demonstrates that there is likely to be a good cause of action, then it will be necessary to make sure that causation can be established. There will be categories of case where causation is likely to be a particular problem, for example in many clinical negligence cases where the cause of an injury is difficult to determine, or in cases of professional negligence case where liability is clear, but there are arguments about whether the negligence caused the particular loss.

Difficulties on limitation

3.15   It is important to beware of limitation periods. It will be necessary to ask whether there is enough time in which to assess a case sufficiently before being forced to issue proceedings. It will be particularly important to be wary of taking on CFA cases which are coming up to their limitation period, especially if they are referred or taken over from other solicitors where there is a lot of sorting-out to do. Care must be taken not to run out of time before it is possible to make an adequate assessment of the critical areas, being forced to issue and serve proceedings before the assessment process is really complete. As all litigators know, this is a weak position for a claimant, who should be taking the initiative from the start. A lawyer should not be panicked or over-eager to take on cases that look superficially attractive but which on closer examination turn out to be potential nightmares.

Impact of pre-action protocols

3.16   The CPR introduced pre-action protocols, at the date of writing, in the areas of personal injury, clinical negligence, defamation and construction and engineering disputes. The protocols are intended to promote openness and settlement. When risk assessing a CFA case, particularly the factors relating to the likely success fee, it is important to remember that, in theory at least, if it is a case where a pre-action protocol applies, settlement may be more likely and more speedy. In *Callery* v. *Gray* [2001] EWCA Civ 1117 the Court of Appeal relied on figures which showed that 90 per cent of personal injury cases can be expected to settle during the protocol period (para.89). It is also important to bear in mind that some after-the-event insurers stipulate that firms must adhere to the terms of the appropriate protocol.

Availability of counsel willing to work on CFA basis

3.17   Since all contentious cases may go to court, which probably means the involvement of a barrister, it is important for a solicitor to know at the outset that he or she can, if necessary, find a suitable advocate to handle the firm's cases on a CFA basis. It will be prudent to develop relationships of mutual trust and confidence with counsel, whether individually or as groups or as sets of chambers, who are committed to making conditional fees work. It will also be necessary to bear in mind that there are differences between the CFA with counsel and that made with the client. It is worth knowing something of how barristers approach CFAs, and Chapter 6 read in conjunction with Appendices 21a to 21h will provide a useful starting-point.

Likelihood of interim payment

3.18   Where clients have no other means of funding disbursements, cases which are likely to have an interim payment will ease pressure on a firm's cash flow.

Likelihood of Part 36 payment or offer to settle

3.19 Similar considerations apply in respect of settlement as they do to pre-action protocols (see 3.16 above). Offers to settle under CPR Part 36 can, and should, be used tactically by the claimant's solicitor to bring the case to a speedy conclusion.

Financial equation

3.20 It may be preferred to set a threshold of likely damages, however arbitrary, below which a firm will not normally take CFA cases.

Funding insurance premiums

3.21 Who will pay the cost of the client's AEI insurance premium? Now that AEI premiums are recoverable from the losing party, this becomes an issue of cash flow rather than of outright expenditure. This means that the recoverability of the insurance premium may open the way for more firms to meet the cost. Firms should be wary of over-extending themselves. An alternative may be one of the increasing number of AEI products which are now linked to disbursement funding schemes which include the insurance premium. Other AEI products are available where the premium is payable only if the case wins. However, it is important to bear in mind that the losing opponent may challenge the cost of the AEI premium. It will be necessary for firms to keep an eye on the premium levels being allowed by the courts in order to avoid having to pay all, or some, of the cost. A record should be kept of why a particular product was chosen.

Formula for calculating the success fee

3.22 It would be meaningless for the authors to try to give even a broad indication of what level of success fee is likely to be appropriate for particular types of cases. In Chapter 4, we set out the components that need to be taken into account to calculate the right success fee for a case (see 4.19ff below). However, you may need to tread carefully as the losing party (who will have to pay the success fee) will be able to challenge the amount if they believe it to be unreasonable. It will be essential to keep records of how a success fee was reached in case of a challenge by the opposition.

Protecting yourself from the worst

3.23   Should a limit be imposed on the number, or size, of CFA cases that can be run at any one time, either within individual departments or across the entire firm, in order to limit the financial knock which a firm could take if the worst happened? It is important for individual firms to reach a decision as to the maximum potential exposure to lost fees, wasted working hours, and unrecovered disbursements which can be risked in the event that a string of CFAs are lost the same financial year.

CFA terms

3.24   Model agreements are available covering different types of cases, but practitioners may wish routinely to vary certain clauses in order to reflect the firm's policy on matters such as interim payments, appeals, and CPR Part 36 payments and offers.

Proportionality and fast-track cases

3.25   The CPR introduced the concept of proportionality to the civil litigation process. Proportionality means maintaining a balance between damages and costs. This is at its most potent in fast-track cases (those worth under £15,000). There are already fixed costs for trial in the fast track. It remains to be seen whether fixed costs will be imposed for preparation work, but the judges are moving towards fixed costs where possible. This creates a problem in the fast track where margins are low, creating a delicate financial equation on the conclusion of the case. Damages for the client must be balanced against costs (including the success fee, insurance premium and disbursements) which are recovered from the losing party. In low margin fast-track cases, it is important to take care that the damages and costs which are recoverable are worth it for the amount of work involved.

Proportionality and the multi-track

3.26   Multi-track cases (worth more than £15,000) poses different dilemmas from the fast track (see above). The fast track is more rigid, but has more certainty over costs. The multi-track relies on judges to manage cases and adopt a flexible attitude, depending on the needs of the case. With flexibility, however, comes unpredictability. The level of discretion available to judges makes it difficult for a firm to assess the financial equation at the outset of a case. Calculations should take into account the judge's discretion in determining the costs at the end of the case, whether by summary or detailed assessment.

Timing of entering CFA

3.27   When is it appropriate to enter into a CFA? The optimum timing for signing the agreement will vary from firm to firm and from case to case, while the policy conditions of the AEI insurer may be critical (see Chapter 7). Some AEI insurers (for example Accident Line Protect) insist on cover being taken out at an early stage as recommended in the Protocols Practice Direction because of concerns over adverse selection (see Chapter 7). In *Callery* v. *Gray* the Court of Appeal has approved the practice, in the bulk of personal injury cases where there are no special risk factors, of entering into a CFA as soon as the client gives instructions to the solicitor. This is to allow the solicitor and the under-writers of after-the-event insurance policies effectively to spread the risks between clients (see section 10). The position may be otherwise in those cases (such as commercial actions) where a more considered view of the individual risks is necessary.

Summary

3.28   The key areas listed above should form a broad template against which individual cases can be measured as they come in. In the next chapter, we look at case-specific criteria and the detailed risk assessment process. These processes will rule a case in or out of a firm's CFA workload, and, if it is ruled in, on what terms. Some firms may well be content to proceed with minimal risk assessment or screening, signing up clients at first interview wherever possible. Others will prefer to investigate rout-inely before committing themselves to CFAs. In some cases, legal support may be available from the Community Legal Service under the provisions in the Funding Code for Investigative and Litigation Support (see Appendix 25).

OTHER FACTORS TO CONSIDER WHEN RUNNING A CFA PRACTICE

Pre-CFA funding arrangement

3.29   Even with the most efficient risk assessment processes it will not always be possible to tell at the outset of a case whether it is safe to proceed on a conditional fee basis. In this situation, rather than turning away the client altogether, or risking taking on an unsuitable case on CFA, it may make sense to agree an alternative form of funding until more is known about the case.

3.30　Alternative funding options include charging on a conventional hourly rate plus disbursements, charging for disbursements only, or charging an up-front fixed fee (set according to the type of case). If the client is charged on an hourly rate, this may be billed either at the time of entering into the CFA, or at the end (win or lose). It is uncertain to what extent it is lawful to be open with the client and to follow an express oral intimation that the case will be run on a 'no win, no fee' basis, with a written CFA once the risks have been properly assessed. Some commentators consider this a breach of the rule against past consideration, since the initial investigative work will have been carried out under an unenforceable *Thai Trading*-style agreement. On the other hand, comments in *Callery* v. *Gray* [2001] EWCA Civ 1117 suggest that this is a legitimate approach.

In-house investigators

3.31　With CFA cases there is a greater need than ever to have all the available evidence to hand as early as possible and promote good risk assessment. Bigger firms which specialise in a particular area of work may want to take on experienced non-lawyer staff to weed out weak cases and to gather evidence on those which may be suitable candidates for a CFA.

Expert witnesses

3.32　In cases where the issues turn on expert evidence, it will be necessary to be cautious about entering into a CFA until a report has been obtained from the expert.

Documentary evidence

3.33　Many types of litigation turn on the documents, so that it will be necessary to locate and obtain vital documents as fast as possible.

Involving counsel

3.34　As has been said, it is important to have a strong relationship with individual barristers, groups of barristers or sets of chambers willing to do

CFA work (see 3.17 above). It may be more satisfactory to seek to screen complicated cases at an early stage on a team basis with counsel you wish to instruct. This will give you input from another experienced practitioner, and you will know from the outset that the barrister is willing to take on the case on a CFA basis.

FINANCIAL MANAGEMENT ISSUES

3.35 Conditional fees reflect a sea-change of approach towards funding litigation. The trend in recent years in publicly funded cases was towards greater payment on account. This followed understandable howls of protest to the Legal Aid Board about firms' cash flow difficulties. However, now that CFAs are expected to replace state funding in all monetary claims, this trend will be thrown into reverse. As well as having to cope without payments on account, firms may also have to meet start-up costs, disbursements and insurance premiums, as well as assuming the risk of not being paid at all at the conclusion of cases.

3.36 Whether or not an individual firm can risk embarking on this kind of work on a widespread basis will depend on the firm's current banking position. The partners need to have a detailed knowledge of patterns in the firms cash-flow. Embarking on CFA work is an investment in the firm's future, so that the overall policy in this area of speculative funding needs to have the backing of all the partners whose money is at risk.

3.37 It is also important to have a clear understanding with the firm's bankers in order to assess the extent to which the firm is financially stable enough to offer conditional fees, if at all. If it is, one way of minimising the risk might be to set up a dedicated fund to cushion the impact of lost cases, paying a set proportion of all success fees in winning cases into such a fund.

How to fund disbursements

3.38 There are many options, depending on the resources of the client, the attitude and resources of the firm, and the type of case. For example, the client may be able to pay these as he goes along (see model agreement), or the firm may pay, either from its own reserves or by borrowing from the bank. The regulations do not permit a lawyer to increase the success fee as compensation for the cost of commercial borrowing.

3.39 Given the withdrawal of legal aid for mainstream personal injury work, and the upsurge in the numbers of cases being funded by CFAs and the profile of the clients involved, there is likely to be a greater role for disbursement funding schemes. There are an increasing number of such schemes around where the disbursement loan only has to be paid if the case is won. That is to say that if the case loses, the client does not have to pay anything; if he wins, the cost is met by the losing party. The winning client will, however, remain liable for the interest on the loan. (See also 7.43ff below.)

How to fund after-the-event insurance

3.40   In theory at least there are many options available. Firms may want to have a policy of paying the premium either in a selection of cases, in all cases, or not at all. Since the AEI premium is now recoverable, the cost of the insurance will ultimately be recovered by whoever paid it if the case wins (although the level of premium paid is of course open to challenge by the other side (see 2.71 above)). Some firms may opt to self-insure in some or all cases. However, self-insurance may be less attractive now that the cost of the AEI premium can be recovered. Although s.30 of the 1999 Act enables prescribed bodies like trade unions to recover a notional premium for self-insurance, it is not clear if this facility will be an option for law firms who self-insure their clients (see 2.41 above).

3.41   If a practice is not paying the premium or otherwise providing cover, the client has various options. These range from going ahead uninsured, paying the cost of the AEI premium himself, or taking out an AEI policy where the premium is payable only if he wins (see Chapter 7). The latter option is likely to increase in popularity as the withdrawal of legal aid prompts more insurers to offer products where the premium is written off if the case loses.

Terms of business with expert witnesses

3.42   It is not permissible to retain experts (or any other member of the litigation support team) on a 'no win no fee' basis. This practice is prohibited by the rules of professional conduct. Principle 21.11 of *The Guide to the Professional Conduct of Solicitors 1999* says: 'A solicitor must not make or offer to make payments to a witness contingent upon the nature of the evidence given or upon the outcome of a case'.

Research by Bond Solon, a company which specialises in training expert witnesses for court, suggests that in fact the practice is not uncommon. What is legitimate is an agreement whereby the expert will defer his fee until the end of the case. Likewise it is permissible for the expert to decide to waive his fee if the case is lost. Provided there is no antecedent agreement that the expert will not charge if the case loses, this does not breach the professional conduct rules.

3.43   It may be that a firm is prepared to meet experts' costs in some circumstances for some types of case. If so, how much up-front funding will the firm be prepared to make, say, over the course of a year? The cost of funding expert witnesses can be substantial burden, with an accountant's report in a big personal injury case costing as much as £5,000. Does a firm's terms of business with accountants and other experts require them to wait for payment until the case is over? A firm needs to decide whether it will rule out cases where the cost of experts is likely to exceed a set amount if the firm has to fund these itself.

Track records

3.44   Closed files of cases previously handled on a non-CFA basis will be a source of invaluable information if CFAs are to be made to work for a firm. Before embarking on conditional fees at all, or in a new area of work, it is strongly advisable to study a representative sample of closed files over the past two or three years. This should make it possible to work out the firm's success rate for particular types of work and the average ratio of compensation awarded to fees in different types of case. (It is important to bear in mind that the costs incurred in a case that loses at trial will generally be higher than the fees which are received on a case which settles.) With the benefit of hindsight, what level of success fee would have been needed to run these cases profitably on a 'no win no fee' basis? Do fee earners have different success rates? Is there a referral source which sends cases which are particularly problematic or particularly successful? Is that source keen for the firm to accept these referrals on a CFA basis?

3.45   Although monitoring existing data will provide invaluable information, past experience with cases funded by other means may not necessarily translate directly across where cases are being funded on CFAs. Defendants, for instance, may be less likely to settle cases funded by CFAs than they are cases funded by legal aid. One AEI provider blames this more bullish attitude of defendants towards CFA cases for its higher-than-expected losses.

OFFICE SYSTEMS

3.46   Once a firm has settled its broad policy towards conditional fees, the information and the procedures for implementing the policy in individual cases must be disseminated to all the relevant fee earners. The appropriate method of doing this will depend largely on the size of the practice. Larger firms may develop a procedural manual and hold in-house lectures for fee earners and other staff. In smaller firms, it may be appropriate for this to be done more informally. Small firms may want to share knowledge, ideas and problems with other friendly firms and to get a second opinion on the merits of a case.

3.47 The manual should cover the firm's policy on the financial and risk-management issues mentioned above, and should include model forms, checklists, client care letters, insurance details and so on. Firms should also develop a computerised case management system to track the progress and costs exposure of CFA cases. This should detect whether the firm is becoming over-exposed financially (because, for instance, it has too many lengthy cases on the go at once, and is carrying too high a level of disbursements); whether success fees are being set appropriately (are anticipated prospects for success reflected in the results of completed cases?); or whether cases are stagnating. If a conditional fee case is lost, the reasons should be carefully examined immediately to see whether any lessons need to be learned in order to avoid a repetition. E-mail is a good forum for internal CFA news and shared experiences.

3.48 Firms may also want to develop an extensive library of non-legal, specialist textbooks in the key areas in which it plans to operate conditional fees. In the case of personal injury cases for instance, this might cover areas like health and safety, and medical and product liability. This will help staff make an initial assessment of cases in-house, without having to pay an external expert to evaluate the cases on the firm's behalf.

3.49 Firms will also need to monitor the progress and outcome of CFA cases continuously. This will ensure that fee earners are not tempted to put the interests of the firm above those of the client, and will provide an early warning if the firm's initial parameters need to be refined in any way.

3.50 Data on the outcome of cases should be fed back into the risk management process to see whether, with hindsight, the assessments were correct, and whether the firm's approach needs to be adjusted.

ATTITUDE OF THE OPPONENT

3.51 Over time, it may also be possible to build up statistics of the results of particular types of CFA cases which make it possible to gauge the reaction of firms which regularly appear for opposing parties, principally defence lawyers.

3.52   There is no reliable evidence to date, but some anecdotal material suggests that defendants are litigating more aggressively in response to CFAs. The leading AEI insurer Accident Line Protect said that one reason for its premium hike in November 1999 was lower than expected success rates caused by the more bullish approach of defence teams.

3.53   With CFAs, a case which was always going to be hard to litigate may be even harder. Defendants who are informed that the claimant's CFA is backed by AEI insurance may be inclined to fight where they would otherwise have settled. If the claimant has AEI insurance, the defendant knows that if he wins he will recover the costs from the AEI provider. The defendant will also know that, if he loses, he may have to pay up to double his opponent's usual costs (because of the success fee), and also the cost of the AEI premium.

3.54   If defendants do react to conditional fees by fighting more cases, this should be factored into the risk assessment process for the firm. For example, it may make CFAs less attractive than Community Legal Service funding with a contribution (where this continues to be available). If cases are being dragged out interminably, the firm may have to revise its guidelines for the cases it accepts to avoid any risk of succumbing to pressure to under-settle. Therefore a CFA case should never be accepted unless the firm is prepared to take it all the way if necessary. It can never be assumed that a case will settle.

3.55   A canny defendant might try to spin out an action in the hope of putting the claimant's firm under financial pressure. If a small firm which is already in financial difficulties has taken on a big CFA case, this could be a startlingly effective tactic. We have to accept that there are ostensible temptations posed by the conflict between, on the one hand, the option of speedy under-settling, and, on the other, jeopardising the firm's financial viability by standing firm in the face of delaying tactics from the other side (see 1.41ff above). This is another reason why only those with sound finances, good risk management and close case control should embark on CFAs. Under-settling that is shown to be due to solicitors putting their interest before that of the client is likely to be a matter of professional misconduct and to lead to a negligence claim.

3.56   An already unclear picture is likely to be muddied even further by the introduction of recoverability of the success fee and AEI premium. Again, no one really knows what the impact of this major funding change is likely to be. Recoverability will make losing a case considerably more expensive. This may make defendants either more determined to take cases all the way to trial, or keener to settle earlier rather than adding to a bill which is already steep.

3.57 There is nothing to stop defendants from acting under CFAs. In this situation, a losing claimant could find himself liable for his opponent's success fee and AEI premium. Indeed, it is known that one City solicitor has advised his clients to respond to CFA claimants by 'upping the ante' and taking out a 'tit-for-tat' CFA themselves. Such a tactic may deter would-be claimants from bringing CFA claims. These extra costs (the winning defendant's success fee and insurance premium) are usually covered by the claimant's own AEI policy. However, if defendant CFAs become common, AEI companies say that they would be likely to respond to this new development by putting up premium rates or by imposing higher success criteria on cases which they are willing to underwrite. What impact changes of this kind will have on an already fluid situation is anybody's guess, but firms would be wise closely to monitor market developments.

CHAPTER 4

Running a conditional fee case

Sallie Booth

INTRODUCTION

4.1   As Chapter 3 shows, the use of conditional fees requires structural and strategic changes to the way in which solicitors' firms run their practices. Similar changes will also be necessary amongst groups of barristers regularly undertaking CFA work. Lawyers will also need to make changes to the way in which each individual case is managed. Once the appropriate office systems have been set up so that the practice as a whole is geared to coping with conditional fees as a method of funding, the next step is to focus on the impact of conditional fees on each particular case. Funding by conditional fees is not just an issue to be dealt with at the outset of a case; it influences the way in which a case is handled from start to finish.

4.2   Good risk management and case screening is vital, and early assessment and regular monitoring of cases in progress will be essential in the interest of the practice and of the client. There are a number of measures which firms can take to improve the prospects of getting the risk assessment right, particularly in larger cases.

4.3   The following information is written specifically with claimants' solicitors in mind. However, much of it will apply equally well to defence lawyers, and the key principles will also be relevant to barristers.

RISK ASSESSMENT

4.4   Firms should make an accurate assessment of all elements of the risk involved in a case before entering into a CFA. This means that more investigative work needs to be done at an early stage. Once a CFA is signed, both parties are likely to be stuck with it and its terms. A solicitor cannot unilaterally pull out, save for a good reason which is clearly provided for in the CFA. Neither will it be possible to be able to change the terms of the CFA, for instance by increasing the success fee to reflect what are subsequently seen as the risks involved. It should be noted, however, that in *Callery* v. *Gray* [2001] EWCA Civ 1117 the Court of Appeal contemplated the development of two-stage success fees allowing for a high uplift substantially discounted in the event of settlement at an early stage (see para.106ff.).

SCREENING

Introduction

4.5   Rigorous, accurate initial screening of cases will be one of the keys to making conditional fees work for firms which handle them. If various different litigation departments are conducting a substantial proportion of their work on CFA terms, a firm cannot afford to waste time on cases which do not ultimately translate into a CFA. Firms need to develop systems to weed out the no-hopers as early as possible.

Questionnaires

4.6   This will involve the earliest possible assessment of the merits of the case. Put simply, is it a good case or not? Depending on the size and structure of the firm, it may be appropriate to devise a questionnaire which guides the fee earners into addressing each key issue. The questionnaire should cover the two key areas: details of the case itself (including any anticipated difficulties with liability, causation or quantum) and the costs/likely return if the case is successful.

4.7   A questionnaire should help identify whether a case has very good, good, fair, or poor prospects for success. Each firm will have to develop its own definition of these terms. For instance, over 90 per cent may represent cases with very good prospects, 75–90 per cent good prospects, and so on. Firms will also have to decide which categories of case they are prepared to take on under CFA terms. It is likely that some types of case, such as clinical negligence, will generally be more difficult to assess accurately at the outset, and may result in a lower percentage prospect for success and a higher success fee.

Is it worth investing time on a case with 'average' prospects of success?

4.8   If, on an initial assessment, a case falls into one of the lower categories, a decision needs to be taken whether it is worth spending valuable time trying to turn, say, a 'fair' case into a 'good' one. In some cases, it may well be. For instance, a solicitor might want to invest more time in assessing a potentially high value case which appears to have only fair prospects than he or she would, say, on a low value case with the same prospects for success. As a rule of thumb, it is likely that firms will be more interested in high value cases with average prospects than in low value cases with average prospects.

Key issues

4.9 The key issues to identify early on are, first, is the evidence strong enough, and secondly, what are the potential pitfalls?

Initial client interviews

4.10 The initial client interview is an opportunity to start gleaning this vital information. Fee earners (prompted by a questionnaire, if appropriate) should keep in mind at all times that the primary aim is to extract enough information to be able to make a rapid, but informed decision. In practice, depending on the complexity of the case, this may take one or more client interviews and may involve consideration of documentary or even expert evidence before a decision whether or not to take the case on a CFA basis can be made.

4.11 There will be different features to consider, both in terms of facts and the law, depending on the particular class of case. One area which will be common to all is assessment of the level of likely damages. The most important task during the interview is to make a quick initial assessment of all the issues that will determine whether a firm should take on a case, and, if so, on what basis.

Key issues: factual

4.12 As to the factual issues, the following issues should be considered:

(1) Are the facts of the case clear-cut, or complicated?

(2) How strong is the client's evidence?

(3) How strong is the evidence of other witnesses, and how available are they?

(4) Will the input of expert witnesses be required in order to establish liability (which will add to the cost), or can the facts be established without recourse to an expert? (If not, it is likely to be a complex case.)

(5) Is the client, and are the other witnesses plausible? Will they go down well with a judge or jury if the case comes to court?

(6) What supporting material is there? How accessible is it? What volume of it is there?

(7) Who are the defendants? Are they insured (or do they have other means)? Where are they?

(8) Is there potentially more than one defendant? Is it the kind of case where there is likely to be a third party notice? If so, tread carefully; in this situation, there is a danger of winning against one but losing against another.

Key issues: legal

4.13 As to the legal issues, relevant issues will include the following:

(1) Does the case turn on an established legal issue?

(2) Are the issues clear cut? Are they novel? If the latter, the solicitor may still want to take on the case if other circumstances prevail, such as the potential for a particularly high return, or the chance to break new legal ground and to help a particular client.

(3) Are the issues complex? (It will be necessary to analyse and research the relevant case law speedily.)

(4) Is the case within the limitation period? Is there enough time to do the work required before issuing proceedings? If the solicitor is not confident that there is, then it may be necessary to turn away the case. If it is a personal injury case and the limitation period has been exceeded, is the case one where it is worth applying to the court for an extension of the time allowed?

(5) Is there likely to be a counterclaim which would reduce the pot of potential damages?

(6) Are there issues as to causation?

Key issues: damages

4.14 As to damage, the following issues may well be relevant:

(1) Are there issues as to foreseeability?

(2) What are the minimum and maximum damages which are likely?

(3) Is the client's loss easy to quantify or are there likely to be problems proving damage? Will the input of an expert be required?

(4) What levels of damages have been awarded in similar cases? What are the guidelines for these awards? (Urgent research may need to be carried out in this area.)

(5) Who sets the level of damages, judge or jury? If the latter, the amount may be less predictable.

(6) Is there scope for aggravated or exemplary damages?

(7) Is there scope for interim payments, which could be used to fund disbursements (if the client has no other means of meeting these costs)?

Key issues: costs

4.15 Questions also need to be asked about the likely costs, in particular:

(1) Is insurance available (and on what terms) to protect the client from having to pay the other side's costs if he loses? Is the level of cover on offer adequate?

(2) What is the likely overall level of disbursements? Who will be funding these, the client or the firm?

(3) If an expert witness is needed, will he have to be paid while the case progresses, or at the end?

(4) How long is the case likely to take to be resolved before getting paid?

(5) What is the likely overall level of financial subsidy for the firm? (This would involve taking into account time lag before payment, payment of disbursements and insurance, and the amount of fee earner time likely to be needed.)

(6) What are the total likely costs on which the success fee will be based (that is, what is the likely overall recovery)?

Key issues: various

4.16 Other factors too need to be considered, for instance:

(1) Will the case qualify for the fast or multi-track if it reaches court? (A fast-track case should mean that the firm gets paid within a reasonable period. If costs are fixed, it should be easier for the firm to assess the likely recovery in advance, although the attractiveness of fast-track cases will obviously depend on costs being set at a realistic level.)

(2) What level of judge will decide the case? (A more junior judge may be reluctant to make a decision which breaks new legal ground.)

(3) Is the client a private individual or company? (A company may be more able to pay disbursements. But, conversely, if company personnel change, it may hinder the handling of the case.)

(4) Are there any other likely claimants with similar cases? (If so, it might be that the work invested in this case could be useful for them, too.) However, multi-party litigation will require special consideration so far as CFA insurance is concerned.

(5) Is the case in an area where the firm already has proven experience and expertise? (A conditional fee case is not a good time to start experimenting in untested areas.)

(6) Is arbitration or mediation an option? (If so, it could mean the case being settled more quickly.)

(7) Is there sufficient expertise available to do the advocacy in-house? (This may be particularly important in a fast-track case with fixed costs.)

(8) Does the firm have the spare capacity in terms of fee earners and support personnel to take on the case?

(9) Can the firm stand the financial strain of carrying the case until its conclusion (always bearing in mind that if the case is lost, payment will not just be delayed, but simply will not happen)?

Key issues: children and adults under a disability

4.17   Special considerations will also apply if the client is a child or an adult under a disability. If the client is a child, then the litigation friend can sign a CFA for the purpose of pursuing the case. The assessment of the prospects of success and the calculation of the success fee should be dealt with carefully and mindful of the fact that at a later stage the court will have jurisdiction to determine whether the success fee was reasonable or otherwise. The level of success fee could be challenged by the opponent, and also by the litigation friend at a later stage during the detailed assessment procedure.

4.18   In the case of an adult who lacks mental capacity to take proceedings on his own behalf, again, the litigation friend can enter into a CFA on behalf of the claimant/patient. If the Court of Protection is already involved, it should be asked to approve the CFA, especially the level of the success fee. It is the Court of Protection in those circumstances which gives the receiver the authority to enter into the agreement. If the Court of Protection has not yet been involved, it will be necessary when an application is eventually made for the appointment of a receiver to bring the matter to the attention of the Court of Protection and seek retrospective approval at that point in time. If the Court of Protection indicated that it was not prepared to approve the CFA because of the level of the success fee, then it will be necessary to adjust the success fee and satisfy the Court of Protection. Ultimately the level of success fee in the CFA could be challenged by the opponent in the litigation and the matter could be considered at the end of litigation by the costs judge dealing with the detailed assessment of costs. However, if the CFA has been signed by the receiver with the approval of the Court of Protection, there should be little difficulty in persuading the costs judge that the level of success fee was reasonably set at the time the agreement was entered into.

CALCULATING THE SUCCESS FEE

Introduction

4.19 Each time that the percentage success fee is calculated, it is important to ensure, so far as possible, that it will translate into an amount of money which adequately rewards the firm for the risk which has been taken. It will be necessary to make a detailed contemporaneous note explaining how the success fee has been calculated since it may subsequently be subject to challenge, either by the defendant or by the client (see 2.33 and 2.68 above). The success fee is calculated as a percentage of the costs recoverable from an unsuccessful defendant, and is payable by the defendant. The client, therefore, will have no financial interest in the level of success fee as such, but it will be necessary to be able to justify it.

4.20 Setting the success fee at an appropriate level in individual cases will be one of the keys to running a profitable litigation practice. However rigorous the screening of cases, and however experienced or methodical members of staff are, setting a success fee can never be a science. Wise firms will do their calculations (see below) and then may add in extra percentage points as a margin of error to represent the ordinary risks of litigation. This will be especially important once a substantial proportion of a firm's litigation is being done on conditional fees. In a class of proceedings where the risks involved in each case are likely to be uniform (such as ostensibly straightforward road traffic claims), the solicitor may find it more difficult to identify individual items of risk since the Court of Appeal has indicated that it is the ordinary risks of such litigation alone which are likely to be the cause of failure (see *Callery* v. *Gray* [2001] EWCA Civ 1117 at para.84, and 4.25 below).

4.21 Setting a realistic and fair level of success fee is an essential, if problematic, element in the equation, both for the firm and the client. Specifying a success fee of, say, 10 or 25 per cent to a lay client is likely to be fairly meaningless without translating this information into a form which he can readily understand. How the success fee has been calculated must be spelt out to each client. This is an express requirement of the Conditional Fee Agreements Regulations 2000, SI 2000/692 (see 2.31 above), and without it the CFA will be unenforceable.

Information for the client

4.22 Before the *client* can decide whether to go ahead with a particular CFA, the most important information which he or she must have is:

(a) the prospects of success;

(b) the likely level of damages;

(c) the percentage success fee to be charged in the event that he or she wins (and how this figure has been arrived at (see below));

(d) the likely level of own solicitor's costs;

(e) approximately how much (in money) the success fee will come to;

(f) the amount which he or she might have to pay to make up the short-fall between the costs and disbursements recovered from the other side and the total amount of own solicitor's costs and disbursements (a shortfall could arise because of differences between the hourly charging rate to the client compared with the rate which can be recovered from the other side (usually on assessment); it could also arise when, on assessment, an amount claimed from the other side is held to be a solicitor and own client item);

(g) whether or not the defendant can pay.

This is not only good sense but it is expressly required by the 2000 Regulations (see 2.28ff above) and is a matter of professional conduct by virtue of Rule 15 of the Solicitors' Practice Rules and the Solicitors' Costs and Client Care Code 1999.

4.23 The solicitor must give the client his best guess of the expected level of damages (with the caveat that this can only be an estimate). To avoid raising a client's expectations unreasonably a conservative approach should be adopted, and, where possible, he or she should be referred to established benchmarks, for example, to the Judicial Studies Board's Guidelines for General Damages in Personal Injuries: a sceptical client may be reassured by seeing some kind of written endorsement of the assessment.

Information for the firm

4.24   To assess the level of success fee, the most important information which the *firm* needs to have is:

(a) the prospects for success and the financial burden the case will place on the firm (see below);

(b) how the risk factors translate into a percentage success fee;

(c) the likely level of its own costs on which the success fee will be based;

(d) how much (in money) the success fee will work out to, using the estimated costs as a basis for calculation;

(e) whether or not the defendant can pay.

Main risk factors

4.25   The are two main elements to be taken into account which fall under the broad heading of risk:

(a) a percentage based on the case's prospects for success;

(b) a percentage to reflect what might be called the 'lightning factor' (see below).

A note of caution must be added in the case of very straightforward cases which fall within a single category and which are handled on a regular basis by the solicitor. This is because of the Court of Appeal ruling in *Callery* v. *Gray* (see 4.20 above). In *Callery's* case the Court of Appeal decided that '20 per cent is the maximum uplift that can reasonably be agreed' in respect of 'modest claims in respect of a road traffic accident, where liability is unlikely to be in issue and the question of damages is unlikely to create complexities'. Lord Woolf stated (para.84) that:

> The risk assessment that results in the determination of the uplift is likely to turn, not on peculiar features of the instant case – for there will be none – but on his experience that in a small minority of such cases, when

the claim is pursued some unforeseen circumstance results in the ultimate failure or abandonment of the claim.

In other words the Court of Appeal considered that there will be classes of case where a very detailed assessment of the risks involved in an individual matter is not as important to the setting of the uplift as the relevant lightning factors.

Assessing the prospects of success

4.26 Solicitors are already used to thinking about litigation in terms of percentage prospects of success. Cases are often assessed, albeit informally, as 50/50, 75 per cent, and so on. Since the use of CFAs means that firms' profitability depends on the accuracy of the assessment, a more considered approach will be required in order to calculate the prospects of success. Nevertheless, the principle remains the same with the advent of CFAs.

4.27 With conditional fees, this prospect for success figure needs to be translated into a percentage that can be charged as a success fee.

4.28 There is no single, definitive, way of arriving at a figure to reflect the 'prospects of success' element of a success fee. Firms will need to develop systems which are fair both to themselves and to their clients, always bearing in mind that the success fee must be justifiable on an assessment of costs (see 2.68ff above).

An 'actuarial' approach

4.29 One option may be to take an actuarial approach to the calculation as a starting point. In simple terms, whether you are a bookmaker calculating the odds for horses in the Grand National, or a solicitor calculating the odds appropriate to be charged in respect of a particular case, the pure mathematical approach is the same.

Law Society 'ready reckoner'

4.30 The Law Society has produced a probability table to help calculate the appropriate success fee in cases run on a conditional basis. It is set out at Appendix 19 and should be used as recommended in the following paragraphs. The table can be routinely used as a 'ready reckoner' by firms, once they are satisfied they have assessed a case's prospects for success. However, for this table to work in practice, the prospects of success and the risk of failure must be accurately assessed at the outset of the case, and this is not an easy exercise, even for the most experienced solicitor.

Using the 'ready reckoner'

4.31 The figures in the table are calculated using the following formula:

$F/S \times 100 = SF$

F = prospects of failure

S = prospects of success

SF = success fee

For example, let us suppose that the chances of success in a particular case are assessed as 75 per cent. According to the table, this produces a success fee of 33.3 per cent. This figure is worked out on the following basis. A case which has a 75 per cent chance of succeeding has a 25 per cent risk of failure. Applying the formula set out above, this produces the following equation:

25 divided by 75, and multiplied by 100, results in a success fee of 33.3 per cent.

One way of making this formula understandable to lay clients may be to explain that if the firm were to take on four cases which each had a 75 per cent chance of success, then on the basis of pure probability, it would lose one of those cases. In order not to be out of pocket, the firm would need to charge an extra third on to each of the three which it won in order to compensate it for the one which it lost (if we assume that the costs in each case are comparable, which of course they are unlikely to be in practice).

4.32 This calculation is complicated in practice by the fact that the costs incurred in each case, and therefore the amount of financial risk being run each time by the firm, will not be identical. Let us suppose, for instance, that a firm takes on two 50/50 cases, and that each case has a success fee of 100 per cent (as set out in the table). If the firm goes on to win that case in which the costs are, say, £100,000, but at the same time it loses the case where the costs are, say, £5,000, then it would follow that the firm would be rather better off than if things had been the other way round.

73

Advantages of the 'actuarial approach'

4.33 As has been said, firms will need to develop their own method of translating 'prospects of success' into a percentage figure. However, by using the formulaic approach set out above (but before adding in other elements, in respect of which see below), then the following advantages are likely to follow:

(a) a good starting point is given from which to calculate the success fee;

(b) the solicitor is able to give the client an estimate of the success fee in money terms, based on the likely costs of the case;

(c) it may help to reassure the client that the success fee is arrived at fairly, rather than on a random basis;

(d) it gives a framework for calculating success fees and, therefore, should lead to consistency of approach;

(e) provided that a firm has assessed the prospects for success fairly, a success fee based on the figures in the chart should be justifiable on a detailed assessment;

(f) the solicitor has a graphic illustration of the risks of running cases which have poor prospects for success. For example, in a case with a 40 per cent chance of winning, then according to the table, it would be necessary to charge a success fee of 150 per cent, which exceeds the maximum permitted by statute. The gap between what should be charged on an actuarial assessment and what can be charged in practice is likely to deter firms from taking on high-risk cases which might threaten their financial stability.

Explaining to the client

4.34 While this formulaic approach has advantages, it is important not to underestimate the risk of blinding the client with science. If this table is going to be used, then the basis on which it going to be used should be explained to the client. This will necessarily involve talking about actuarial principles and probability theory. At the same time, use of the table does have the benefit of being quick and easy to explain, which may make it suitable in some limited circumstances. However, even if it were acceptable for routine, low value cases, we suggest that it is likely to be inappropriate for rather more complex cases, say, those over £10,000 in value. Clients in such cases may merit a rather more considered approach to the way their success fee is calculated.

'Lightning' factors: special risks

4.35 Litigation is a notoriously uncertain business. Every litigator will have experience of cases which, on the law and the facts, should have succeeded, but which failed for extraneous reasons. For instance the judge may take against a client, or an experienced expert witness may suddenly unravel in the witness box.

4.36 There is clearly no way of predicting when such unexpected events might strike, which is why we have termed it the 'lightning factor'. It is, however, a fact of life for litigators. Because of the potential impact on a firm's finances when the lightning factor strikes in a conditional fee case, it is appropriate routinely to add extra percentage points to each success fee to provide for a kind of margin for error. It is worth noting that in *Callery* v. *Gray* Lord Woolf stated that: 'We do not consider that it can ever be said a case is without risk' (para.103).

4.37 It is important that the client understands how the proposed success fee has been calculated, and this needs to be explained in some detail (see 4.22 above). What is it about the case that makes it relatively risky? If it is such a strong case, why is the solicitor asking for this level of success fee, and why does the client need insurance?

A case by case process

4.38 Any firm taking on a CFA case will understandably want to know how much money it stands to receive if the case is won, and, conversely, how much it is likely to lose if the case fails. To do this, the firm needs to estimate both the percentage success fee and the likely costs, which enables it to calculate likely earnings. This crucial earnings figure will be wholly dependent on these two factors. It is essential that the level of earnings should be determined by the costs and success fee, and not the other way round. A firm must emphatically not decide how much it would like to earn from a case and then set the success fee accordingly to try to ensure that it achieves this figure. Nor, of course, can the firm's costs be altered as the case progresses in order try to achieve the same effect.

4.39 The respective exercises of estimating costs and determining success fee must be kept entirely separate from any assessment of how much money the firm would like to earn from the case. It is, of course, entirely reasonable for a firm to work out what its earnings would be and to decide not to offer a CFA if these are not acceptable. It is not permissible to try to make the figures more acceptable by tinkering with other elements in the equation. Unless the success fee arrived at is defensible on its own merits, it may be reduced on an assessment, and the firm could find itself in breach of the Law Society's rules.

Altering the success fee

4.40 As with any contract, however, if both sides agree, then the terms may be altered and a new agreement signed (but see 2.39 above). There may be situations when a change is justified. However, it is necessary to consider carefully before trying to alter the success fee, even where this would be to the client's advantage.

4.41 For example, supposing that a client comes to his solicitor with what is an apparently difficult case. After going through the initial screening process, the solicitor offers to take it on with a success fee of 75 per cent. The next week, a surprise witness appears, greatly strengthening the case. If the case were being assessed now, then a success fee of, say, 10 per cent would be more appropriate. Although it might be tempting in this situation to offer the client a new agreement with a lower success fee, it should be remembered that if the situation were reversed, say an apparently certain case which suddenly becomes much more difficult, then the solicitor would be bound by the original CFA.

4.42 In practice, success fees can only be amended one way – downwards. No right-thinking client is likely to agree to a higher success fee when he has a contract binding a solicitor to the lower one, no matter how much the circumstances of the case may have changed. In these circumstances the solicitor will have to live with the consequences of the initial assessment. He may well feel, therefore, that it is equally legitimate for the same to be true when circumstances change in his favour. In reality, an element of 'swings and roundabouts' is an inevitable part of the CFA mix. It is important to note, however, that on assessment of costs, the success fee will always be considered in respect of the individual circumstances of the case. In *Callery* v. *Gray* the Court of Appeal suggested that 'once the necessary data is available' there may be occasions (in respect of straightforward cases at least) when a two-stage success fee can be agreed at the outset of a claim.

Is the success fee vulnerable on an assessment?

4.43 So long as the initial assessment is made in good faith and on the basis of information available at the time, a success fee which turns out to be generous is unlikely to be successfully challenged subsequently.

The client's perspective

4.44   We are not suggesting that weighing up the suitability of a complex case is ever easy but, once a solicitor has assessed the case to a firm's satisfaction and is willing to offer the client a CFA, from the client's point of view, there is unlikely to be much of a decision to be made between doing nothing or going ahead with a CFA (particularly if it is combined with after-the-event insurance protecting him from the other side's costs should he lose). However, the client still needs to decide whether he is happy with the specific terms of the contract being offered, particularly the success fee, hourly rates, likely level of disbursements, potential damages and the costs of insurance.

Wealthy clients

4.45   We believe that, where a CFA is available together with after-the-event insurance, then the CFA route is likely to be the best option for the wealthiest client. Even in a case which has a strong prospect for success and the client is rich enough to meet both sides' costs should he lose, then on a bald statistical basis, the client will get a better deal with a CFA in every case.

Relevance of the availability of after-the-event insurance?

4.46   Whether insurance cover is available obviously has a major bearing on whether a case is suitable to be run on a CFA basis. The client who enters into a CFA without the benefit of insurance cover is leaving himself open to having to pay thousands of pounds in the other side's costs if he or she loses.

4.47   The Law Society's approved insurance product, Accident Line, is not available to cover medical negligence, pharmaceutical, drug, or tobacco-related claims. Many CFA insurance products are now available, the terms of which do vary considerably from one to another (see Chapter 7).

4.48   However, where a client with some means is bringing a conditional fee case without the protection of after-the-event insurance, it is important to make sure that he fully understands that the arrangement is not 'no win no fee'. He must be given as accurate a picture as possible of what the other side's costs and his solicitor's disbursements are likely to be, and therefore the level of financial risk to which he is exposing himself.

The reaction of defendants

4.49 One historical advantage of being on legal aid was that defendants who knew that they were unlikely to recover their costs were more inclined to settle cases which they might otherwise fight. The CFA client with an AEI product behind him or her may well be at a relative disadvantage, in that defendants may take a harder line, knowing that if they win, their costs will be met by the insurers (see 3.51ff above).

The model conditional fee agreement: using the Law Society model CFA

Gareth Phillips

ABOUT THIS CHAPTER

5.1 This chapter is intended to offer a detailed commentary on the Law Society model CFA and accompanying Law Society Conditions which have been produced by the Law Society in response to the changes to the statutory regime effected by the Access to Justice Act 1999 and subsequent amendments to the Civil Procedure Rules and Costs Practice Direction.

5.2 The model CFA and Conditions are reproduced at Appendix 20 with a series of numerical notations which should be used to cross-refer to the commentary provided below. The overall aim of the commentary is to highlight points of particular interest or importance in the model CFA and those points which need to be spelled out especially carefully to the client. It is suggested that the solicitor conduct a similarly detailed exercise to the one undertaken in the commentary with the client, running through the contract line by line and dealing with queries as they arise.

5.3 Before setting out the commentary we provide below some introductory remarks, some observations on whether it is appropriate to depart from the wording of the model agreement, and some guidance on the need to explain the contents of a CFA to a client.

INTRODUCTION

The Law Society and model agreements

5.4 Once a firm has covered the matters discussed in Chapters 3 and 4 (running a litigation practice on conditional fees and running a conditional fee case) and having decided both that CFAs are right for the firm and that such an arrangement is appropriate to the particular case, it is necessary to enter into a formal CFA.

5.5 The Law Society first produced a model conditional fee agreement in response to the Conditional Fee Agreements Regulations 1995, SI 1995/1675. This original model was aimed specifically at personal injury cases and has been rendered obsolete by the Conditional Fee Agreements Regulations 2000, SI 2000/692. It will not be enforceable if entered into after 1 April 2000. In revising the original model as a result of the later Regulations, the Society was caused a great problem by the fact that the changes to the CPR were not published until July 2000, accompanied by a new and substantial Costs Practice Direction. Consequently, the Society suggested that during this period of uncertainty practitioners should not enter new agreements until the legislative background was finalised. However, the Society was also mindful of the need of some practitioners to enter agreements due to limitation problems. Accordingly, the Society produced a 'running repair' model agreement which sought to amend the original model and make it compliant with the minimum requirements of the new Regulations. However, that 'running repair' was never intended as a long term solution to the issues raised by the new regime. The revised model conditional fee agreement was finalised in July 2000 following consultation within the profession in the light of the CFA Regulations 2000, CPR Costs Rules and Costs Practice Direction. The revised model agreement is again aimed at personal injury matters, but can be amended to cover other types of case. It is this latest model which is set out at Appendix 20.

DEPARTING FROM THE MODEL

5.6 Use of the model is not mandatory. Firms are free to develop their own document if they wish. Indeed, those wishing to use conditional fee agreements for cases other than personal injury will inevitably have to amend the wording in certain areas. The Law Society is considering producing model agreements for other subject areas where there may be a demand, but in the meantime those wishing to enter non-personal injury agreements can use the model as a base, bearing in mind the matters that follow. To be an effective agreement, drafters will need to comply with:

- the legislative framework of Regulations, Rules and Practice Direction;
- the indemnity principle;
- the general law of contract;
- the requirements of after-the-event insurers.

Consequently, those wishing to depart from the model should be cautious for the following reasons. First, it was produced after wide consultation among the profession and consumer groups, is written in plain English and went through many drafts before being finalised. Secondly, parts of the model are based directly on the requirements of the CFA Regulations 2000, and in particular the specific requirements to provide information to clients. If a solicitor fails to deal with these elements in an amended version, the CFA may be unenforceable. Thirdly, where the CFA is linked to after-the-event insurance (which is likely in the vast majority of cases), practitioners may be required by the insurers to use a contract containing many of the Law Society Conditions.

5.7   The model agreement incorporates the basic changes from the previous conditional fee scheme as set out in Part II of the Access to Justice Act 1999. As has been said (above), the model agreement further incorporates the essential elements of the CFA Regulations 2000. The model agreement also incorporates an essential provision from the Conditional Fee Agreements Order 1998, SI 1998/1860, which states that the maximum permitted percentage increase on fees is 100 per cent. In addition, the model CFA incorporates matters contained in the revised CPR, including matters set out in CPR Rules 44.3 B(1)(a), 44.15 and 44.16 (see Chapter 2).

Compulsory and recommended clauses

5.8   At the same time, the Law Society's model agreement includes some clauses which are recommended rather than compulsory. Some clauses are open to possible variations. This chapter will seek to clarify which elements are set down by regulations and those which can be varied.

Transitional provisions

5.9   Finally, those solicitors who entered into the old style model agreement prior to 1 April 2000 should resist the temptation to tear up those agreements and enter fresh agreements under the new Regulations in the hope of switching responsibility for paying the success fee. The Costs Practice Direction specifically makes it impossible to enter into a further CFA after 1 April 2001 which purports to allow for the recovery of an additional liability.

EXPLAINING THE AGREEMENT

5.10 The CFA is an important document and it is essential that both solicitor and client fully understand its implications. The serious nature of the contract which the client is entering into must be stressed. It is a legally binding document, signed by both parties, which commits *both* to taking a particular course of action and imposes duties on both. The arrangement required by the regulatory framework is complex and poses certain difficulties which have taxed the minds of experienced lawyers in the field (see Chapter 2). At the same time it must be made comprehensible to the lay client. It is essential that the full cost implications are made clear to the client, but the client will not want to be baffled with an explanation so complex that he has no real understanding of what is going on.

Conditional Fees Explained

5.11 Before attempting to explain the full intricacies of the agreement it may be as well to run through the Law Society's revised leaflet *Conditional Fees Explained*. This attempts to explain the essential elements of the agreement but in a less legalistic fashion. Again, as with the agreement itself, practitioners should ensure that they utilise the latest version of the leaflet. The new leaflet, as with the agreement, has been written in plain English, and is designed to be a gentle introduction to the subject for the client. However, it is no substitute for a proper explanation, and the solicitor must remember that he will have specifically to advise on certain aspects of this agreement under the CFA Regulations 2000, reg.4. *Conditional Fees Explained* is an aid rather than a substitute for a proper oral explanation. The solicitor should bear in mind that if a disgruntled client brought his or her discontent to the attention of the court, the entire agreement might be rendered unenforceable if it is shown that the solicitor has not discharged the duty imposed by the 2000 Regulations. At the time of writing the leaflet is available from the Law Society's Business Centre (020 7320 5640), £11 per pack of 50.

COMMENTARY ON THE MODEL CFA

Structure of the model CFA

5.12 The model CFA comes in two parts. The first part consists of the formal contract which both the solicitor and client have to sign, together with a schedule containing information specific to the particular case. The latter section consists of the Law Society's Conditions on which the contract is based.

5.13 The 'you' in the contract is a reference to the client throughout.

The Law Society Conditions

5.14 To understand the agreement fully, the client must understand the Conditions. In a detailed explanation of the agreement the solicitor should continuously cross-refer to the Conditions where appropriate. In particular, condition 3 defines a number of terms, several of which (for instance disbursements, basic costs, lien) will be unfamiliar to the client, and the solicitor should take care to ensure he has explained them carefully. It is important for the solicitor to remember that he is under a duty under the CFA Regulations 2000 to explain the effect of the agreement both orally and in writing. Whilst the Law Society Conditions constitute a written explanation of much of the agreement the solicitor cannot merely rely on handing over a copy of the Regulations to a client, tell him to read it and believe that his duties are discharged. The solicitor should suggest to the client that if there are any particular aspects of the agreement which he finds unclear from the text the solicitor will explain them to him orally.

Note reference: cross-referencing with Appendix 20

5.15 As we have said above the Notes referred to in the paragraphs below are references to the annotations appearing in the text set out at Appendix 20.

WHAT IS COVERED BY THE MODEL CFA

Identifying the opponent

Note 1

5.16 Regulation 2(1)(a) of the CFA Regulations 2000 requires the solicitor to identify the proceedings to which the agreement relates (see 2.29 above). This may be done to some extent by identifying the proposed opponent. However, this may not be straightforward if the investigations are at an early stage, particularly if there is potentially more than one opponent. There is also a question mark as to whether the solicitor should have a separate agreement for each potential opponent where there is more than party on the other side. The solicitor must think carefully through the implications dependent on the nature of the case. In particular he will have to consider this question in the context of the after-the-event insurance arrangements. If it is impossible to identify the opponent at the time of entering the agreement it will be necessary to identify the nature of the proceedings in another manner, although it may well have implications for the risk assessment process if the solicitor enters into an agreement without knowing the precise identity of the opponent. It is questionable as to whether it is wise to enter such an agreement if the solicitor does not know whether the proposed opponent is likely to either be insured or have sufficient means to meet a judgment. In such circumstances can the solicitor be truly confident of being paid if the client is successful?

'Damages'; 'personal injury'

Note 2

5.17 Damages are defined at condition 3(e) of the Conditions. The model agreement does not give a definition of 'personal injury', but implicitly relies on the definition given in the former RSC at Order 1(4)(1)), namely:

> Proceedings in which there is a claim for damages in respect of personal injuries or in respect of a person's death, and 'personal injuries' includes any disease and any impairment of a person's physical or mental condition.

Identifying the date of the injury

Note 3

5.18 Care needs to be taken in specifying an accurate date. If the client has a series of claims, for instance a car crash followed by allegedly negligent medical treatment, is the agreement to cover both? It must be remembered that if both claims are to be made under the same agreement, then the after-the-event insurance position will need to be considered. Separate cover will probably be required for each aspect of the claim. In the case of an industrial disease a range of dates will probably need to be inserted.

WHAT IS NOT COVERED BY THE MODEL CFA

Counterclaims

Note 4

5.19 The limitations on the scope of the agreement should be explained to the client. The standard terms exclude *defending* a counterclaim brought by a defendant. But if the solicitor is prepared to act for a client on a conditional fee basis if there is a counterclaim, this is a variation which could be incorporated at the outset. Alternatively it would be possible to agree to amend the CFA if a counterclaim arises. However, the standard terms cover a defendant *bringing* a counterclaim for personal injury damages against a claimant, for instance a road traffic accident where there is an element of blame on both sides. Again, it will be necessary to check the position carefully as to whether the after-the-event insurance is valid for a counterclaim.

Appeals

Note 5

5.20 Appeals by the client are not covered in the standard terms of the model. If the standard version is used, the agreement would end when the case is lost. If the client wants to take it to appeal, then it will be necessary to negotiate a new agreement. Alternatively, this is a clause which could be varied, if, at the outset of the CFA, it is agreed to build in a liability on the part of the lawyer to take the case to appeal. However, the AEI policy must extend to the appeal in these circumstances. It should be remembered that the definition of 'win' (as given in condition 3(n)) means that the defence of appeals by the other side are included as standard (see explanation below). Interim appeals by the client during the case (before final judgment) are included in the model.

PAYMENT OBLIGATIONS

Paying the solicitor's own costs

Note 6

5.21   This clause reflects the requirements of the CFA Regulations 2000, reg.2(1)(b),(c),(d), and reg.4(2)(a) (see 2.29 and 2.36 above). Cross-reference needs to be made to conditions 4 and 5. This constitutes an important part of the duty of explanation under the Regulations since the duty of oral explanation under reg.4(2)(a) is mandatory.

5.22   This clause is likely to cause a great deal of difficulty when it comes to setting out clearly to clients the position as to potential costs liabilities. At face value it hardly seems consistent with the idea of a 'no win no fee' agreement, i.e. that the client might expect to be spared the worry of bearing the costs of a case in any circumstances. Accordingly it presents a difficulty in that having attracted the client on the premise that the solicitor is sharing the risk, the solicitor is immediately duty bound to inform the client that he is liable for the solicitor's costs! The clause exists because the liability needs to be incorporated into the CFA in order to comply with the indemnity principle. If the client were not liable in the first instance, then the principle would operate so that that the other side would not be liable for the costs either, since their liability only extends to costs for which the client is liable. Many would argue that the indemnity principle is an anachronism which has no place in the modern world of litigation, and that it is as much honoured in the breach as observed. Litigation is littered with anomalous situations which appear to breach the principle. However, until it is either abolished or abrogated we have to live with its existence and agreements must be drafted accordingly. Nevertheless, it has to be said that the message to be given to clients by their lawyers is confusing. One can well imagine the potential for a client to be at total cross-purposes over what is really going to happen, and a lawyer needs full powers of explanation in order to try to avoid this.

Paying the disbursements

5.23   The model agreement is silent as to the precise method by which the client funds disbursements. For reasons of cash flow solicitors may seek funding from the client as the case progresses. If this is the intention, then this must be specified in the agreement. However, payment arrangements for disbursements is an area with potential for considerable flexibility. For example, for clients with limited means, the solicitor may opt to fund the disbursements throughout the life of the case, being reimbursed at the end either by the other side or by insurers. Because of the scope for flexibility there is also scope for misunderstanding. Whatever option is chosen it needs to be fully explained and understood by both sides, and set out in the CFA.

Recovery from the opponent

Note 7

5.24 One of the principal differences between the current form of the model agreement and the original is the removal of the cap on the success fee. The cap was never a statutory or common law requirement, but merely a recommendation by the Law Society. It acted as a measure of consumer protection when, under the old Regulations, the success fee was payable out of a client's damages. Now that the success fee is recoverable from the other side, and reg.3(2)(b) provides protection to the client from a solicitor who tries to recover the balance of a success fee deemed unreasonably high on assessment (see 2.33 above), the cap does not have the same importance. There may be certain small claims where full recovery of the entire success fee from the other side may not be anticipated, but a court might allow it against the client. In such circumstances it may be deemed appropriate as a gesture of goodwill to the client to impose a cap. In practice such circumstances are unlikely to be a common occurrence.

Note 8

5.25 This sentence reflects the 'loser pays' principle, subject to the caveat of what is allowed on assessment if there is a dispute. It also reflects the major change brought about under the 1999 Act whereby success fees and insurance premiums are recoverable from the other side.

CPR Part 36 offers

Note 9

5.26 It might be argued that, in practical terms, this is one of the most important clauses in the agreement. Statistically, the vast majority of personal injury claims are brought to a conclusion with a payment in the claimant's favour. Critics of conditional fees argue that the risk for the lawyer ceases when an open admission of liability is made, and that he could cynically run up extra costs (plus a success fee on top) by allowing matters to proceed to trial, for example a trial on quantum, irrespective of the real issues in the case. Leaving aside issues such as professional negligence, breach of the Solicitors' Practice Rules, and the process of assessment of costs, the agreement provides a further disincentive to a solicitor who fails to respond properly to a reasonable offer of settlement.

5.27   This clause seeks to continue the sharing of risk in circumstances where the opponent has 'put their money where their mouth is' and made a Part 36 payment. If a solicitor wrongly advises continued prosecution of a claim where what proves to be a reasonable CPR Part 36 offer has been made, he will not be able to claim a success fee on the base costs incurred after the date of the Part 36 offer. This clearly acts as a disincentive to a cavalier approach to Part 36 offers. Solicitors will have to consider and judge Part 36 offers carefully, for if they fail to react to a good offer, not only will their client suffer in costs, but they will lose in fees.

5.28   This approach can be varied at the outset. For instance, an alternative which is set out in Accident Line Protect's *User Manual* is that the lawyer waives his right to any fees for work done between the date of the Part 36 offer and an award of lower damages. The choice of clause may have a bearing on the amount of insurance cover available to the client, and the solicitor should check the position carefully with the AEI insurers before finalising this clause.

5.29   If the CFA fails to address the issue of Part 36 offers at all, then the solicitor would, in theory, be entitled to both the base costs and the success fee if the offer was not beaten. However, the client would be unlikely to find this acceptable.

Interim damages and disbursements

Note 10

5.30   Cash-flow will represent a serious issue for many firms undertaking work under CFAs. Previously, most firms would fund disbursements either by seeking payments on account from the former Legal Aid Board (in publicly funded cases), or from the privately paying client. The former is impossible under the new regime, and the latter unlikely to be feasible with a less well-healed client. Some insurance products may allow for payment of disbursements in certain circumstances, but this will vary. One method of obtaining funds to cover disbursements in more complex cases is to make sufficient provision when applying for interim payments also to cover disbursements to date, and estimate likely future disbursements. The agreement provides for the deduction of such amounts from any interim payments received.

Provisional damages

Note 11

5.31 Where the client successfully obtains an order for provisional damages the solicitor will be entitled to receive payment in full, including a success fee for work carried out up until that point. If the client goes on to obtain a further payment at a later stage the solicitor will be entitled to levy further base charges and a further success fee thereon under the terms of the original agreement. A solicitor should beware if approached by a client about taking over a claim for a further hearing where there has been a previous award of provisional damages. He should check carefully whether there is a subsisting CFA in force with the previous solicitors, check the terms of the same, and advise the client of the full implications.

Payment of the opponent's costs of an interim hearing by an otherwise successful client

Note 12

5.32 This clause emphasises to clients that success is not always unequivocal. Sometimes an ultimately successful client will lose an interim hearing. Any adverse costs order will still hold good notwithstanding that the client is successful overall.

Note 13

5.33 This clause specifically allows the solicitor to make base charges in relation to a successful interim hearing prior to the final order in the case. The costs regime introduced with the Civil Procedure Rules allows for summary assessment of costs on an interim hearing (see 2.59–2.60 above), and those costs are normally payable before the other side is allowed to continue to defend. This clause allows the solicitor to receive those costs, obviously an aid to cash-flow. The costs received in this way, however, are in the short term limited to base charges, as the success fee does not become payable until the case overall is won. In any event, a solicitor would not normally want to reveal the level of the success fee to an opponent until there has been a final order on liability. Further, the court cannot summarily assess a success fee until the conclusion of the case. However, the success fee will ultimately be payable on the base costs of the interim hearing.

Payment of the opponent's costs if the client loses

Note 14

5.34 The client will be liable for the losing side's costs and disbursements (plus potentially a success fee if the other side are also operating on a CFA). It should be pointed out that these will be subject to the scrutiny of assessment. Further, the solicitor is under a duty under the Regulations to advise the client as to the availability and suitability of insurance products to cover such potential liabilities. It is important that the client understands what liabilities there will be in the event of him or her losing. This is a specific duty under reg.4(2)(b) of the CFA Regulations 2000 (see 2.36 above).

Note 14

5.35 The model agreement makes provision for the solicitor to recover his disbursements from the client in the event that the case does not succeed. In practice this may be wholly impractical since the client may not have any worthwhile income or assets. Further, many solicitors may feel it undesirable to acquire the reputation for enforcing such liabilities, particularly if their competitors are known to swallow the loss. Solicitors may feel that to enforce such a liability would go against the spirit of 'no-win no-fee' agreements. If a solicitor agrees to vary this condition it will have to be specifically dealt with. Again, some insurance products make provision for payment of such disbursements, and these should be investigated and discussed with your client at the outset to satisfy your obligations under the Regulations.

Payment of own solicitor's costs in the event of termination of the agreement

Note 15

5.36 The agreement may be ended early either by the solicitor or the client. Whereas the solicitor can end the agreement only in the limited circumstances set out in condition 7, the client can end it at any time. However, the client must understand the consequences of his terminating the agreement before the case is won or lost. Condition 7 needs to be explained in detail, and indeed the possible consequences of the client terminating (i.e. becoming liable for base charges, success fee and disbursements depending on circumstances) should be explained as part of the duty under reg.4(2)(a) (see 2.36 above).

Basic charges

Note 16

5.37 Basic charges as defined by condition 3(b) are to be calculated by reference to work actually carried out, i.e. time spent or items incurred, and have no relation to the amount at issue in the case. The success fee is calculated as a percentage of those base charges on top. The hourly rate (which has to be set out in the agreement) should be based on the solicitor's normal charging rates to privately-paying clients, not the expense rates. The charging rate may not be the same across the board, but may need to be adjusted to reflect the complexity of the case in question. It is this figure which should go into the agreement. Under condition 4, if there is a shortfall between what the solicitor recovers by way of base costs inter partes and the specified hourly rate, the client is liable to make up the difference. (The situation is more complex regarding shortfalls in the success fee rate.) Some firms will charge this to the client in a successful case but others will not. However, even if the solicitor has no intention of claiming the difference in costs from the client, this technical liability for that shortfall should not be removed from the CFA. Under the indemnity principle the solicitor can only recover costs from the other side which the client would otherwise be liable to pay. If the client has been formally exempted in advance from his liability to pay a proportion of the costs, but then tries to recover the full amount from the other side, the other side can refuse to pay the extra amount. They will not be liable for more than you could recover from the client yourself.

Review of solicitor's rates

Note 17

5.38 The solicitor is allowed under the agreement to review his rates annually by no more than the Retail Price Index (RPI). This provision could be amended to allow more regular reviews and greater increases. However, any variation needs to comply with the relevant European Directive, Council Directive 93/13/EEC (codified in the Unfair Terms in Consumer Contracts Regulations 1994, SI 1994/3159) and the Unfair Contract Terms Act 1977, both of which govern fairness of contracts between professional advisers and consumers. In particular, clauses which give freedom unilaterally to increase charging rates with no agreed reference point will almost certainly fall foul of such legislation.

Success fee

Note 18

5.39 The success fee is a percentage of the solicitor's base costs and is not related to disbursements. Matters relevant to calculation are dealt with at note 24 below and at Schedule 1 to the agreement (see note 37).

5.40 The previous version of the model agreement included a 'cap' which limited the amount of a client's damages that could be paid in lawyer's fees. As the success fee is now recoverable from the other side the cap is no longer deemed appropriate in the majority of cases, although there may be certain limited circumstances where it could be used (see note 10).

5.41 As under the previous conditional fee agreement scheme, the solicitor is limited under the new statutory regime to a maximum success fee of 100 per cent.

Reasons for calculating the success fee

Note 19

5.42 The solicitor is under a duty under reg.3 of the 2000 Regulations to specify the reasons for setting the success fee. The solicitor needs to explain to the client that the level of the success fee is related specifically to the merits of his particular case. This provision confirms that the solicitor has not adopted a blanket approach. The solicitor should explain the way that the success fee has been calculated by reference to two discrete components: the assessment of risk, and the level of financial subsidy that the solicitor will have to make to run the case. Regulation 3(1)(b) states that the part of the success fee which relates to the cost of postponement of payment of fees must be stated separately. Under CPR Rule 44.3B(1)(a) this amount cannot be recovered against the other side (see 2.61 above). In other words, it will never be possible to recover 100 per cent of the success fee against the other side. The 'financing' element of the success fee will always be payable by the client. Whether the solicitor would wish to enforce this element against the client will again be a question of judgement (not to mention marketing) for the solicitor. Common sense suggests that if the solicitor wants to recover as much of the success fee as is possible against the other side the solicitor should not over-emphasise the financing element.

VAT

Note 20

5.43   The success fee is based on the basic charges before addition of VAT.

Law Society Conditions

Note 21

5.44   The Law Society Conditions are part of the agreement, should be appended to it, and fully explained to your client.

Other points: further information

Note 22

5.45   This section fulfils two functions. First it should be used to double-check that the solicitor has covered all the necessary points and that the client fully understands the agreement. Secondly, it confirms that the solicitor has fulfilled the specific duties and requirements of reg.4 of the 2000 Regulations. In particular, paragraphs (a)–(e) echo reg.4(2)(a)–(e) which require the information to be explained orally to the client (see 2.36 above).

Note 23

5.46 It is important that client is clear about when he or she would have to pay the solicitor's costs and disbursements and that he or she understands what is meant by disbursements. If necessary, cross-refer to conditions 3(f), 4, 5 and 7.

Note 24

5.47 It is also important that the client understands what an assessment is and when it can be used. The CPR and Costs Practice Direction have been substantially amended and specific provisions introduced to deal with the revised CFA scheme (see 2.49ff above). It should be noted in particular that if the court disallows any part of the percentage uplift as against the other side, it cannot automatically be charged to the client. The solicitor will need to refer the issue to the court, and unless the client consents, the court will determine how much it is appropriate for the client to be charged (see 2.72ff above).

Note 25

5.48 This duty, imposed by the 2000 Regulations and echoing Practice Rule 15, is crucial. If the client already has a legal expenses insurance policy which would cover the proposed proceedings there will be implications if the solicitor ignores the policy and proceed on a CFA. If the existence of the policy comes to light the solicitor is unlikely to recover the cost of the AEI policy, nor any success fee. There may be other adverse cost implications if it is thought that proceeding under the CFA resulted in costs over and above those that would have been incurred had the case been brought under the legal expenses insurance. The solicitor should not, therefore, wilfully ignore the existence of such policies. The client should specifically be asked whether such a policy exists. Even if the client is not aware that he has a specific policy, it is important that checks are carried out to ensure that other common insurance products do not carry legal expenses as an added extra. Many household contents or motor policies now include such cover.

Note 26

5.49 Again, the solicitor should explore other funding possibilities with the client. In certain instances private funding may be a real option, particularly if married to an AEI policy. From the solicitor's point of view, the solicitor may lose the possibility of a success fee but may be able to agree a higher basic charge with the client. The client may in certain instances prefer such an arrangement, particularly if tied in to a '*Thai Trading*'-style reduced fee CFA (i.e. £x in the event of success, but a reduced fee in the event of failure). Community Legal Service funding may be an option in certain types of cases, and where available the solicitor is required to explore the option with the client, albeit that it has not been available from 1 April 2000 for the vast majority of personal injury cases. Legal expenses insurance is dealt with at note 25 above. This list is not exhaustive, and any other options which are open to the client should be explored.

Note 27

5.50   This is arguably the most difficult of the duties imposed by the 2000 Regulations. Regulation 4(2)(e) requires the solicitor to advise on whether he considers any particular method or methods of financing costs is appropriate, and if the solicitor considers that a contract of insurance is appropriate or recommends a particular such contract, the reasons for so doing (see 2.36 above). At first sight this appears a fairly onerous duty and appears to put the solicitor in the role of insurance broker, giving detailed advice on competing financial products. Unsurprisingly, this has caused a great deal of concern to many solicitors. The Law Society view is that the requirements in the Regulations cannot mean that the solicitor must offer advice or the merits of various insurance products and arrange 'the best' (even if it is possible to decide which is 'the best'). The solicitor is not required to act as an insurance broker. The reasoning behind this view is that consultation made it clear that the government was drawing on the obligations in the current Solicitors' Cost Information and Client Care Code (see 2.87 above). It envisaged general information being given about types of alternative products. The reference in the Regulations is in fact no different from previously existing obligations. Solicitors arranging after-the-event insurance have always been acting as 'independent intermediaries' (in insurance language). Such intermediaries duty is simply to ensure that any contract of insurance is appropriate to their client's needs. Provided that the solicitor is satisfied that the policy covers the client's likely risks at a reasonable premium, it is likely to be appropriate to the client's needs. Where the Regulations go further is in requiring the solicitor to give reasons. This will depend on the solicitor's judgement, but, for example, the solicitor may wish to point out where appropriate that:

95

(a) with a delegated authority scheme the solicitor (rather than insurance company) retain professional judgement in the conduct of the case;

(b) the insurer is reputable and the scheme well-established;

(c) the premiums are reasonable.

The solicitor should make it clear to the client that he is not acting as a broker. He should also declare any personal financial interest (i.e. commission) if appropriate. The solicitor will need to be aware of the types of product available and be aware that the market is likely to be fast-moving.

Signature

Note 28

5.51 There is no recommendation that the client take independent advice before signing the agreement. This assumes that by using the plain English version of the model, its terms will have been fully explained. It is, therefore, reasonable to expect the client to be able to determine unaided whether to go ahead. If the solicitor uses a different version, particularly one that is not in plain English, the solicitor should consider whether the client can make an informed decision about its terms without independent advice. It may be useful to run through the checklist in the Law Society's leaflet *Conditional Fees Explained* prior to signature.

Parties' endorsement

Note 29

5.52 In addition to the parties' signatures to the substantive agreement, the model includes an endorsement by both the solicitor and the client confirming that the solicitor has fulfilled his duties of explanation under the Regulations. It is important to remember that if the 2000 Regulations are not complied with the agreement is likely to become unenforceable. The endorsement is designed to draw attention to the specific duties under the Regulations and requires the client specifically to confirm that explanations have been given. Hopefully this should head off any future disputes.

The Schedules

Note 30

5.53 Due to the complexity of certain duties under the Regulations and the amount of detailed information specific to the particular case which must potentially be provided, it was felt more appropriate for much information to be set out in separate schedules rather than by clogging up the body of the agreement.

Schedule 1 success fee

Note 31

5.54 As indicated above, the new statutory regime prohibits the success fee from being greater than 100 per cent. The solicitor should carry out a specific risk assessment in each particular case and set out his reasons for setting the percentage uplift at which it is set. It must be remembered that the percentage uplift is not the same as the solicitor's assessment of the percentage chances of success (see Chapter 4). The reasons set out in the model are suggestions and should not be followed slavishly. In particular, the matters to be set out at paragraph (d) will vary from case to case. It should also be remembered that the 'financing' element will fall to be paid by the client, and this liability should be emphasised (see 2.31 above).

Note 32

5.55 As discussed at note 25 above, the part of the success fee which relates to the 'financing' element needs to be shown separately in order to comply with the Regulations. This element is not recoverable from a losing opponent.

Schedule 2 insurance policy

Note 33

5.56 The nature of the duty to explain the nature of available insurance products is set out in detail at notes 25 and 27 above. The solicitor's reasons for his advice are to be set out at this point.

Note 34

5.57 The model confirms specifically that the solicitor is not a broker (see note 27 above).

LAW SOCIETY CONDITIONS

Solicitor's responsibilities

Note 35

5.58 The CFA imposes no new or especially onerous duties on a solicitor. This condition simply summarises the normal professional responsibilities of a solicitor in a personal injury case. To emphasise the mutually binding nature of the agreement, the solicitor should run through each point with his client, giving examples if appropriate, and checking that he or she fully understands what the solicitor is committed to doing for him or her.

Client's responsibilities

Note 36

5.59 This sets out the client's responsibilities towards the solicitor. The solicitor should run through each of these responsibilities and use them to stress that the CFA is a serious undertaking. Unless the client keeps to his side of it, it can be terminated (with the cost consequences that would follow (see note 15)). However, the solicitor will also need to reassure the client that his or her obligations are not unfair or particularly onerous. It may, therefore, be helpful to give the client examples of, say, the kind of co-operation which the solicitor will expect: 'we cannot demand you to attend our office at a moment's notice; but you should co-operate if we reasonably ask you to attend a medical examination'.

Explanation of words used

Note 37

5.60 Many of these words will be unfamiliar to the client, and as the words appear in various parts of the agreement, they should be explained carefully.

'Advocacy'

Note 38

5.61 'Advocacy' is particularly important in the context of condition 6.

Basic costs

Note 39

5.62 Condition 3(b) defines basic costs for the client, and should be read in the context of the appropriate section of the main agreement (see note 16).

'Disbursements'

Note 40

5.63 The standard disbursements in a personal injury case are defined in condition 3(f). These disbursements will be familiar to the solicitor, but probably not to the client. The solicitor should therefore take the client through the list, explaining each in turn. Fees for advocacy may or may not be treated as disbursements, depending on whether a barrister is used, and whether the advocate is working under a CFA (see note 72). This condition emphasises the client's liability to pay these disbursements win or lose, giving the solicitor protection under the indemnity principle. It also re-iterates that 'no win no fee' doesn't mean no win no costs.

'Interim damages'

Note 41

5.64 The solicitor can use interim damages to fund future disbursements or reimburse ones already paid. Neither the basic fee or the success fee can be taken out of out of these payments. (See also note 10 above.)

'Interim hearing'

Note 42

5.65 See notes 12 and 13.

'Lien'

Note 43

5.66 Many clients will be unfamiliar with the term 'lien'. The solicitor should therefore explain both its meaning and its implications. Although the papers relate to the client's case, the solicitor has legal rights over them. If the client arbitrarily decides to switch firm, you could, if you chose, decide to exercise those rights until payment arrangements for the work you have done have been agreed.

'Lose'

Note 44

5.67 The definition of 'lose' should be carefully explained to the client.

'Part 36 offers or payments'

Note 45

5.68 CPR Part 36 offers and payments are a complex area in themselves which the solicitor will need to explain carefully to the client. If a Part 36 offer is not beaten, under the model CFA the solicitor will be entitled to his base costs (but not a success fee) for the work done after the date of the offer. (See also note 9.)

'Provisional damages'

Note 46

5.69 See note 11.

'Success fee'

Note 47

5.70 See note 18.

'Win'

Note 48

5.71 The definition of 'win' needs to be explained carefully. Note that the client is not deemed finally to have won until an appeal by the opponent has either been ruled out or been decided in the client's favour. Thus the CFA covers the defence of an appeal by the opponent.

5.72 Generally, it will be obvious whether a case has been won, and therefore whether the solicitor is entitled to a success fee. However, the position may be less clear cut if the court orders a split trial and at the first trial on liability judgment is given in favour of the client. This amounts to a win. At that stage there will often be an interim payment of damages from which the solicitor may wish to recoup disbursements (see notes 12, 13 and 41). However, if after the success on liability, no damages are paid to the client until settlement of the second trial of quantum, it would not be appropriate for the solicitor to take his disbursements at this stage.

Payment if the client wins

Note 49

5.73 The solicitor will need to take the client carefully through condition 4 which sets out what happens if he wins the case. For a definition of 'win', see notes 5.71–5.72 above.

Note 50

5.74 If the client wins he is responsible for the disbursements, base costs and success fee. This liability must be incorporated in the agreement to comply with the indemnity principle.

Note 51

5.75 This sentence refers to the 'loser pays' principle. If the client wins, then his costs will be paid by the other side. The solicitor could use this as an opportunity to stress that, conversely, if he or she loses, the client will be responsible for the opponent's costs and the possibility of insuring against this risk.

Note 52

5.76   This sentence refers to the assessment procedure. The solicitor must also stress that if there is a discrepancy between the amount allowed on taxation and the solicitor's costs, the client is responsible for the difference.

Note 53

5.77   This sentence reflects CPR Rule 44.3.B(1)(a) (see 2.61 above). It will need to be explained to the solicitor's client that this will be his liability.

Note 54

5.78   This sentence reflects reg.3(2)(a)(ii) of the 2000 Regulations which requires the agreement to provide for disclosure of this information (see 2.32 above).

Note 55

5.79   This sentence reflects reg.3(2)(b) (see 2.33 above). If the court disallows any part of the percentage uplift on the basis that it is unreasonable, the solicitor cannot merely turn around and ask the client to meet the shortfall. If the solicitor believes that it is reasonable for the client to pay the shortfall then the solicitor will need to apply to the court under CPR Rule 44.16 (see 2.72–2.74 above). This provides a measure of consumer protection in cases where the solicitor has not set an unrealistically high success fee. As to cases where the court might feel it appropriate to allow the shortfall to be recovered, one can envisage instances, for example, where a client has been particularly difficult or misleading.

Note 56

5.80   It is open for the solicitor to negotiate a settlement of the costs by agreeing a lower rate of success fee. However, once this has been done this, then under reg.3(2)(c) the solicitor cannot recover the shortfall without reference to the court (see 2.32 above). Similar considerations apply as at note 61, save that logically it is likely to be a more uphill task to persuade the court that the shortfall should be payable by the client where the solicitor has agreed to a lesser sum.

Note 57

5.81 This sentence attempts to safeguard against the position where the solicitor is on the verge of settling the claim, the general level of damages has been agreed, but there is an issue as to costs, and in particular, the level of the success fee. The client cannot insist that the solicitor accepts such an offer in this instance, even though the client might be happy with the level of compensation he or she is to receive. This avoids a situation where the lawyer is put into a corner by an opponent's representative who offers a reasonable level of compensation, but who seeks drastically to attack the success fee. Generally the solicitor is bound to follow the client's instructions, potentially leaving the success fee decimated and profitability threatened. This clause seeks to offer the solicitor protection in those circumstances.

Note 58

5.82 The solicitor must explain to his client that despite the 'loser pays' principle, if the opponent is publicly funded, the client may be very unlikely to be able to recover his costs. He will therefore have to pay the base costs, disbursement, and success fee out of any damages. The solicitor may therefore wish to think hard before taking on a CFA case where the opponent is receiving Community Legal Service funding.

Note 59

5.83 See notes 6 and 47.

Note 60

5.84 This ensures that any costs not payable by the other side can be recovered from the client.

Note 61

5.85 The solicitor will need to get the client's agreement that the solicitor can keep any interest paid by the opponent on the costs.

Note 62

5.86 See condition 6 and notes 70–73 below.

If the client's opponent fails to pay

Note 63

5.87 This gives the solicitor the right of subrogation to enforce payment of costs.

Payment if the client loses

Note 64

5.88 The solicitor will need to take the client through condition 5, which sets out what happens if he loses.

Note 65

5.89 If the solicitor is protected by after-the-event insurance this will normally cover him for disbursements and the other side's costs. The definition of 'lose' is given at condition 3(j), which also needs to be explained. The opening sentence encapsulates the essence of conditional fees: if the client's case is lost he does not have to pay the solicitor's fees.

Note 66

5.90 However, it is equally important that clients understand both what they will not have to pay and what they will have to pay. The client should therefore make sure that he understands what his liabilities will be in the event that he loses. Under the standard terms the client is liable to pay the solicitor for any disbursements (unless otherwise agreed) in the event of a loss. Some solicitors believe that it is against the spirit of 'no win no fee' agreements to enforce this liability, and that the lawyer will bear the loss. In a competitive market-place it may be unattractive to clients to have to bear this potential liability. If a decision is taken to vary the term, then the solicitor must make sure that the indemnity principle is not breached. The disbursements must definitely remain part of the client's liability in the event of a win. Alternatively, the solicitor may be able to take advantage of the developing insurance market to guard against this potential liability. Lawyers will need to consider such options in order to discharge their duties to advise on insurance products under the 2000 Regulations (see 5.50 above).

Note 67

5.91 The client will be liable for the other side's costs and disbursements unless protected by insurance. However, solicitors should point out that these will be subject to the scrutiny of assessment. The client will not just be liable for the other side's costs if the entire case is lost. He may also have to pay costs if any minor battles are lost along the way, for instance interim hearings, judgments on a counterclaim, or a failure to beat a CPR Part 36 offer. There are extra costs which may have to come out of the client's damages if he is not covered by insurance.

Note 68

5.92 The solicitor can use this clause to reassure his client that if the client has an insurance policy in force, then, although in theory he may be personally liable for the disbursements and his opponent's fees and disbursements, these will be met by the insurers.

Note 69

5.93 If the case is lost overall, but an interim hearing has been won along the way at which the client was awarded costs, those costs will fall to be carried by the solicitor.

Advocacy

Note 70

5.94 The advocate can be an in-house solicitor, solicitor's agent or a barrister. Where advocacy is undertaken by the firm or another solicitor, the cost cannot be treated as a disbursement for the purpose of recovery or insurance. This means that it forms part of the firm's base costs and will not be recovered if the case is lost, but a success fee is payable on it if the case is won. Where the advocacy is performed by a barrister the fees are described as a disbursement whether the case is won or lost. Whether or not the fees can be recovered under an insurance policy will vary according to the product.

Barristers

Note 71

5.95   The solicitor will need to notify the client of the basis upon which the barrister's fees are payable (e.g. are they also on a CFA?), since this is clearly capable of affecting a client's liability.

Barristers working under a CFA

Note 72

5.96   At the time of signing the CFA with the client the solicitor may not know whether he can find a suitable barrister to act on a CFA basis or not. The solicitor should therefore explain to his client what would happen in both situations.

5.97   If the barrister is instructed on a CFA basis, the client benefits from not having to pay the barrister's fees as the case goes along, and not being liable for those fees if the case is lost. If he wins there will be two success fees payable, one to the firm and one to the barrister (although payment of the barrister's fees remains ultimately the responsibility of the solicitor, see below). Because of the additional expense to the losing party, the opponent is likely to take an aggressive stance toward any unnecessary use of counsel, and the solicitor will need to be able to justify the same.

5.98   If the barrister is working under CFA terms, there will be a separate agreement between the solicitor and the barrister (there is no direct agreement between the barrister and the client). Although most of the terms which will be agreed with the barrister will not concern the client, the Law Society's model agreement requires the solicitor to inform the client of the level of the barrister's success fee.

Barristers not working under a CFA

Note 73

5.99   If the barrister is not working on a conditional fee basis, this has the disadvantage for the client that he would have to pay these costs if the case were lost. With a non-CFA barrister, the solicitor's partnership remains professionally responsible for his fees, win or lose, in the usual way. Under the standard terms of the model CFA the client is made liable for this amount. Again, it is a matter for the solicitor whether to enforce such a liability or bear it as an operating cost. Further, the solicitor should monitor developments in the AEI market which may cover such outgoings. If the solicitor has varied the model and agreed to bear these fees if the case is lost, this added financial risk should be reflected in a higher success fee.

Early termination

Note 74

5.100 This condition covers a crucial area of the agreement. The respective rights of client and solicitor if the CFA is terminated early is a complex area and one which is ripe for misunderstanding. The solicitor must be sure that both he or she and the client fully understand what would be involved before signing the agreement. If, however, the stage is reached where an existing agreement is about to be ended, the solicitor and the client will need to refer back to this condition in far greater detail.

Payment if the client terminates the CFA

Note 75

5.101 As discussed at note 15 the client has greater freedom to end the agreement than the solicitor. The client can end it without having to give any reasons, whereas the solicitor can only do so if certain conditions are met. This reflects the relationship between solicitor and client, as set out in *The Guide to the Professional Conduct of Solicitors 1999* which states that a solicitor must not terminate his retainer with the client except for good reason and upon reasonable notice. In the event that the client does end the agreement early the solicitor has two options:

(a) to take his costs immediately (in which case the right to a success fee should the case be won is forfeit)

(b) to wait and see whether the case ultimately succeeds (either under another solicitor or with the client as a litigant in person) and agree to wait until the case is won, in which case the solicitor is entitled to his basic costs, disbursements and success fee. If the case is not won then the solicitor will not be entitled to any of these payments.

When deciding which option to choose, the solicitor should consider the following:

(1) Does the client intend to continue the case himself or to use another solicitor, or to abandon it altogether?

(2) If the client plans to act for himself, what are the prospects of success?

(3) If the client plans to use another solicitor, how does the solicitor rate the firm?

(4) How strong is the case overall?

(5) What stage has been reached?

(6) What is the solicitor's firm's cash-flow position?

(7) What is the likely level of base costs, disbursements and success fee?

(8) Does the client have the means to pay immediately?

Whichever option the solicitor chooses, the decision should be recorded in writing. If the solicitor has decided to wait in the hope of a successful outcome, then the solicitor's lien over the papers should be preserved until the usual undertaking from the former client's new firm that the solicitor's entitlement to costs, disbursements and success fee will be preserved when these items are dealt with at the end of a successful case.

Payment if the solicitor terminates the CFA

Note 76

5.102 Whereas the client can end the agreement at will, the solicitor can end it if the client is in breach of one of his or her responsibilities under the agreement (see condition 2). If the solicitor ends the agreement because the client is in breach, the solicitor can decide whether:

(a) to take basic costs and disbursements straight away but sacrifice any success fee; or

(b) to wait until the case is won before taking the basic costs and disbursements, plus the success fee.

If the latter option is chosen and the case is lost, then the solicitor forfeits the right to any of these payments.

Note 77

5.103 The solicitor can also end the agreement unilaterally if he thinks that the case will not succeed. In this situation the client is not liable for the solicitor's fees but may have to pay the disbursements. Whether this is the case depends on the insurance position and on whether the solicitor had agreed to fund the disbursements on the client's behalf in the event that the case be lost.

Note 78

5.104 If the solicitor ends the agreement because the client rejects the advice to accept an offer of settlement, the client must pay the solicitor's base costs and disbursements immediately because the solicitor has effectively 'won' the case. As and when a final order is made the success fee can be claimed. Again, the solicitor would be right to preserve his lien over the papers until he has received the necessary undertakings about receiving payment. If the solicitor and the client disagree over whether to accept an offer of settlement, the client is entitled to a second opinion. This is the only area of the agreement which gives the client the right to insist on a formal review of the solicitor's decision, albeit at the client's own expense.

Death

Note 79

5.105 The consequences of death before the case is finally dealt with under the CFA should be carefully explained to the client, particularly, for example, in industrial disease cases where this could be a genuine possibility. Death automatically brings the agreement to an end and base charges should be recovered from the deceased's estate. If the deceased's personal representatives wish to continue with the claim, they will need to enter a fresh conditional fee agreement which makes special provision for payment of a success fee not only on the base charges incurred during the currency of that agreement, but also on base charges incurred under the existing agreement.

What happens after the CFA ends

Note 80

5.106 If the client terminates the CFA and retainer, then the solicitor will still be on the court record until an application is made to be removed.

Accident Line rider

Note 81

5.107 This clause should be added into the main body of the agreement in cases covered by the Accident Line AEI package. This clause can also be amended and inserted to cover cases insured with other AEI products.

CHAPTER 6

The Bar

Gordon Wignall

INTRODUCTION

6.1 CFAs present particularly acute challenges of a practical nature to the Bar as an independent referral profession. The effect of CFAs on the structure and management of chambers has not been fully worked out. The Bar Council has recently made extensive practical guidance for barristers and their clerks immediately accessible on its website (www.barcouncil.org.uk), but, as the Bar Council itself says, this guidance is not intended to be prescriptive (see Appendices 21a–h for extracts). Under the Bar Code of Conduct barristers are 'individually and personally' responsible for their own practices (see para.306). Whilst there is a duty on heads of chambers to ensure the efficient operation of chambers as a whole and the effective collection of fees, it is up to individual practitioners to ensure that they manage their affairs so that the fee arrangements into which they enter, and the practical steps which they put in place to manage them, are both commercially sound and enforceable (see Part IV).

6.2 So long as there is nothing in a CFA which might make a barrister uninsured (which would become a breach of the Code of Conduct), barristers are free to make what agreements they will. As to the Bar's mutual insurer (BMIF) its practical concern is not the mechanics of a CFA, but the danger that barristers may expose them to express liabilities to solicitors to which they are not ordinarily exposed. So long as these are capped (the current acceptable cap is £25,000), BMIF is likely to approve CFAs submitted to it for scrutiny (see 6.14–6.15 below). At present there are two model barrister CFAs in existence which have been approved by BMIF and which are available for general use, the first being the model personal injury agreement negotiated between the Association of Personal Injury Lawyers (APIL) and the Personal Injury Bar Association (PIBA) (the version available at the time of writing being version 5), and the second the terms of engagement prepared by the Chancery Bar Association (ChBA). (The model agreements will be found at Appendices 22 and 23a–b.)

6.3   The new system put in place by Part II of the Access to Justice Act 1999 (which is considered in detail in Chapter 2) will probably make CFAs between barristers and solicitors more common than they were under the old regime. This is because of the impact of the Courts and Legal Services Act 1990, s.58A(6), which allows for costs orders to include the success fee payable under a CFA. The previous system (under the un-altered 1990 Act) meant that success fees were recoverable only from a claimant's damages, and this was subject to a voluntarily imposed maxi-mum cap on the amount of the damages which could be appropriated in this way. The solicitor's profession imposed a 25 per cent cap, whilst the Bar applied a 10 per cent limit (the solicitor's 25 per cent cap included the barrister's uplift). This had two consequences. First, a solicitor was less likely to want to involve a barrister if it meant that the capped proportion of the damages available to meet success fees had to be apportioned between both solicitor and barrister. Secondly, CFAs were unlikely to be used to fund any party other than claimants seeking awards of damages.

6.4   Whilst the 1999 Act has removed some of the economic disincentives in the way of funding advocacy and other services provided by barristers, a solicitor still needs to ask whether the client is in fact better off by the instruction of counsel on a CFA basis at all. Appropriate use of a bar-rister under an ordinary retainer allows the client and solicitor to ensure that no conflicts can arise as a direct result of the CFA. This may be particularly valuable, for instance, where a settlement is proposed or a CPR Part 36 payment is made, the acceptance of which guarantees the payment of the lawyers' fees. If the client can afford to do so, the use of a barrister as a disbursement in the ordinary way may assist the soli-citor in relieving the client of any residual doubts which the client may have over the independence and objectivity of any advice to settle. The sophistication of combined loan and after-the-event insurance products can enable clients effectively to make use of the Bar's services on a refer-ral basis (see Chapter 7), and this method of funding is likely to repres-ent the most attractive way forward to many members of the Bar. Some AEI insurers insist that barristers are retained on non-CFA terms.

6.5   The Bar, especially its senior members, has not responded enthusiasti-cally to CFAs. This is probably, in part, because barristers would simply rather not share the risks of the litigation, the attendant perils being more acute when the fees are high, the caseload relatively low and the bulk of the barrister's fees are incurred towards the end of the case once key strategic decisions have already been taken. It is also because barristers tend to be particularly nervous about the effect of CFAs on their relationship with the judges, and about any imputation that their independence is compromised by the nature of the funding. Some barristers see CFAs as a direct affront to their status as providers of independent, objective advice. This reaction may or may not be understandable, but it has led to wider concerns, especially amongst the solicitor's profession, about the Bar's willingness fully to play its part in providing advocacy services under CFA terms. On occasions the Bar has shown itself too ready to assume an ethical responsibility for matters which are beyond its remit, particularly the way in which the instructing solicitor has complied with the onerous responsibilities placed on him under the Conditional Fee Agreements Regulations 2000 to give certain advice and information to the client. (Ethical considerations are considered in more detail at 6.58 below.)

6.6 From a purely commercial point of view, CFAs are not always attractive to the Bar. Although they are ostensibly well-suited to claimant personal injury cases where liability is unlikely to be in issue, there is not much of a financial uplift to be gained in such cases if the matter does not proceed to trial. In commercial cases, 'differential' or 'mixed' fee agreements are likely to be more attractive to the Bar, and they do not carry all the risks usually associated with failure. Under the terms of such agreements the barrister agrees to receive his normal fees if the case succeeds (with or without a percentage uplift) and a reduction of his or her normal fees in the event of failure.

6.7 The risks to which barristers are particularly exposed when working under CFA terms arise first, because each member of chambers carries his or her own losses (as well as successes) and secondly, because counsel cannot scrutinise what is happening on a day-to-day basis with the proceedings. Both individual barristers and their chambers must be alert to the need to minimise the financial risks to which barristers are likely to be exposed as a result of entering into CFAs. Procedures need to be put in place to ensure that these risks are controlled and that the outcomes are monitored. This will require the resolution of difficult questions within chambers as to how (if at all) such procedures are to be enforced against individuals.

6.8 This chapter is concerned with CFAs which are entered into after 1 April 2000, being the date on which the Access to Justice Act 1999 came into force. CFAs entered into before 1 April 2000 cannot be assessed as funding arrangements for the purposes of the CFA regime as it exists as a result of the 1999 Act (see 2.3 above).

THE LEGISLATIVE FRAMEWORK AND THE BARRISTER/ SOLICITOR RELATIONSHIP

6.9   The legal framework which permits the engagement of barristers on a conditional fee basis after 1 April 2000 is no different from that which governs the relationship of solicitor and lay client, save that some of the formalities designed to protect the lay client are not required to be observed as between solicitor and an 'additional legal representative' (see 2.38 above).

6.10   In outline, a solicitor/barrister CFA is only enforceable if it is caught by the provisions of the Courts and Legal Services Act 1990, ss.58, 58A (as substituted and inserted by Part II of the Access to Justice Act 1999) (see 2.1–2.2 above). This means that the agreement must be in writing (s.58(3)(a)), and it must 'not relate to proceedings which cannot be the subject of an enforceable conditional fee agreement' (s.58(3)(b)) (see 2.16–2.18 above). Further, any CFA between a solicitor and counsel must comply with any relevant regulations prescribed by the Lord Chancellor (s.58(3)(c)). The effect of ss.58, 58A, is that there must be strict compliance with both the Act and the relevant regulations for a CFA to be enforceable (see 2.2 above for the consequences of unenforceability).

6.11   To date, the relevant regulations which have been prescribed are set out in the Conditional Fee Agreements Regulations 2000, SI 2000/692 ('the CFA Regulations 2000') (see 2.28ff above). Regulation 1(3) is so worded as to define counsel's instructing solicitor as the 'client' and the barrister as the 'legal representative'. The Regulations do not affect the normal relationship between solicitor and counsel (save perhaps when it comes to the recovery of a success fee which has been disallowed on an assessment (see 6.54–6.55 below)). It is the solicitor who remains personally liable to pay counsel, whether under the usual Terms of Work on Which Barristers Offer Their Services to Solicitors or under any variation recorded in writing (see para.8 of the Terms of Work). This means that the agreement between counsel and solicitor can be said to have an effective life of its own. It follows that whilst the barrister is exposed to any act or omission on the part of the solicitor which may result in there not being a 'success' which entitles counsel to his or her fees, if there has been any act or omission on the solicitor's part which renders the agreement between solicitor and lay client unenforceable as to the solicitor's costs, counsel can still look to his instructing solicitor to pay his fees. It should be noted, however, that the Bar Council believes that there may be dangers in a barrister entering into a CFA with a solicitor if the solicitor has agreed to represent a client under the terms of a non-contentious business agreement, for instance in employment tribunal or CICA proceedings (see paras 11.4–11.5 of Part 2 of the Practical Guidance and see 1.2–1.4 above).

6.12 The relevant provisions under the CFA Regulations 2000 which concern the Bar are the general regulations (reg.2) and the requirements for CFAs which provide for a success fee (reg.3). These regulations also apply as between the solicitor and his or her client, and a detailed discussion of their contents is set out at 2.28ff above. The regulations which expressly do not apply as between counsel and solicitor are reg.4 (see reg.4(6)) and also reg.5(1) (see reg.5(2) and see 2.38 above). When lawyers become more familiar with CFAs it is likely that chambers, or that certain members of chambers, will enter into collective conditional fee agreements with firms of solicitors with whom they work, in which case the Collective Conditional Fee Agreements Regulations 2000, SI 2000/2988 will be the relevant statutory instrument (see 2.43ff above).

Notification and the recoverability of counsel's success fee

6.13 Barristers need to be aware of CPR Rule 44.3B(1)(c), which prohibits a party from recovering an additional liability (in this instance the success fee) where the party has failed to provide information about a CFA (see 2.54–2.57, 2.63 above). The CPR do not require separate notification to be given of the existence of a barrister/solicitor CFA in addition to the existence of a solicitor/client CFA. In practical terms, a solicitor can generally be relied on to provide sufficient information about funding arrangements when he has entered into a CFA with the client. But if there is no solicitor/client CFA, then counsel should ensure that the solicitor does provide effective notification as required to allow the barrister to recover his success fee as provided by the CPR Costs Rules and Costs Practice Direction (see Chapter 2, especially 2.49 and 2.54–2.57 above). If notification is not given within the rules then counsel can probably still recover the success fee from his instructing solicitor, since the solicitor remains professionally liable to pay counsel's fees. If not, then counsel may be able to fall back on any express indemnity set out in the CFA. A healthier approach would be to make sure at the outset that sufficient information has been provided as required by the CPR. (It should also be remembered that if there is a failure to notify the other side as required by the rules, then it is possible to apply for relief from sanction under section 10 of the Costs Practice Direction (see 2.65 above).)

BMIF

6.14   Rule 10.1.1 of the rules of BMIF, the Bar's mutual insurer, states that:

> BMIF shall indemnify the Insured against claims by a solicitor for payment of all or part of the solicitor's fees under a conditional fee agreement between the Insured Barrister and that solicitor, only if and to the extent that:
>> the conditional fee agreement entered into by the Barrister and the solicitor is in a form previously approved in writing by the Directors.

Privately, senior figures at BMIF have expressed concern that the wording of this rule might lead to an influx of divergent CFAs being sent to BMIF for formal approval. BMIF is not concerned with the general provisions of CFA agreements and does not want to be seen to have given approval to anything other than the express indemnity clause usually prevalent in a CFA. Such clauses are properly inserted at the insistence of solicitors. In the normal way, if an error or omission on the part of a barrister leads to the failure of a claim, the solicitor would recover his fees as part of the damages sought by the client. Since carelessness on the part of a barrister where the solicitor represents his client under CFA terms makes the recovery of fees more difficult to assess (the solicitor having to demonstrate the extent to which it was likely that success would have been achieved), an express indemnity on the part of the barrister is a standard part of a barrister/solicitor CFA. In turn the solicitor can also expect to have to provide such an express indemnity in the agreement (see for instance APIL/PIBA 5 at para.22(1)).

6.15   In practice BMIF has not been overwhelmed with applications for the approval of CFA agreements. This is probably because barristers have preferred to work on the standard models drawn up by those professional bodies which have received BMIF approval (see below). However, there are certain CFAs in existence between barristers' chambers and solicitors' practices which do not conform with the model agreements. Barristers need, at the very least, to ensure that where there is an express indemnity that this is capped at £25,000, since it is the extent of the cap which is of concern to BMIF. The amount of £25,000 is the maximum liability to which, at the time of writing, BMIF is willing to expose itself.

MODEL AGREEMENTS AND CLAUSES OF PARTICULAR CONCERN TO BARRISTERS

6.16   As has been said above, there are currently only two model agreements available which have BMIF approval. One is the joint APIL/PIBA agreement (APIL/PIBA 5, see Appendix 22), and the other is the Chancery Bar Association terms of engagement (see Appendices 23a to 23d). The first represents a compromise reached between personal injury solicitors and barristers. In certain critical areas it contains alternative provisions, and counsel should be careful to ensure that any agreement entered into is entered into on the appropriate clauses. APIL/PIBA 5 was drafted specifically with personal injury and clinical negligence proceedings in mind where the solicitor is also working under CFA terms with his client (on the Law Society model agreement, see Chapter 5 and Appendix 20). It is an industry-wide agreement and there is little prospect of a prudent personal injury solicitor departing from its key clauses. The ChBA agreement is a much more flexible instrument and is more effective at protecting the interests of barristers. Whilst further agreements are expected, for instance from COMBAR and ELBA, the ChBA terms of engagement can be easily adapted to cover a very wide range of circumstances.

6.17   The following paragraphs consider and summarise some of the key provisions of the model agreements. Barristers (and solicitors) need to familiarise themselves with all of the contents of these agreements in order to ensure that they understand the nature of the terms into which they are entering.

The 'proceedings' to be covered by a CFA: enforcement: appeals

6.18   Regulation 2 of the CFA Regulations 2000 requires a CFA to specify the particular proceedings or parts of them to which the agreement relates (reg.2(1)(a)). This provision requires some thought on the part of both solicitor and barrister. Whilst most agreements are entered into at the commencement of instructions and are intended to run to the conclusion of the action, there is no reason why a barrister cannot be brought in in a complex case as and when required under new agreements for limited purposes on each occasion. Such a procedure requires the barrister to embark on a new risk assessment on each occasion when he or she is presented with a new CFA. At the same time it confers benefits on the barrister as well as on the solicitor and client. For the solicitor and client, a CFA restricted to part of the proceedings allows use to be made of a barrister under an ordinary retainer where appropriate (for instance advice as to settlement), but it also gives the barrister the power to limit his or her commitment to the CFA. What may appear an attractive commercial risk when first taken on may become less so some years down the line once the matter is booked in for trial. In a complex case counsel should have reservations about entering into an open-ended CFA, especially where it may be prudent to revisit the appropriate percentage uplift at a later date. The current legislation does not provide a mechanism for a revision of the measure of the success fee after the original agreement, save that the court has power to reduce an unreasonably high percentage uplift down, having regard to the factors known to the legal representative at the time at which the CFA was made (see 2.67–2.70 above).

6.19 Consideration also needs to be given to the extent to which the proceedings specified in the CFA by virtue of reg.2 are to include any appeal or enforcement or any interlocutory proceedings. Regulation 2 expressly requires the CFA to state whether the proceedings include 'any appeal, counterclaim or proceedings to enforce a judgement or order' (reg.2(1)(a)).

6.20 The ChBA terms of engagement offer complete flexibility in the extent to which they allow counsel to select the proceedings to be covered by the agreement. APIL/PIBA 5 is restricted to claims for 'damages for personal injuries' and categorises nine substantive and procedural areas to which it relates. These include 'any appeal by the client's opponent(s)', 'any appeal by the client against an interim order', 'any appeal by the client advised by counsel', and 'any proceedings to enforce a judgment or order'. By agreeing at the commencement of a CFA to accept an open-ended commitment to enforcement the barrister is exposed to risks which in some cases it might have been prudent to be able to reassess at a later date. He or she will not be able to increase either the original success fee or the rates of remuneration set out in the CFA.

Interim hearings

6.21 APIL/PIBA 5 states that counsel is not required to accept instructions to appear at an interim hearing if it would be reasonable (a) to assume that counsel's fees would not be allowed on an assessment or (b) to instruct a less experienced barrister, provided that counsel has 'used his best endeavours' to ensure that another barrister will accept instructions under the same CFA terms (para.9). The ChBA terms of engagement contain a similar provision (para.4).

Returns of work

6.22 Counsel needs to be extremely cautious about para.25 of APIL/PIBA 5 which sets out the obligations of counsel where he has to return work. Paragraph 25(1) requires him to ensure that he 'will use his best endeavours' to find an 'appropriate' replacement who will act for the client on the same CFA terms. If not, then according to which sub-paragraph has been deleted from the agreement, either (a) he becomes personally responsible for any additional fees which are reasonably incurred, or (b) he does not become responsible for the fees. Counsel needs to ensure that (a) rather than (b) has been deleted from the agreement. The ChBA terms require a barrister who is obliged to return work to 'endeavour' to find an acceptable replacement, but if such a barrister cannot be found then this does not constitute a breach of the agreement (para.5).

6.23 Chambers will have to find solutions where possible to the problem of organising alternative counsel. In areas where chambers rely on bulk supplies of similar work, notably personal injury work, it would be unsatisfactory commercially for instructing solicitors to have to accept disclaimers of the type set out in the ChBA agreement. There is no doubt that notwithstanding that barristers generally do their best to avoid returning cases, the system of returns is highly unpopular with solicitors, and solicitors are particularly concerned about difficulties which may arise in the case of returned CFA instructions. This is one issue where chambers need to devise effective policies to enable returned cases to be covered and where chambers need to take decisions on how these procedures can be enforced (see 6.48 below).

Specifying the circumstances in which fees are payable: 'success'

6.24 Regulation 2 of the CFA Regulations 2000 requires the CFA to provide a comprehensive account of the circumstances in which the legal representative will be paid his or her professional fees and expenses, or any part of them (reg.2(1)(b)).

6.25 The definition of 'success' in most CFAs may well overlap with the way in which 'proceedings' are defined and counsel must decide the appropriate standard by which success is to be determined. The easiest method, it is suggested, is to determine success by reference to the relief granted by the court (or as set out in any compromise agreement). Another method could be to determine success by reference to the question whether any costs are to be awarded by the court. In cases where the relief sought is equitable in nature it is more likely that the description of success will need to have some reference to the facts in issue.

6.26 As to the model agreements, the ChBA terms leave success to be defined by reference to the relief sought (see para.20(1)). This is required to be set out in an annex to the agreement. At the other extreme, the APIL/PIBA model defines success as 'the same as "win" in the Conditional Fee Agreement between the Solicitor and Client' (para.19(1)). In most cases the solicitor/client CFA will be based on the Law Society model, which defines 'win' as a claim for damages which is 'finally decided in [the client's] favour' (see Chapter 5 and Appendix 20).

Early termination and payment obligations

6.27 Regulation 2(1)(c) requires a legal representative clearly to set out what payment is due in the event of part-success and on early termination of the agreement. A barrister will need to have an eye to the possibility of termination prior to final disposal in a number of distinct circumstances. The first is where the solicitor is entitled unilaterally to terminate the CFA. The second is where there is some settlement or compromise of the proceedings. The third is where counsel is entitled to terminate the agreement. The fourth is where some prescribed event occurs which enables, or requires, termination of the CFA.

Early termination by the solicitor

6.28 Both APIL/PIBA 5 and the ChBA model agreements give the solicitor a right to terminate the barrister/solicitor CFA in certain circumstances. Under APIL/PIBA 5 a solicitor can terminate an agreement where the client or litigation friend instructs him to do so (para.12). Under the ChBA terms a solicitor can terminate the agreement either without cause (para.8), or in the event that counsel has become unavailable for trial, or the solicitor has 'good reason to believe' that the relation of trust has irretrievably broken down, or the solicitor believes that counsel has manifested incompetence justifying termination of his retainer (para.9). Where the solicitor terminates APIL/PIBA 5, the barrister has to choose whether to accept payment of his normal fees within three months without an uplift, or whether to wait and see if the case succeeds, in which case he can claim both his normal fee and his percentage uplift (para.23(4)). Under the ChBA terms, counsel becomes 'immediately' entitled to his base fees where the agreement is terminated without cause, or where the solicitor believes that there is a breakdown in the relationship between the two parties; he is also entitled to his success fee in the event of subsequent success (para.26). Where the solicitor terminates the agreement because counsel is unavailable for trial or because the solicitor has good reason to suppose that counsel has been incompetent, the matter is initially treated as though the proceedings have failed. That is to say that counsel is entitled only to any reduced rate which may have been agreed in the event of failure, but if the proceedings subsequently succeed, then he is also entitled to the full uplifted rate (paras.27, 28).

Settlement

6.29   Special provisions are needed to cover what happens in the event of a compromise of the proceedings. This is because the provisions in the agreement will be varied to accommodate what happens when a CPR Part 36 payment or offer is made (the definition of 'success' being unlikely to be entirely appropriate to determine whether or not the lawyers are entitled to their fees). Under both APIL/PIBA 5 and the ChBA terms, if the amount of damages and interest awarded by the court is less than a Part 36 payment or offer, counsel is entitled to both his normal and success fees if he advised its acceptance; but if he advised its rejection, then he is entitled to his normal fees and percentage uplift up to the date of receipt of the Part 36 notice, but only to his normal fees for any subsequent work (APIL/PIBA 5, para.20 and, ChBA terms, para.21).

6.30   Counsel needs to ensure that he or she is actively engaged in the settlement process. That is to say that the CFA must be drafted so that he or she is made aware of any Part 36 offer or payment in sufficient time to consider the merits of the offer of payment. The CFA should also require the solicitor promptly to pass any formal advice which counsel has given about the offer or the payment to the client (a provision which is set out in the model agreements in current use).

Termination by counsel: general

6.31   Since the payment of fees is dependent on 'success' as defined by the barrister/solicitor CFA, counsel will need to do what he can to ensure that his financial interest in the proceedings are as secure as possible when the matter is not within his control. This requires a degree of caution when he is first presented with the case, but it also means that the barrister must do what he can to be involved in critical decisions about the subsequent conduct of the proceedings. He will also need ultimately to reserve to himself the ability to be able to withdraw from the CFA so far as possible.

Termination by counsel on the grounds of non-disclosure of relevant material

6.32 When the barrister first receives the papers he needs to ensure that he is presented with all the material relevant to (a) his decision whether to accept the case at all and (b) what percentage uplift is appropriate. APIL/PIBA 5 contains a recital that counsel has been sent 'all relevant papers and risk assessment material' and 'any offers of settlement already made' (para.5(4),(5)). The ChBA terms contain similar provisions at para.7. Compliance with these provisions is thought to be somewhat patchy. Both model agreements allow counsel to terminate the CFA if there has been a breach of the obligations relating to disclosure (see para.11). If the barrister is being instructed by a solicitor whose reliability and competence are entirely unknown, then the need for such protection is particularly important. It is also worth pointing out that counsel's instructing solicitor and counsel are both exposed to the risk that the remedy sought by a client is caught by the principle in *Henderson* v. *Henderson* (1843) 3 Hare 100, so that, for instance, a client who wishes to seek damages for a whiplash injury may already unwittingly have accepted a small sum in settlement of all his causes of action at the instigation of insurers seeking the recovery of compensation for damage to the client's vehicle (see *Talbot* v. *Berkshire County Council* [1993] 3 WLR 708 and *Sheriff* v. *Klyne Tugs (Lowestoft) Ltd* [1999] ICR 1170 for applications of the *Henderson* v. *Henderson* principle (noting also *Johnson* v. *Gore Wood & Co* [2001] 2 WLR 72, HL).

Termination by counsel because of matters arising during the conduct of the proceedings

6.33 What protection can the barrister seek in respect of a termination arising as a result of what may occur during the currency of the agreement? Both APIL/PIBA 5 and the ChBA model agreement impose obligations on the solicitor to seek the advice of counsel at pre-determined moments during the course of litigation (see APIL/PIBA 5, para.10(5) and ChBA terms para.7(5)). The ChBA document probably gives greater protection to counsel since it obliges the solicitor to consider *with counsel* whether a written advice is needed at a variety of stages. Both agreements contain catch-all provisions designed to require the solicitor (a) to bring relevant or material information to counsel's attention and

(b) to conduct the case diligently and in such a way that there is no danger of the matter falling foul of any procedural rules. The sections of the two models dealing with the solicitors' obligations are also worded to ensure that (a) counsel is involved as fully as possible in any settlement discussions, (b) counsel's views about the prospects of success are brought to the attention of the client and (c) counsel is given as much notice as possible of forthcoming hearings.

6.34 Where there is a breach by the solicitor of the obligations as set out in the CFA, then a right of termination by counsel is reserved in both APIL/PIBA 5 and the ChBA terms (see para.11). There is also a right of termination by counsel in the event that counsel's advice about settlement or the prospects of success is rejected. Detailed provisions as to payment of counsel's fees in the event of termination are contained in both documents, and barristers should make themselves aware of these prior to entering into either of the two agreements. The main difference between the two is that under APIL/PIBA 5 counsel has to elect whether to receive his basic fees within three months of termination, or to await the outcome in order to be able to claim his full fees (including a percentage uplift) in the event of success; under the ChBA terms the right to payment of the percentage uplift follows in any event if the proceedings are successful.

Termination in prescribed circumstances

6.35 A solicitor is required as part of his professional duties to ensure that his or her client is made aware that state funding is available if that should be the case. In order to be able to supply funding at state expense the solicitor generally has to have a contract with the Community Legal Service. The position is complicated because there are circumstances under the Funding Code in which a lay client may be entitled to public assistance with certain parts of proceedings or with certain disbursements without being entitled to the equivalent of a full legal aid certificate (see Appendix 25). Both APIL/PIBA 5 and the ChBA terms provide that the barrister/solicitor CFA automatically terminates where state funding becomes available.

6.36 In circumstances where the client either dies or goes bankrupt or an IVA is approved, or, in the case of a corporate client, if it becomes subject to a winding-up order, or if an administration order is made, or similar, then counsel may or may not necessarily want to terminate the retainer. Further, the barrister/solicitor CFA needs to specify what consequences are to follow if junior counsel becomes a Queen's Counsel, or if a barrister retires, or is unable to practise through some disciplinary sanction, or accepts a full-time judicial appointment. The consequences in terms of payment need to be spelled out as appropriate, and in the latter set of circumstances (those affecting the barrister's ability to practise) chambers needs to adopt a policy whether or not the set will be able to assist the solicitor with an alternative.

STATEMENTS OF REASONS AND RISK ASSESSMENTS

6.37   The risk assessment process is of course vital for the purposes or recovering the success fee at all, since reg.3(1)(a) of the CFA Regulations 2000 requires the CFA 'briefly to specify the reasons for setting the percentage increase at the level stated in the agreement'. Regulation 3(2)(b) also requires the CFA to state how much of the percentage uplift relates to the cost to the legal representative of the postponement of his fees and expenses, this latter sum not being recoverable from the losing side in any circumstances (see 2.61 above). The risk assessment must be undertaken when the decision as to the appropriate success fee is made. Barristers who think that they can conjure up a proper risk assessment at a later stage – perhaps from some contemporaneous jotting – are likely to come unstuck.

6.38   APIL/PIBA 5 sets out a simple formula at para.17(2) which states the basic reasons why the percentage uplift is set at the specified level. This is the sum of (a) the appropriate percentage increase (Y per cent) reflecting the prospects of success (X per cent) (the latter said to be 'more fully set out in counsel's risk assessment'), together with (b) the cost of postponement of fees and expenses. The Bar's CFA Panel has prepared a Protocol for use with APIL/PIBA 5 described as 'Counsel's Risk Assessment to Help Counsel make a Risk Assessment and give a Statement of Reasons for Conditional Fees in Personal Injury Cases' (see Appendix 21g). The advice from PIBA has been to hold back the full risk assessment on the basis that it may contain material which the barrister does not wish the solicitor to see. For instance, it is common practice for barristers to incorporate an estimate of the risks of working for the particular solicitor if there is concern about the way in which that solicitor has previously handled cases. The CFA itself therefore will contain a summary of the reasons for setting the percentage uplift at the level at which it was set only in numerical (percentage) terms. We suggest that where counsel fails to make it clear in the body of the CFA what the risk elements are, then this deficiency is unlikely to be cured by the subsequent disclosure of a risk assessment which was not seen by the solicitor at the time at which the CFA was made. The result could cause problems for the solicitor, since the solicitor may find that he is liable for the barrister's percentage uplift without being able to recover that success fee from the losing side. This is because of CPR Rule 44.3B(1)(d) and the fact that the 'reasons' for the percentage uplift have not been stated in the CFA. On the other hand, the solicitor will have a good argument that the percentage uplift is not payable at all because of non-compliance with reg.3(1)(a). The CFA Regulations 2000 exist in order to provide a client with information relevant to his decision whether to enter into the CFA, and they apply as much between a barrister and solicitor as between a solicitor and lay client. The practice of withholding reasons for setting the percentage uplift at the level claimed from a CFA is contrary to the practice adopted by solicitors, the Law Society's model CFA anticipating that the solicitor will spell out his assessment of the risks to the client (see Schedule 1 at app.20 and also 4.37 above). The ChBA terms require simply that the reasons for the uplifted rate should 'briefly' be set out (para.15).

6.39   The risk assessment protocol drafted by the Bar's CFA Panel is worth reading in full, setting out as it does some of the details to be considered by counsel when assessing the risks. As the protocol points out, a risk assessment is 'not a science but the application of knowledge and experience to the facts as known at the time'. It is a mixture of the main risk factors special to the risks of the case and the ordinary risks of litigation and includes a 'ready reckoner' similar to that in use by solicitors (see Appendix 19). Counsel's approach in estimating the risks will be similar to that adopted by solicitors, consisting of an actuarial approach based on the special risks applicable to the individual proceedings, combined with an allowance for the ordinary perils of litigation. The discussion at Chapter 4 provides useful guidance for barristers as well as for solicitors, especially the considerations set out at 4.19ff above (see in particular 4.25–4.33 and 4.35–4.36 above).

6.40   It is important that the risk assessment is personally prepared by counsel and that it reflects what was known to counsel at the time at which the CFA was entered into. What the risk assessment must not do is slavishly follow the risk assessment prepared by the instructing solicitor. The facts known to the solicitor at the time at which he entered into the solicitor/client CFA are likely to be very different from those known to counsel when counsel was instructed.

CHARGING FOR THE INITIAL ADVICE

6.41　The risk assessment process faced by a barrister presents him or her with special difficulties which are unlikely to be faced by the solicitor who first receives the case. Solicitors in firms where conditional fee work is the norm, that is to say those which have busy personal injury departments, are more likely to be used to taking an informed view about the likely success and complexity of a matter at an early stage. They may well have a brief statement from the client, some details of what witnesses are going to say and some photographs of the scene of the accident. All of this material may even have been prepared by an agent and not by the solicitor, who, on a conventional approach to CFA risk assessment, is likely to have made a speedy assessment of the merits prior to embarking on further investigative costs and the expense of complying with the pre-action protocols.

6.42　In the case of a barrister, a full set of papers is more likely to be received with instructions perhaps to advise on merits, evidence and quantum. The decision whether to accept a case on CFA terms may well require hours of preparation. The ChBA has prepared a document entitled 'Terms of Engagement for Preliminary Work where Retainer on a Conditional Fee Basis is Contemplated' (see Appendix 23b), and these terms allow for payment of fees in a variety of circumstances once the preliminary work has been completed. For instance, it requires fees to be paid on an ordinary hourly basis if a CFA is subsequently not entered into, alternatively that the fees should be added to the fees due under the full CFA. The ChBA model agreement for use in relation to preliminary work is a useful response to the request to undertake what may be a long and complicated case under CFA terms, albeit that it comes with a warning that it may not be enforceable, if the fees are added to the main CFA.

MANAGING CFAs IN CHAMBERS

6.43　Neither individual barristers nor their chambers should allow themselves to run a significant CFA caseload without adopting procedures which allow them to control the potential risks of losing income. This means that barristers should do the best which they can to make prudent decisions about whether to accept instructions under CFA terms. It also requires careful monitoring of cases which have been already been commenced under CFAs.

Screening procedures

6.44   Individual barristers need to ensure that there are colleagues in chambers with whom they can screen cases prior to taking them on. The nature of the arrangements made between individual members will vary from chambers to chambers. In a busy set where a great deal of CFA work is undertaken in personal injury cases, chambers may need to set up regular procedures, and a panel which is required to examine the potential risks of each case. It is more likely that individual members will want to form themselves into smaller groups, and they may only discuss those cases where the prospects of success are considered by the individual who has received a particular brief to be below a particular percentage. Small groups are more likely to be the norm since different members of chambers will be more likely to trust the judgement of like-minded individuals, and there will be collections of barristers who are agreed about those solicitors from whom they will, and from whom they will not, accept CFA work. On the other hand, individuals will need to adopt close working relationships with a reasonable number of colleagues at the screening stage in order to ensure that there is sufficient cover available in the event that a brief has to be returned. It is not conducive to good commercial relationships either with solicitors, or within a set of chambers, to discover that when a brief has to be returned there is no-one available who is willing to take on the case. There may be questions of client confidence which need to be addressed if a second barrister is to be asked to examine another's set of instructions.

Monitoring outcomes

6.45   Monitoring the outcome of a CFA caseload is important to gauge the accuracy of barristers' decisions when agreeing to undertake CFA work. Proper monitoring ensures that screening practices are working correctly, that barristers are making the right decisions about the firms from which it is safe to accept CFA instructions, that they are making accurate assessments of risk, and that chambers is not over-exposed to the possibility of losing an unacceptably large number of CFA cases.

6.46   The Bar's Practical Guidance (Part 2) at paras.39–46 (see Appendix 21c) sets out a variety of steps which chambers can take to facilitate effective monitoring. These include establishing a log of CFA cases, a contemporaneous record for production in the event of assessment, an individual log for each member of chambers, and both chambers' and individuals' records of CFA cases. Barristers are advised to maintain a file in respect of each case which should become available to barristers to whom a case has to be returned.

6.47 Many of the suggestions made in the Practical Guidance constitute something of a counsel of perfection, and they require intensive labour on the part either of barristers or of administrative staff. They also add to the financial burdens on chambers, and in a highly competitive market-place, the increased fees required to ensure the adoption and maintenance of such systems run the risk of making chambers commercially unattractive. Good monitoring records on the other hand are vital, and those chambers which are most likely to accommodate such records are those which are most IT-minded. In chambers where members have access to a shared hard-drive, whether from home or at work, joint access to data files in CFA cases will assist in sharing, and in assessing, CFA information. The costs of running a CFA practice can be incorporated in counsel's basic fees, but can play no part in determining the success fee.

Enforcement of chambers' policies

6.48 Practical measures which might be taken on a chambers or group basis to ensure uniformity of approach are set out in the Bar's Practical Guidance (Part 2) at paras.33–37 (see Appendix 21c). They include consideration of the extent to which screening procedures need to be adopted throughout chambers, and whether chambers' policies (such as that relating to the return of work) should be published. What is likely to be much more difficult in practice is for chambers to be able to 'police' such agreed policies internally. What happens, for instance, if barrister X simply refuses to take any returns from barrister Y because he does not trust Y's judgement about screening, or if barrister Z refuses, against chambers' published criteria, to accept any returns from a certain firm of solicitors because he believes that that particular firm does not always make proper disclosure of the materials necessary adequately to screen the risks? The answers to such questions are generally being worked out on an ad hoc basis, but chambers need to consider whether rules of conduct in relation to CFA work need to be incorporated within their constitutions and what steps can legitimately be taken to enforce such rules.

RECOVERABILITY OF COUNSEL'S FEES AND ASSESSMENTS

6.49 Notwithstanding that when working under CFA terms the solicitor remains liable in the ordinary way to pay counsel's fees (save for the question of payment of a disallowed percentage uplift), barristers should be familiar with those parts of the CPR and Costs Practice Direction which are relevant to CFAs. They are discussed in detail at 2.49ff above, and will be found at Appendices 11 and 12 respectively. There is a useful discussion in Part 2 of the Bar's Guidance (app.21(c)).

Notification of CFAs entered into between 1 April and 2 July 2000

6.50 Importantly, the opposing side needs to be notified of the existence of CFA funding in order for the success fee to be recoverable. As has been said (see 6.13 above), there may be a problem in obtaining payment of a percentage uplift from an instructing solicitor if that solicitor is not engaged on CFA terms and has not notified the opposing side of the existence of the barrister/solicitor CFA. A discussion of the legislative provisions as to notification are set out at 2.54–2.57 above, including those provisions relating to CFAs entered into between 1 April and 2 July 2000 (requiring information to have been provided before 31 July).

Time and procedure of assessments

6.51 The process of assessment is considered at 2.58–2.60 above, the rules being designed to prevent the disclosure of the receiving party's assessment of the risks involved in the litigation. The notion is that if the paying party knew the details of the success fee claimed by the receiving party's lawyers, for instance at an interim stage, then the paying party would be better placed to determine whether to fight the proceedings or to settle the matter in a manner which the funded party would not be able to resist.

Limits on recovery under funding arrangements

6.52 Above at 2.61–2.66 is set out the provisions of CPR Rule 44.3B which imposes limits on the recoverability of success fees under funding arrangements, and also the contents of section 10 of the Costs Practice Direction which allows a solicitor to obtain relief from sanctions imposed by Rule 44.3B.

Factors to be taken into account in deciding whether a percentage uplift is reasonable

6.53 The factors which the court will take into account in deciding whether a percentage uplift is reasonable are set out above at 2.67–2.70. The discussion at 6.38 about the extent to which 'reasons' need to be contained in the body of counsel's CFA should be read in this context.

'Disallowed' uplifts in the barrister/solicitor relationship

6.54 Regulation 3(2)(b) of the CFA Regulations 2000 provides that where part of a percentage uplift is disallowed on the basis that the level at which the increase was set was unreasonable in the light of the facts known to the lawyer at the time at which the increase was set, then that amount is 'not payable under the agreement'. A similar provision applies where there is a compromise of an action. CPR Rule 44.16 allows for the legal representative to apply to the court that the full amount should 'continue to be payable by his client', and the detailed procedure is set out at section 20 of the Costs Practice Division (including steps to be taken by counsel, for instance at para.20.4 and 20.7(2)).

6.55 The combined effect of these provisions on the solicitor's liability to pay an agreed uplift is unclear. In the ordinary way a solicitor is required to pay counsel's reasonable fees, and any such fees which have been expressly agreed in writing are deemed to be reasonable and therefore due from the solicitor, whether or not they can be recovered from the client. In the case of CFAs it seems that the effect of reg.3(2)(b) is that counsel does have to persuade the court that that part of the agreed percentage uplift which has been disallowed was reasonable, notwithstanding that the instructing solicitor may have agreed to it in writing in the body of the CFA. The solicitor is very unlikely not to make a simultaneous application that the disputed part of counsel's uplift should be paid by the client if the court has held that it was unreasonable, but if the solicitor does not do so, then it is possible that the solicitor may have to meet a fee which the client is not obliged to pay. Further discussion of the procedural steps required to be taken by a solicitor to notify counsel that his fees have been disallowed is set out at 2.72–2.74 above.

CAN A BARRISTER TURN DOWN A CFA CASE?

6.56   Para. 604 of the Code of Conduct ('the Code'), provides an exception to that part of the Code which appears under the heading 'acceptance of instructions and the "cab-rank rule" ':

> a barrister in independent practice is not obliged to accept instructions . . .
> (c) to do any work under a conditional fee agreement.

In other words a barrister can turn down any case offered to him or her which is to be funded by way of a CFA. If a barrister refuses to take on a case on a CFA basis then he or she must take this decision speedily, since not to do so is to run the risk of falling foul of para.701 of the Code (requiring instructions to be read expeditiously and to be returned promptly).

FOREIGN PROCEEDINGS

6.57   The Code itself contains no other express reference which specifically refers to barristers and the use of CFAs, save that it must be remembered that in relation to work falling within certain criteria set out in Annex D, a barrister is permitted to work for a 'conditional or contingent fee where this is permissible under the laws or rules of the place where the services are to be provided'.

ETHICAL CONSIDERATIONS

6.58   The Bar's CFA Guidance contains an extensive discussion of the ethical considerations perceived by the Bar Council to apply to instructions accepted on CFA terms (app.21(b)). Relevant parts of the Code include the following:

> 303 A barrister:
> (a)   must promote and protect fearlessly and by all proper and lawful means the lay client's best interests and do so without regard to his own interests or to any consequences to himself or to any other person (including any professional client or other intermediary or another barrister);
> (b)   owes his primary duty as between the lay client and any professional client or other intermediary to the lay client and must not

permit the intermediary to limit his discretion as to how the interests of the lay client can best be served;

307 A barrister must not:
(a) permit his absolute independence integrity and freedom from external pressures to be compromised; . . .
(c) compromise his professional standards in order to please his client the Court or a third party.

There has been some discussion amongst senior figures in the profession as to the extent to which these extracts of the Code require a barrister to concern himself with the question whether the client has had a fair deal in the financial arrangements made at the commencement of the CFA entered into between the solicitor and lay client. It would seem very unlikely indeed that these parts of the Code do make it any part of a barrister's function to satisfy himself that the funding arrangements in place are satisfactory. Barristers are ill-equipped to determine the competing merits of different AEI products and loan arrangements.

6.59 Model CFA agreements currently circulating require the solicitor to disclose a copy of his CFA with the client and any AEI product (even though the 2000 Regulations themselves require the CFA between the instructing solicitor and lay client to state on its face that the information required by reg.4 has been supplied by the solicitor). It is questionable whether counsel needs to have sight of the solicitor/client CFA, or of any AEI policy, given that the validity of the agreement with counsel is not dependent on the validity of the solicitor/client relationship. The APIL/PIBA model as currently drafted makes it necessary for the barrister to see the contents of the solicitor/client CFA since the meaning of 'success' is imported into the barrister/solicitor CFA from the solicitor/client agreement. There is the added complication that, once supplied with such material, counsel may find himself in the invidious position of having to form a view about the quality of the products in place and the circumstances in which the client was advised to make use of them in the light of the provisions of the Code of Conduct set out above (see the discussion in Chapter 4 of *The Ethics of Conditional Fee Arrangements* (The Society for Advanced Legal Studies, January 2001)). The Bar Council should perhaps consider whether changes need to be made to the Code of Conduct and the Terms of Work in order to make it clear that when undertaking CFA work, counsel does not, as part of his normal duties, have any obligation to comment on the adequacy of any financial, or AEI, provision which may already have been put in place.

6.60 From a commercial point of view there is something to be said for demanding suitable reassurance that after-the-event insurance is in place if it is intended to cover some or all of the barrister's own fees (that is if the barrister is being engaged on a non-CFA or a mixed CFA basis). On the whole, however, it is our view that counsel should require as much material as possible to assist him with the question whether the risks of entering into a CFA are acceptable, but as little as possible which might result in having to consider issues on which he or she is not required to comment relating to the potential advantages (or disadvantages) of the commercial products which have been acquired by the client.

6.61 A further matter which does need to be considered is the potential conflicts of interest which may arise in chambers as a result of CFA instructions. Barristers will want to avoid any hint of impropriety where two counsel are instructed in a case and one is CFA-financed and another is not. If the financial stability of chambers is threatened by the failure of the CFA party, questions may be asked about the objectivity and independence of the non-CFA funded barrister. Similar issues may also arise if the judge is a Recorder and one of the barristers appearing before him is from his chambers and is CFA-funded.

CHAPTER 7

After-the-event insurance explained

Emmanuel Gilbert

INTRODUCTION

7.1 If ever something was designed to confuse, then after-the-event insurance (AEI) is it. Try and explain it to your average man in the street and you will get a very blank look. 'How can you take out insurance for something that has already happened?' is the common response.

7.2 Any solicitor who conducts litigation needs to know about after-the-event insurance. This chapter is intended to give the reader a good introduction and to help in dealings with the AEI providers. It is designed to be readily understood, and to speak directly to the lawyer. At the same time, it should be of assistance to the non-lawyer reader who is concerned about AEI products.

7.3 In the rest of this chapter, the companies that provide the insurance backing for AEI are referred to as 'underwriters' and the insurers that are on the receiving end of AEI are referred to as 'defendant insurers'.

7.4 So what is AEI? It is legal expenses insurance. It is not, however, like the legal expenses insurance that is commonly found as part of a household or motor insurance policy, and is now conventionally known as 'before-the-event' insurance. The three main differences are:

(a) an AEI policy covers a specific legal action for which a solicitor has already been instructed;

(b) an AEI policy lasts as long as the legal action;

(c) the premium charged for AEI is very expensive when compared to traditional before-the-event legal expenses insurance.

7.5 The term 'after-the-event' was coined because the 'event' that has given rise to the legal action has already taken place. This has led to the traditional annual legal expenses policies being labelled 'before-the-event' (BEI). BEI policies are cheap because many are taken out but comparatively few claims are made. Conversely, AEI policies have a higher incidence of claims so the premiums are higher. When cases are lost, the costs can be high. So how are premiums calculated? Basically, underwriters set premiums at levels to ensure, as far as possible, that the total premium income from all policies issued is sufficient to cover the cost of claims, as well as leaving something over for profit. In the five years since the first edition of this book, AEI premium rates have increased sharply. In 1995, a client pursuing a high value claim for personal injuries caused by an industrial disease could have purchased an Accident Line Protect policy from Abbey Legal Protection for £85 including tax. At the time of writing, the same policy will cost him £3,045. If this rate of increase continues, in the year 2005 the policy will cost nearly £110,000! Clearly this is not going to happen. There are a number of well-documented reasons why premiums have risen so dramatically and there are now arguments to support the reduction of premiums. However, there is likely to be continued volatility until the position over recoverability is clarified. Claims results will also need to be analysed by the underwriters to see whether premiums have been set at correct levels.

7.6 So, since 1995, AEI has changed substantially, and particularly during the last two years. The Conditional Fee Agreements Order 1998, SI 1998/1860 (since replaced by the Conditional Fee Agreements Order 2000, SI 2000/823) effectively extended the use of CFAs to all damages claims. However, the main driving force behind the explosive growth of the AEI industry was the implementation of the Access to Justice Act 1999 and more particularly s. 29, which allows for the recoverability of AEI premiums from the losing opponent.

7.7 With s.29 of the Access to Justice Act, the main reason not to take out AEI was removed, and AEI providers have sprung up to take advantage of the increase in demand. Some of these AEI providers have an established record in the provision of legal expenses insurance, many others do not.

7.8 Forecasts on the size of the market in the future vary hugely. One key factor will be how the defendant insurers react to the premiums they are asked to pay. If they are successful in restricting both the size of premiums and number of policies they have to pay for, this will have a direct impact on the number of insurance providers as there will be less business to go around.

AEI FOR DEFENDANTS

7.9 While the AEI market has its roots firmly in the claimant camp, policies for defendants are slowly becoming more common. As the market continues to mature, AEI providers are likely to embrace defendant cases as they seek to attract new business.

POLICY ANALYSIS

7.10 For the purposes of this chapter, it is not possible to pore over the minutiae of all the policies. There are essentially three types of AEI cover: CFA cover, 'both sides' costs' cover (which is generally an alternative to CFAs) and hybrid cover (which is a mixture of both types).

CFA cover

7.11 Typically, these policies provide cover to pay for the opponent's costs and disbursements and the client's own disbursements. The client's own solicitor's fees are not usually covered. There are some differences between the various CFA policies on offer. These are:

(a) whether the policy covers costs and disbursements already incurred (known as retrospective cover);

(b) whether the policy covers own counsel's fees;

(c) what cover the policy provides in the event of a failure to beat a CPR Part 36 payment. Usually, the client's costs and/or damages would first be used to satisfy an adverse costs award with the insurer paying any amount left over. It is possible to find AEI providers that will make no deductions from the client's damages in this event, although this is currently the exception rather than the rule.

'Both sides' costs' cover

7.12 As the name suggests, all costs on both sides are covered. Usually, own costs incurred prior to the issue of a policy are not insured. If premiums for 'both sides' costs' policies are recoverable when they are taken out prior to the issue of proceedings, solicitors are likely to recommend to clients that a policy is taken out at a relatively early stage. This will minimise the uninsured costs. However, it should be pointed out that 'both sides' costs' policies are usually more expensive than CFA policies, for two reasons:

(a) the amount of cover required is greater (the policy covers own costs as well as the opponents');

(b) the premium rating applied to these policies is usually greater than with CFA policies.

As an example, imagine a clinical negligence case where the total potential costs are £100,000, broken down as follows:

Own costs:	£30,000
Own disbursements:	£20,000
Opponent's costs:	£30,000
Opponent's disbursements:	£20,000

7.13   A CFA policy will cover all the above costs, *excluding* own costs (as the solicitor is acting under a CFA). Therefore the amount of cover required is £70,000. A 'both sides' costs' policy on the other hand will cover all of the above costs, so the amount of cover required is £100,000. At the time of writing, AEI premiums for CFA clinical negligence cases are charged at around 10 per cent of the amount of cover required, so that in this example, the premium will be approximately £7,000. However, AEI premiums for 'both sides' costs' clinical negligence cases are charged at around 25 per cent of the amount of cover required, so that here the premium will be approximately £25,000, some £18,000 more than the CFA premium.

7.14   Admittedly, under the 'both sides' costs' option, there is no success fee for the opponent to pay. In some cases it may be that this will be a cheaper option for the opponent than a CFA premium and success fee of up to 100 per cent of the basic costs. What is curious is that the assessment process adopted by the AEI provider is usually identical for both CFA and 'both sides' costs' policies, but the percentage charged for the premium is higher if cover is required for all costs. If the AEI providers are right to do this, it must mean the success rate for CFA cases is higher than for non-CFA cases. This must mean that solicitors handle cases differently if their own costs are at risk than if they are paid in any event. If this assertion is incorrect, either the premiums for 'both sides' costs' are too high, or the premiums for CFA cases are too low. Time will tell.

Hybrid cover

7.15   This is where complications start creeping in. A small number of AEI providers offer a mix of the two options above, CFA insurance but with own solicitor's costs also insured. This seems a fantastic option. It means that a solicitor can act under a CFA, be paid a success fee if the case wins, and be paid by the AEI policy if the case loses. While this does sound like the perfect solution, the reality is a little different. The premiums charged for these policies are broadly similar to the premiums charged for 'both sides' costs' insurance. This being so, when a solicitor seeks to recover a success fee and this type of AEI premium, the opponent is unlikely to agree to pay the full cost as the other two options are bound to be cheaper (CFA premium plus success fee or an AEI policy covering both sides' costs with no success fee being claimed). First Assist, part of the Royal and Sun Alliance, get around this problem by separating the two elements of the premium. The solicitor chooses a percentage of his own costs to insure (which can be anything from 0 to 90 per cent) and this element of the premium is payable by the solicitor, not the client, at the end of the case. For commercial solicitors wanting to try out CFAs, this may be the best way to put a toe into the water. Premiums are payable at the end of the case, and are calculated as a percentage of own costs at the time of settlement. As with any insurance policy, the amount of the premiums charged and how they compare to others available will be a key factor.

Making the choice

7.16   So what is the best choice? Clearly it is for individual firms to decide when to offer CFAs to clients, and there is no shortage of AEI providers ready and willing to insure the cases. This is particularly true outside personal injury where the premiums (and potentially the profits) are much higher. Cases where the costs involved are likely to be high are perhaps those where the 'both sides' costs' option is more attractive. Although firms will be missing out on a lucrative success fee, the comfort of having one's own costs paid in any event may appeal. A run of losses of CFA cases could be catastrophic to a smaller firm, so a mixed approach to insuring cases may be better.

CURRENT PROVIDERS

7.17   A table of the AEI providers at the time of writing is included in Appendix 24. Contact details and brief summaries of the types of policies on offer are also listed. It should be stressed that this is a list of AEI providers offering cover to solicitors in respect of the solicitors' own clients. The list does not include organisations which exclusively arrange AEI cover for clients before referring them on to a solicitor.

One exception to this is Claims Direct, which offers insurance under its Accident Assist brand to all clients of personal injury solicitors in addition to referring claimants to its own panel of solicitors.

7.18 When examining AEI, it is interesting that some of the underwriters behind the AEI providers are also defendant insurers (although different divisions of the insurer will be involved). This means that not only are insurers supporting and funding litigation against themselves, they are also seeking to recover the cost of the policies and seem likely to dispute the cost of AEI premiums presented to them.

AEI PREMIUMS AND RECOVERABILITY

7.19 If an AEI provider's premiums are too expensive and not recoverable, the AEI provider will not survive in the market. Solicitors are not likely to choose these policies, as it will be the clients who pay the unrecovered premium out of damages (unless the solicitor bears the loss on the client's behalf).

7.20 Early indications from the defendant insurers are that AEI premiums will be strongly contested. Arguments over the availability of BEI are likely to be a central theme until the courts clarify the position. At least one defendant insurer is giving away BEI as part of motor and household policies and other insurers are bound to follow suit. The points of attack for the defendant insurers are numerous and most commentators agree that there will be chaos, at least initially. When choosing AEI, solicitors will increasingly be drawn to policies where the premiums are most likely to be recoverable, or find a way to obtain competitive quotations to present to the client. These are difficult issues for solicitors to consider. If a firm is committed to a particular policy which it knows to be more expensive than others and which is routinely reduced by opponents, can the solicitor pass the unrecovered cost on to the client? Some clients may not be prepared to accept this cost, thinking that the solicitor should have recommended a cheaper alternative. It is true that solicitors are not insurance brokers, although knowingly choosing policies where the premiums are not recoverable in full is another matter. Quoting from the 'Other Points' section of the Law Society's model CFA:

> In all the circumstances, on the information currently available to us, we believe that a contract of insurance with [. . .] is appropriate. Detailed reasons for this are set out in Schedule 2.

In Schedule 2, the solicitor has to set out the reasons for the choice of

AEI product. This part of the agreement could become significant in the event that the losing party challenges the level of AEI premium being reclaimed. A CFA premium known to be significantly more expensive than the premiums for similar policies which are available cannot be described as appropriate.

HOW AEI PROVIDERS OPERATE

7.21   AEI providers offer a variety of schemes and assess cases in different ways. This section looks at the options open to solicitors and examines the assessment process to help solicitors obtain insurance for their clients.

Delegated authority

7.22   If an AEI policy scheme is 'delegated authority' it means that the authority to accept cases for insurance is delegated by the underwriter to the solicitor. This is a big attraction for firms, as it removes the AEI provider from the decision-making process in whether or not to insure a particular client. One big issue is how much control the AEI provider exercises over the case after a policy has been issued. Most AEI providers require the solicitor to report material developments, for example the issue of proceedings, a Part 36 offer being made or the case being set down for trial. Many solicitors tell of being forced by AEI providers to accept offers they felt could be bettered. This is bound to continue.

7.23   One possible solution to this problem is to choose a delegated authority scheme where there is minimum interference by the AEI providers. These schemes are rare but are becoming more common as solicitors demand to be allowed to handle cases from beginning to end, without having to obtain permission from the AEI providers to continue, when, for example, an offer of settlement is received.

7.24   Under delegated authority schemes, the AEI providers insist that all qualifying CFA cases are included to ensure that they have a good spread of risk. Put simply, the 'cast-iron' as well as the more complex cases are insured. But how does this sit with the solicitor's responsibilities to the client? With the position on recoverability unresolved, courts may occasionally take the view on assessment that no AEI premium is recoverable in a 'cast-iron' case.

7.25   So while the law firm has contractual obligations to the AEI provider, it is the obligations to the client that are causing concern among many solicitors. This is where delegated authority schemes start to lose some of their appeal. They remove the solicitor's freedom to give any kind of choice of AEI policy to the client, or indeed use the AEI premium as a negotiating tactic. For example, in quantum negotiations, solicitors could stress to defendant insurers that a failure to reach agreement will mean that an AEI policy costing, for example, £2,000 is taken out. This very real threat to defendant insurers of increased costs could mean that the clients are the happy beneficiaries of earlier, and possibly slightly increased, settlements.

Individually underwritten

7.26 Where cases are assessed by the AEI providers (or by an external assessor on the AEI providers' behalf) the solicitor is effectively passing the decision as to whether or not the case will proceed to the AEI providers. This makes the AEI providers the new gatekeepers to access to justice. Criteria for accepting cases varies between AEI providers and are often based on the crude and subjective 'percentage prospects of success'. It is apparently not unheard of for AEI providers to say that they will insure cases where the prospects of success are in excess of 50 per cent, but then reject them, despite both the solicitor and barrister stating that the prospects exceed this figure. AEI providers will always have the right to take a different view from solicitors of percentage prospects, although the proposal that a subjective percentage can be used as a yardstick for accepting cases looks increasingly questionable. The same case may be assessed as having a 50 per cent chance of success by a pessimist and 80 per cent by an optimist.

Rejected cases

7.27 When AEI providers reject cases, solicitors face a difficult situation: are they to trawl the case round the insurance market trying to get cover for the client? With possible assessment fees payable each time this could be an expensive exercise, and AEI providers will be nervous of insuring cases that have been rejected by others. If solicitors do not do this, the case cannot proceed so they may have no choice. Easier access to the AEI market through the use of the Internet, together with competition between AEI providers should help alleviate this problem.

Assessors and assessments

7.28 As touched on earlier, the assessment process can be fraught with uncertainty and inconsistency. The AEI providers have to strike a balance between attracting business, not cherry-picking the best cases, and taking on cases that will make a profit for the underwriters. Spread of risk is also important. The AEI provider will consider the types of cases already on cover when deciding whether to offer an AEI policy. For example, if a large number of high value clinical negligence cases are already insured, the AEI provider may well refuse further similar cases, preferring to 'balance the book' and insure other types of cases.

7.29 In such a young industry there can be a cross-over between the marketing, assessing and underwriter liaison roles within the AEI providers. The following is a hypothetical example taken as an illustration.

7.30 Someone managing the personal injury division for an AEI provider is set sales targets for premium income so that he telephones and writes to solicitors, encouraging them to submit cases for insurance. The cases which are subsequently submitted are assessed, premiums are paid and are passed on to the underwriters. This process continues and the sales targets are exceeded. One year later, a higher than expected number of cases are lost and claims are made on the policies. What looked like a profit a year ago has turned into a large loss for the underwriters. The personal injury manager at the AEI provider gives assurances to the underwriters that the success rate of cases insured will go up. Gradually, the assessment of cases becomes stricter and more cases are rejected. Fewer claims are made and the underwriters claw back the losses and start to show a small profit.

7.31 What this example shows is that the merits of the case are potentially only one aspect at play when the AEI provider decides whether or not to offer insurance to the client. If one AEI provider is sitting on a large underwriting loss then it is naturally going to be more cautious than an AEI provider who is sitting on a large profit.

7.32 What of the assessors who work for the AEI providers? The range of qualifications of these assessors ranges from none, through to solicitors and barristers. External solicitors and barristers are also used in certain circumstances to provide an independent opinion. When this happens, the client is expected to pay the cost, which can easily reach several hundred pounds for each assessment. If assessment fees are charged, clients will be understandably reluctant to 'shop around' for competitive premiums. Where the AEI providers reject cases, and the client has paid a hefty assessment fee, the decision to approach a different AEI provider and pay a further assessment fee must be taken carefully. In certain clinical negligence schemes the charity AVMA (Action for Victims of Medical Accidents) assesses some cases on behalf of the AEI providers and receives a percentage commission for those cases that are subsequently insured. Some may mischievously point out that there is a financial disincentive for AVMA to reject cases (as they receive no payment for these), although there is no evidence to suggest that this arrangement affects AVMA's recommendations.

7.33   What can we glean from the assessment process? What is certain is that a rejection from an AEI provider is not necessarily the final word. After all, AEI providers are sensitive (or should be) to criticisms of insuring only the best cases and reducing access to justice, especially as some have assured the Lord Chancellor's Department that they can provide an effective replacement to legal aid. So, if a case is rejected, try appealing to the AEI provider. It might just work. Failing that, there are plenty of other AEI providers looking for new business at the right premium.

AEI POLICIES IN MORE DETAIL

7.34   When recommending a policy to clients there are many areas to consider. Aspects of the policies are analysed here to assist solicitors in making that recommendation.

Premium cover

7.35   Premium cover is now a common feature of many AEI policies. This works as follows:

(a)   the client takes out a policy;

(b)   if the client wins, the opponent pays the premium;

(c)   if the client loses, the premium is repaid by the policy.

Whatever happens, the insurance will cost the client nothing. At least that is the theory. This is a fairly bizarre concept. Can you imagine getting a refund on your car insurance if you have an accident? It means that the insurer only receives a premium for the successful cases. Clearly, the amount charged includes an element to pay for the premiums in the losing cases. Will defendant insurers challenge policies that include this cover? This is an area that is known to be under scrutiny. If premium cover survives it is certainly something solicitors should be recommending to their clients if attached to an appropriate policy. The promise to the client that if the case loses there will be nothing whatsoever to pay is certainly attractive. A bank can usually be found to fund premiums so affordability is no longer a problem, although solicitors must keep in mind that the interest on any loan is not recoverable. At the time of writing, one of the AEI providers arranges finance for the client's disbursements at nearly 20 per cent APR. A certain amount of shopping around for finance schemes may be a wise move.

Deferred premiums

7.36 Royal and Sun Alliance introduced deferred premiums, which are also only payable if the case is successful, in 1999 as part of its pursuit policy. This model has been adopted by a number of AEI providers since. The attraction to a potential client is obvious. The client is told what the premium will be (or in Royal and Sun Alliance's case, how the premium payable will be calculated) but pays nothing until the end of the case with no interest charges being added. The policies include premium cover (see above), so that the premium is both deferred and only payable in the event of success. If the premium is recovered in full from the opponent in a successful case, the client will not have paid a penny. The ultimate cover is where an AEI provider guarantees that, in the event of the premium amount being reduced by the opponent, only the reduced amount is payable. If the defendants have significant success in challenges to the recoverability of AEI premiums, this will undoubtedly play havoc with the underwriting profitability of such a scheme. However, where this cover is available, it certainly represents a 'no lose' situation as far as the client is concerned.

STABILITY OF UNDERWRITERS

7.37 Most AEI providers are actually insurance agencies which design, market and administer insurance policies and take a commission from the premium paid. The remainder of the premium is then passed to the underwriters. The underwriter is the insurance company (or Lloyd's syndicate) which pays any claims under the policy and will either make a net profit or loss on the premiums received.

7.38 Attracting underwriters to a new market has its difficulties. The usual statistics to help set insurance premiums are not available on the AEI market, so premium setting has been, in many cases, educated guesswork. How good these guesses have been will become apparent in years to come. The potential for instability in the market is very real. Underwriters who were quick to join the AEI market may be just as quick to leave if results of cases do not go as expected. There have already been changes in the underwriting of some of the most established policies, and predicting which underwriters and AEI providers are likely to be around in years to come is difficult.

7.39 One final word on this topic: to issue policies for AEI, insurers have to be UK-authorised. There have been instances of AEI providers using insurers based offshore and solicitors should think carefully before accepting policies from such insurers. Taking the Isle of Man as an example, the Financial Services Authority says: 'a company is not permitted to carry on insurance business in the UK on the strength of its Isle of Man authorisation'. The definition of 'carrying on insurance business' is key and there are grey areas. Solicitors would do well to err on the side of caution or to take expert advice if a non-UK backed AEI policy is offered. A dispute with an offshore insurer over the payment of a claim may not be as easy to resolve as a dispute with a UK insurer.

TIED INSURANCE POLICIES

7.40 These are policies that have grown in popularity on the back of the success initially enjoyed by Claims Direct, the personal injury claims management company. The recent collapse in their share price may have a lot to do with adverse publicity from both BBC TV's 'Watchdog' and the *Sun* newspaper. There may also be wider concerns about the make up of the AEI policies, which if successfully challenged will impact on other claims management companies who have copied Claims Direct's lead. The policies are usually linked to referring organisations and are issued to every client before being referred to a solicitor firm which handles the claim.

7.41 The reason these AEI policies have been so popular with claims management companies is that they receive large commissions/contributions to costs from the gross premium. This arrangement has enabled them to abandon the traditional contingency fee deduction from damages. While this may be very attractive to the claims management companies, the defendant insurers are known to be unhappy both with the size of the commissions and the size of the premiums.

7.42 There is, however, a wider question. If solicitor firms on claims management company panels act for clients who are insured by AEI policies known not to be recoverable in full from the opponent, should it be these firms, and not the client, who are to bear any shortfall in unrecovered premium? This argument applies not only to insurance policies which are 'tied' to claims management companies, but also to other delegated authority schemes to which solicitor firms may have signed up. The fact that AEI providers prevent shopping around for alternative quotes will not impress clients if they are asked to pay the shortfall out of their damages.

FUNDING OPTIONS

7.43 The funding of litigation is one of the key issues for solicitors to consider. This has not been lost on the AEI providers who now have a range of funding options as part of the various packages. The issue is complex and is dealt with in very broad terms here.

Premium funding

7.44 When AEI was first introduced with personal injury premiums at £85, funding the premium was not a big problem. Now that premiums are substantially higher, funding has become a big issue. There are various options to enable clients to pay for AEI policies; either the premium is deferred, or a bank provides a loan, only requiring repayment of the capital plus interest at the end of the case. Usually, no repayments are made while the case is proceeding. The funds are advanced to the solicitor firm or to the client (depending on the arrangements the AEI provider has made). These loans are usually linked to premium cover with the AEI policy, and are repaid to the bank either out of the damages awarded to the client or by the proceeds of a claim under the policy. With the former scenario, the solicitor then attempts to recover the AEI premium from the opponent. If the AEI premium is recovered in full, the client or solicitor is left to pay any interest charges. Either way, the banks are guaranteed repayment of the loan which enables interest rates to be set at very competitive levels. Where interest rates charged by the banks are higher than the average, it may mean the AEI provider is earning a commission on the loan interest, providing them with an additional source of revenue. The funding of litigation is big business.

Disbursement funding

7.45 Bank disbursement funding is available through AEI providers on similar terms to premium funding. The loan is repaid out of damages or by a claim under the policy. Where disbursement funding is not secured by the policy it is secured on the solicitor's practice. Limits on lending will be set using usual banking criteria. As an alternative, firms should consider approaching their own bank in the first instance, since lower interest rates may be available.

147

Work in progress funding

7.46 For a firm dealing with a large volume of CFA cases, the funding of work in progress is a big issue. Banks have recognised this and a range of solutions is beginning to appear. As with finance for disbursements, solicitors can make arrangements with the banks direct, or go through one of the AEI providers.

Self-insurance

7.47 This must be an attractive option to some firms. After all, if they know they win most of their cases, why not set up an insurance company, take advantage of recoverability under the revisions to the Courts and Legal Services Act 1990 brought about by the 1999 Act, and participate in the underwriting profits? While this may be appealing in theory, an investment of several hundred thousand pounds is required, so that it is likely to appeal only to the largest firms. Further, with the position on recoverability so unclear, it would be a brave solicitor's practice which went down this route. Perhaps firms will look at self-insuring when (or if) things settle down. If firms want to explore the possibility there are a number of specialist insurance brokers who are expert in this field. Perhaps a simpler solution, already under consideration by some firms, would be for solicitors to be permitted to group together and act as membership organisations, and recover a self-insurance premium from the losing opponent. While AEI providers will recoil in horror at such a suggestion, many firms conducting high volumes of cases under a CFA would no doubt be keen to capitalise on the opportunity.

7.48 Some firms consider another type of self-insurance. The arrangement goes something like this:

(1) The AEI provider agrees a premium for clients of a particular firm and offers the firm delegated authority to issue policies.

(2) The solicitor collects premiums from the clients.

(3) The solicitor passes the premiums on to the AEI providers.

(4) The AEI providers rebate the majority of the premiums to the solicitor in return for a guarantee that no claims under the policy will ever be made.

(5) In the event that any cases are lost, the solicitor meets the costs of claims.

(6) In the unlikely event that the solicitor goes out of business and a claim is subsequently made under the policy, the underwriter that is named on the insurance certificate is responsible for payment.

7.49   Such deals used to be fairly commonplace, although recoverability changes the situation. The advice from most insurance professionals is not to enter into such schemes. Because there is no transfer of risk to the underwriter such an arrangement is unlikely to be acceptable to the Financial Services Authority. Should the detail of these arrangements come to light then at the very least the premiums will not be recoverable from the opponent. The consequences for the firm may be far more serious.

BROKERS AND COMMISSIONS

7.50   AEI is a complicated area and there are few insurance brokers actively operating. The ones that are operating seem to be affiliated to a small number of AEI providers and in some cases are acting as 'tied agents', offering AEI policies from a single AEI provider. The AEI providers are not necessarily supportive of independent brokers, fearing that premium rates will be reduced as brokers take a case from one AEI provider to the next. Instructing a broker to find cover for a particular case may be an option for high value/high premium cases but if brokers are only obtaining quotes from AEI providers who are prepared to pay commissions, the most 'appropriate' policy for the client may be overlooked.

7.51   AEI providers generally derive their revenue from commission payments, usually a fixed percentage of the gross premium, as opposed to a fixed amount per policy. This percentage varies, but it is typically between 20–40 per cent. The AEI providers are insulated from the risk of paying claims, although in a strange 'no lose' situation many also earn commissions on any profits the underwriters make (without sharing the losses). This does not apply to the small number of AEI providers which are also insurance companies in their own right.

7.52   When solicitors are negotiating insurance premiums for their clients it pays to bear these commissions in mind. Where the premium is several thousand pounds, it may be possible to negotiate a reduction. AEI providers would, in many cases, prefer to take a smaller percentage commission and reduce the premium than lose the business to a competitor.

THE FUTURE

7.53   The AEI market is potentially enormous and the current AEI providers are all hoping that they will be offering AEI for a long time to come and making a profit for the underwriters.

7.54   It is interesting that volatility in premiums has centred on personal injury, being the area where there is the most experience in underwriting AEI. As the claims have come in, AEI providers have realised that the premiums were initially under-priced. If the same mistakes are made with other areas of litigation (clinical negligence is probably the next area to receive a wake-up call), volatile premiums are going to be a part of the AEI market for quite some time. Assuming that at least a few AEI providers have set some premiums at unrealistic levels, and this is certain to be the case, it will be interesting to see whether the underwriters backing the schemes will stay in the market in an attempt to claw back the losses, or quietly retire. There is bound to be a shake out. Perhaps the future major players have yet even to enter the market, preferring others to make mistakes before launching their own policies.

7.55   The last five years in AEI have been characterised by innovation and pace of change. The next five years will determine whether AEI is here to stay, or whether it will be viewed as an experiment that went horribly wrong.

Appendices

Appendices

Courts and Legal Services Act 1990, section 58: Conditional fee agreements (prior to 1 April 2000)

58. – (1) In this section 'a conditional fee agreement' means an agreement in writing between a person providing advocacy or litigation services and his client which –

(a) does not relate to proceedings of a kind mentioned in subsection (10);

(b) provides for that person's fees and expenses, or any part of them, to be payable only in specified circumstances;

(c) complies with such requirements (if any) as may be prescribed by the Lord Chancellor; and

(d) is not a contentious business agreement (as defined by section 59 of the Solicitors Act 1974).

(2) Where a conditional fee agreement provides for the amount of any fees to which it applies to be increased, in specified circumstances, above the amount which would be payable if it were not a conditional fee agreement, it shall specify the percentage by which that amount is to be increased.

(3) Subject to subsection (6), a conditional fee agreement which relates to specified proceedings shall not be unenforceable by reason only of its being a conditional fee agreement.

(4) In this section 'specified proceedings' means proceedings of a description specified by order made by the Lord Chancellor for the purposes of subsection (3).

(5) Any such order shall prescribe the maximum permitted percentage for each description of specified proceedings.

(6) An agreement which falls within subsection (2) shall be unenforceable if, at the time when it is entered into, the percentage specified in the agreement exceeds the prescribed maximum permitted percentage for each description of proceedings to which it relates.

(7) Before making any order under this section the Lord Chancellor shall consult the designated judges, the General Council of the Bar, the Law Society and such other authorised bodies (if any) as he considers appropriate.

(8) Where a party to any proceedings has entered into a conditional fee agreement and a costs order is made in those proceedings in his favour, the costs payable to him shall not include any element which takes account of any percentage increase payable under the agreement.

(9) Rules of court may make provision with respect to the taxing of any costs which include fees payable under a conditional fee agreement.

(10) The proceedings mentioned in subsection (1)(a) are any criminal proceedings and any proceedings under –

    (a) the Matrimonial Causes Act 1973;

    (b) the Domestic Violence and Matrimonial Proceedings Act 1976;

    (c) the Adoption Act 1976;

    (d) the Domestic Proceedings and Magistrates' Court Act 1978;

    (e) sections 1 and 9 of the Matrimonial Homes Act 1983;

    (f) Part III of the Matrimonial and Family Proceedings Act 1984;

    (g) Parts I, II or IV of the Children Act 1989; or

    (h) the inherent jurisdiction of the High Court in relation to children.

Courts and Legal Services Act 1990, sections 58 and 58A: Conditional fee agreements (from 1 April 2000)

(as substituted and inserted by Access to Justice Act 1999, s. 27)

58. – (1) A conditional fee agreement which satisfies all of the conditions applicable to it by virtue of this section shall not be unenforceable by reason only of its being a conditional fee agreement; but (subject to subsection (5)) any other conditional fee agreement shall be unenforceable.

(2) For the purposes of this section and section 58A –

    (a) a conditional fee agreement is an agreement with a person providing advocacy or litigation services which provides for his fees and expenses, or any part of them, to be payable only in specified circumstances; and

    (b) a conditional fee agreement provides for a success fee if it provides for the amount of any fees to which it applies to be increased, in specified circumstances, above the amount which would be payable if it were not payable only in specified circumstances.

(3) The following conditions are applicable to every conditional fee agreement –

    (a) it must be in writing;

    (b) it must not relate to proceedings which cannot be the subject of an enforceable conditional fee agreement; and

    (c) it must comply with such requirements (if any) as may be prescribed by the Lord Chancellor.

(4) The following further conditions are applicable to a conditional fee agreement which provides for a success fee –

    (a) it must relate to proceedings of a description specified by order made by the Lord Chancellor;

    (b) it must state the percentage by which the amount of the fees which would be payable if it were not a conditional fee agreement is to be increased; and

    (c) that percentage must not exceed the percentage specified in relation to the description of proceedings to which the agreement relates by order made by the Lord Chancellor.

(5) If a conditional fee agreement is an agreement to which section 57 of the Solicitors Act 1974 (non-contentious business agreements between solicitor and client) applies, subsection (1) shall not make it unenforceable.

58A. – (1) The proceedings which cannot be the subject of an enforceable conditional fee agreement are—

    (a) criminal proceedings, apart from proceedings under section 82 of the Environmental Protection Act 1990; and

    (b) family proceedings.

(2) In subsection (1) 'family proceedings' means proceedings under any one or more of the following –

    (a) the Matrimonial Causes Act 1973;

    (b) the Adoption Act 1976;

    (c) the Domestic Proceedings and Magistrates' Courts Act 1978;

    (d) Part III of the Matrimonial and Family Proceedings Act 1984;

    (e) Parts I, II and IV of the Children Act 1989;

    (f) Part IV of the Family Law Act 1996; and

    (g) the inherent jurisdiction of the High Court in relation to children.

(3) The requirements which the Lord Chancellor may prescribe under section 58(3)(c) –

    (a) include requirements for the person providing advocacy or litigation services to have provided prescribed information before the agreement is made; and

    (b) may be different for different descriptions of conditional fee agreements (and, in particular, may be different for those which provide for a success fee and those which do not).

(4) In section 58 and this section (and in the definitions of 'advocacy services' and 'litigation services' as they apply for their purposes) 'proceedings' includes any sort of proceedings for resolving disputes (and not just proceedings in a court), whether commenced or contemplated.

(5) Before making an order under section 58(4), the Lord Chancellor shall consult –

    (a) the designated judges;

    (b) the General Council of the Bar;

    (c) the Law Society; and

    (d) such other bodies as he considers appropriate.

(6) A costs order made in any proceedings may, subject in the case of court proceedings to rules of court, include provision requiring the payment of any fees payable under a conditional fee agreement which provides for a success fee.

(7) Rules of court may make provision with respect to the assessment of any costs which include fees payable under a conditional fee agreement (including one which provides for a success fee).

Courts and Legal Services Act 1990, section 58B: Litigation funding agreements

(as inserted by Access to Justice Act 1999, s. 28)

58B. – (1) A litigation funding agreement which satisfies all of the conditions applicable to it by virtue of this section shall not be unenforceable by reason only of its being a litigation funding agreement.

(2) For the purposes of this section a litigation funding agreement is an agreement under which –

(a) a person ('the funder') agrees to fund (in whole or in part) the provision of advocacy or litigation services (by someone other than the funder) to another person ('the litigant'); and

(b) the litigant agrees to pay a sum to the funder in specified circumstances.

(3) The following conditions are applicable to a litigation funding agreement –

(a) the funder must be a person, or person of a description, prescribed by the Lord Chancellor;

(b) the agreement must be in writing;

(c) the agreement must not relate to proceedings which by virtue of section 58A(1) and (2) cannot be the subject of an enforceable conditional fee agreement or to proceedings of any such description as may be prescribed by the Lord Chancellor;

(d) the agreement must comply with such requirements (if any) as may be so prescribed;

(e) the sum to be paid by the litigant must consist of any costs payable to him in respect of the proceedings to which the agreement relates together with an amount calculated by reference to the funder's anticipated expenditure in funding the provision of the services; and

(f) that amount must not exceed such percentage of that anticipated expenditure as may be prescribed by the Lord Chancellor in relation to proceedings of the description to which the agreement relates.

(4) Regulations under subsection (3)(a) may require a person to be approved by the Lord Chancellor or by a prescribed person.

(5) The requirements which the Lord Chancellor may prescribe under subsection (3)(d) –

157

    (a) include requirements for the funder to have provided prescribed informa-
tion to the litigant before the agreement is made; and

    (b) may be different for different descriptions of litigation funding agreements.

(6) In this section (and in the definitions of 'advocacy services' and 'litigation services' as they apply for its purposes) 'proceedings' includes any sort of proceedings for resolving disputes (and not just proceedings in a court), whether commenced or contemplated.

(7) Before making regulations under this section, the Lord Chancellor shall consult –

    (a) the designated judges;

    (b) the General Council of the Bar;

    (c) the Law Society; and

    (d) such other bodies as he considers appropriate.

(8) A costs order made in any proceedings may, subject in the case of court proceedings to rules of court, include provision requiring the payment of any amount payable under a litigation funding agreement.

(9) Rules of court may make provision with respect to the assessment of any costs which include fees payable under a litigation funding agreement.

APPENDIX 3

Access to Justice Act 1999, sections 29, 30 and 31: Recovery of insurance premiums and other provisions as to costs

Recovery of insurance premiums by way of costs

29. Where in any proceedings a costs order is made in favour of any party who has taken out an insurance policy against the risk of incurring a liability in those proceedings, the costs payable to him may, subject in the case of court proceedings to rules of court, include costs in respect of the premium of the policy.

Recovery where body undertakes to meet costs liabilities

30. – (1) This section applies where a body of a prescribed description undertakes to meet (in accordance with arrangements satisfying prescribed conditions) liabilities which members of the body or other persons who are parties to proceedings may incur to pay the costs of other parties to the proceedings.

(2) If in any of the proceedings a costs order is made in favour of any of the members or other persons, the costs payable to him may, subject to subsection (3) and (in the case of court proceedings) to rules of court, include an additional amount in respect of any provision made by or on behalf of the body in connection with the proceedings against the risk of having to meet such liabilities.

(3) But the additional amount shall not exceed a sum determined in a prescribed manner; and there may, in particular, be prescribed as a manner of determination one which takes into account the likely cost to the member or other person of the premium of an insurance policy against the risk of incurring a liability to pay the costs of other parties to the proceedings.

(4) In this section 'prescribed' means prescribed by regulations made by the Lord Chancellor by statutory instrument; and a statutory instrument containing such regulations shall be subject to annulment in pursuance of a resolution of either House of Parliament.

(5) Regulations under subsection (1) may, in particular, prescribe as a description of body one which is for the time being approved by the Lord Chancellor or by a prescribed person.

Rules as to costs

31. In section 51 of the Supreme Court Act 1981 (costs), in subsection (2) (rules regulating matters relating to costs), insert at the end 'or for securing that the amount awarded to a party in respect of the costs to be paid by him to such representatives is not limited to what would have been payable by him to them if he had not been awarded costs'.

Conditional Fee Agreements Order 1995, SI 1995/1674

Made 4th July 1995
Coming into force 5th July 1995

Whereas a draft of the above Order has been laid before and approved by resolution of each House of Parliament:

Now, therefore, the Lord Chancellor, in exercise of the powers conferred on him by sections 58(4) and (5) and 120 of the Courts and Legal Services Act 1990, having consulted in accordance with section 58(7) of that Act, hereby makes the following Order:

Citation and commencement

1. This Order may be cited as the Conditional Fee Agreements Order 1995 and shall come into force on the day after the day on which it was made.

Specified proceedings

2. – (1) The proceedings specified for the purpose of section 58(4) of the Courts and Legal Services Act 1990 (conditional fee agreements in respect of specified proceedings not to be unenforceable) are the following:

(a) proceedings in which there is a claim for damages in respect of personal injuries or in respect of a person's death, and 'personal injuries' includes any disease and any impairment of a person's physical or mental condition;

(b) proceedings in England and Wales by a company which is being wound up in England and Wales or Scotland;

(c) proceedings by a company in respect of which an administration order made under Part II of the Insolvency Act 1986 is in force;

(d) proceedings in England and Wales by a person acting in the capacity of –

   (i) liquidator of a company which is being wound up in England and Wales or Scotland; or

   (ii) trustee of a bankrupt's estate;

(e) proceedings by a person acting in the capacity of an administrator appointed pursuant to the provisions of Part II of the Insolvency Act 1986;

(f) proceedings before the European Commission of Human Rights and the European Court of Human Rights established under article 19 of the Convention for the Protection of Human Rights and Fundamental Freedoms opened for signature at Rome on 4th November 1950, ratified by the United Kingdom on 8th March 1951, which came into force on 3rd August 1953,

provided that the client does not have legal aid in respect of the proceedings.

(2) Proceedings specified in paragraph (1) shall be specified proceedings notwithstanding that they are concluded without the commencement of court proceedings.

(3) In paragraphs (1)(b) and (1)(d) 'company' means a company within the meaning of section 735(1) of the Companies Act 1985 or a company which may be wound up under Part V of the Insolvency Act 1986.

(4) Where legal aid in respect of the proceedings to which a conditional fee agreement relates is granted after that agreement is entered into the proceedings shall cease to be specified from the date of the grant.

(5) In this article, 'legal aid' means representation under Part IV of the Legal Aid Act 1988.

Maximum permitted percentage increase on fees

3. For the purpose of section 58(5) of the Courts and Legal Services Act 1990 the maximum permitted percentage by which fees may be increased in respect of each description of proceedings specified in article 2 is 100%.

APPENDIX 5

Conditional Fee Agreements Order 1998, SI 1998/1860

Made 29th July 1998
Coming into force 30th July 1998

The Lord Chancellor, in exercise of the powers conferred on him by sections 58(4) and (5) of the Courts and Legal Services Act 1990, having consulted in accordance with section 58(7) of that Act, makes the following Order, a draft of which has been laid before and approved by resolution of each House of Parliament:

Citation, commencement and interpretation

1. – (1) This Order may be cited as the Conditional Fee Agreements Order 1998 and shall come into force on the day after the day on which it is made.

(2) In this Order 'the Act' means the Courts and Legal Services Act 1990.

Revocation of 1995 Order

2. The Conditional Fee Agreements Order 1995 is revoked.

Specified proceedings

3. – (1) All proceedings are proceedings specified for the purposes of section 58(3) of the Act (conditional fee agreements in respect of specified proceedings not to be unenforceable).

(2) Proceedings specified in paragraph (1) shall be specified proceedings notwithstanding that they are concluded without the commencement of court proceedings.

Maximum permitted percentage increase on fees

4. For the purposes of section 58(5) of the Act the maximum permitted percentage by which fees may be increased in respect of any proceedings designated by article 3 as proceedings specified for the purposes of section 58(3) of the Act is 100%.

Conditional Fee Agreements Regulations 1995, SI 1995/1675

Made 4th July 1995
Coming into force 5th July 1995

Whereas a draft of the above Regulations has been laid before and approved by resolution of each House of Parliament:

Now, therefore, the Lord Chancellor, in exercise of the powers conferred on him by sections 58(1) and 119 of the Courts and Legal Services Act 1990, hereby makes the following Regulations:

Citation, commencement and interpretation

1. – (1) These Regulations may be cited as the Conditional Fee Agreements Regulations 1995 and shall come into force on the day after the day on which they are made.

(2) In these Regulations –

'agreement', in relation to an agreement between a legal representative and an additional legal representative, includes a retainer;

'legal aid' means representation under Part IV of the Legal Aid Act 1988;

'legal representative' means a person providing advocacy or litigation services.

Agreements to comply with prescribed requirements

2. An agreement shall not be a conditional fee agreement unless it complies with the requirements of the following regulations.

Requirements of an agreement

3. An agreement shall state –

(a) the particular proceedings or parts of them to which it relates (including whether it relates to any counterclaim, appeal or proceedings to enforce a judgment or order);

(b) the circumstances in which the legal representative's fees and expenses or part of them are payable;

(c) what, if any, payment is due –

    (i) upon partial failure of the specified circumstances to occur;

    (ii) irrespective of the specified circumstances occurring; and

    (iii) upon termination of the agreement for any reason;

(d) the amount payable in accordance with sub-paragraphs (b) or (c) above or the method to be used to calculate the amount payable; and in particular whether or not the amount payable is limited by reference to the amount of any damages which may be recovered on behalf of the client.

Additional requirements

4. – (1) The agreement shall also state that, immediately before it was entered into, the legal representative drew the client's attention to the matters specified in paragraph (2).

(2) The matters are –

(a) whether the client might be entitled to legal aid in respect of the proceedings to which the agreement relates, the conditions upon which legal aid is available and the application of those conditions to the client in respect of the proceedings;

(b) the circumstances in which the client may be liable to pay the fees and expenses of the legal representative in accordance with the agreement;

(c) the circumstances in which the client may be liable to pay the costs of any other party to the proceedings; and

(d) the circumstances in which the client may seek taxation of the fees and expenses of the legal representative and the procedure for so doing.

Application of regulation 4

5. Regulation 4 shall not apply to an agreement between a legal representative and an additional legal representative.

Form of agreement

6. An agreement shall be in writing and, except in the case of an agreement between a legal representative and an additional legal representative, shall be signed by the client and the legal representative.

Amendment of agreement

7. Where it is proposed to extend the agreement to cover further proceedings or parts of them regulations 3 to 6 shall apply to the agreement as extended.

Conditional Fee Agreements Order 2000, SI 2000/823

Made 20th March 2000
Coming into force 1st April 2000

The Lord Chancellor, in exercise of the powers conferred upon him by section 58(4)(a) and (c) of the Courts and Legal Services Act 1990, and all other powers enabling him in that behalf, having consulted in accordance with section 58A(5) of that Act, makes the following Order, a draft of which has been laid before and approved by resolution of each House of Parliament:

Citation, commencement and interpretation

1. – (1) This Order may be cited as the Conditional Fee Agreements Order 2000 and shall come into force on 1st April 2000.

(2) In this Order 'the Act' means the Courts and Legal Services Act 1990.

Revocation of 1998 Order

2. The Conditional Fee Agreements Order 1998 is revoked.

Agreements providing for success fees

3. All proceedings which, under section 58 of the Act, can be the subject of an enforceable conditional fee agreement, except proceedings under section 82 of the Environmental Protection Act 1990, are proceedings specified for the purposes of section 58(4)(a) of the Act.

Amount for success fees

4. In relation to all proceedings specified in article 3, the percentage specified for the purposes of section 58(4)(c) of the Act shall be 100%.

Dated 20th March 2000   *Irvine of Lairg, C.*

APPENDIX 8

Conditional Fee Agreements Regulations 2000, SI 2000/692

Made 9th March 2000
Coming into force 1st April 2000

The Lord Chancellor, in exercise of the powers conferred on him by sections 58(3)(c), 58A(3) and 119 of the Courts and Legal Services Act 1990 and all other powers enabling him hereby makes the following Regulations:

Citation, commencement and interpretation

1. – (1) These Regulations may be cited as the Conditional Fee Agreements Regulations 2000.

(2) These Regulations come into force on 1st April 2000.

(3) In these Regulations –

'client' includes, except where the context otherwise requires, a person who –

(a) has instructed the legal representative to provide the advocacy or litigation services to which the conditional fee agreement relates, or

(b) is liable to pay the legal representative's fees in respect of those services; and

'legal representative' means the person providing the advocacy or litigation services to which the conditional fee agreement relates.

Requirements for contents of conditional fee agreements: general

2. – (1) A conditional fee agreement must specify –

(a) the particular proceedings or parts of them to which it relates (including whether it relates to any appeal, counterclaim or proceedings to enforce a judgement or order),

(b) the circumstances in which the legal representative's fees and expenses, or part of them, are payable,

(c) what payment, if any, is due –

(i) if those circumstances only partly occur,

(ii) irrespective of whether those circumstances occur, and

(iii) on the termination of the agreement for any reason, and

(d) the amounts which are payable in all the circumstances and cases specified or the method to be used to calculate them and, in particular, whether the amounts are limited by reference to the damages which may be recovered on behalf of the client.

(2) A conditional fee agreement to which regulation 4 applies must contain a statement that the requirements of that regulation which apply in the case of that agreement have been complied with.

Requirements for contents of conditional fee agreements providing for success fees

3. – (1) A conditional fee agreement which provides for a success fee –

(a) must briefly specify the reasons for setting the percentage increase at the level stated in the agreement, and

(b) must specify how much of the percentage increase, if any, relates to the cost to the legal representative of the postponement of the payment of his fees and expenses.

(2) If the agreement relates to court proceedings, it must provide that where the percentage increase becomes payable as a result of those proceedings, then –

(a) if –

(i) any fees subject to the increase are assessed, and

(ii) the legal representative or the client is required by the court to disclose to the court or any other person the reasons for setting the percentage increase at the level stated in the agreement,

he may do so,

(b) if –

(i) any such fees are assessed, and

(ii) any amount in respect of the percentage increase is disallowed on the assessment on the ground that the level at which the increase was set was unreasonable in view of facts which were or should have been known to the legal representative at the time it was set,

that amount ceases to be payable under the agreement, unless the court is satisfied that it should continue to be so payable, and

(c) if –

(i) sub-paragraph (b) does not apply, and

(ii) the legal representative agrees with any person liable as a result of the proceedings to pay fees subject to the percentage increase that a lower amount than the amount payable in accordance with the conditional fee agreement is to be paid instead,

the amount payable under the conditional fee agreement in respect of those fees shall be reduced accordingly, unless the court is satisfied that the full amount should continue to be payable under it.

(3) In this regulation 'percentage increase' means the percentage by which the amount of the fees which would be payable if the agreement were not a conditional fee agreement is to be increased under the agreement.

Information to be given before conditional fee agreements made

4. – (1) Before a conditional fee agreement is made the legal representative must –

   (a) inform the client about the following matters, and

   (b) if the client requires any further explanation, advice or other information about any of those matters, provide such further explanation, advice or other information about them as the client may reasonably require.

(2) Those matters are –

   (a) the circumstances in which the client may be liable to pay the costs of the legal representative in accordance with the agreement,

   (b) the circumstances in which the client may seek assessment of the fees and expenses of the legal representative and the procedure for doing so,

   (c) whether the legal representative considers that the client's risk of incurring liability for costs in respect of the proceedings to which agreement relates is insured against under an existing contract of insurance,

   (d) whether other methods of financing those costs are available, and, if so, how they apply to the client and the proceedings in question,

   (e) whether the legal representative considers that any particular method or methods of financing any or all of those costs is appropriate and, if he considers that a contract of insurance is appropriate or recommends a particular such contract –

      (i) his reasons for doing so, and

      (ii) whether he has an interest in doing so.

(3) Before a conditional fee agreement is made the legal representative must explain its effect to the client.

(4) In the case of an agreement where –

   (a) the legal representative is a body to which section 30 of the Access to Justice Act 1999 (recovery where body undertakes to meet costs liabilities) applies, and

   (b) there are no circumstances in which the client may be liable to pay any costs in respect of the proceedings, paragraph (1) does not apply.

(5) Information required to be given under paragraph (1) about the matters in paragraph (2)(a) to (d) must be given orally (whether or not it is also given in writing), but information required to be so given about the matters in paragraph (2)(e) and the explanation required by paragraph (3) must be given both orally and in writing.

(6) This regulation does not apply in the case of an agreement between a legal representative and an additional legal representative.

Form of agreement

5. – (1) A conditional fee agreement must be signed by the client and the legal representative.

(2) This regulation does not apply in the case of an agreement between a legal representative and an additional legal representative.

Amendment of agreement

6. Where an agreement is amended to cover further proceedings or parts of them –

(a) regulations 2, 3 and 5 apply to the amended agreement as if it were a fresh agreement made at the time of the amendment, and

(b) the obligations under regulation 4 apply in relation to the amendments in so far as they affect the matters mentioned in that regulation.

Revocation of 1995 Regulations

7. The Conditional Fee Agreements Regulations 1995 are revoked.

Access to Justice (Membership Organisations) Regulations 2000, SI 2000/693

Made 9th March 2000
Coming into force 1st April 2000

The Lord Chancellor, in exercise of the powers conferred on him by section 30(1) and (3) to (5) of the Access to Justice Act 1999 and all other powers enabling him hereby makes the following Regulations:

Citation, commencement and interpretation

1. – (1) These Regulations may be cited as the Access to Justice (Membership Organisations) Regulations 2000.

(2) These Regulations come into force on 1st April 2000.

Bodies of a prescribed description

2. The bodies which are prescribed for the purpose of section 30 of the Access to Justice Act 1999 (recovery where body undertakes to meet costs liabilities) are those bodies which are for the time being approved by the Lord Chancellor for that purpose.

Requirements for arrangements to meet costs liabilities

3. – (1) Section 30(1) of the Access to Justice Act 1999 applies to arrangements which satisfy the following conditions.

(2) The arrangements must be in writing.

(3) The arrangements must contain a statement specifying –

    (a)   the circumstances in which the member or other party may be liable to pay costs of the proceedings,

    (b)   whether such a liability arises –

        (i)   if those circumstances only partly occur,

        (ii)   irrespective of whether those circumstances occur, and

        (iii)   on the termination of the arrangements for any reason,

(c)   the basis on which the amount of the liability is calculated, and

(d)   the procedure for seeking assessment of costs.

(4) A copy of the part of the arrangements containing the statement must be given to the member or other party to the proceedings whose liabilities the body is undertaking to meet as soon as possible after the undertaking is given.

Recovery of additional amount for insurance costs

4. – (1) Where an additional amount is included in costs by virtue of section 30(2) of the Access to Justice Act 1999 (costs payable to a member of a body or other person party to the proceedings to include an additional amount in respect of provision made by the body against the risk of having to meet the member's or other person's liabilities to pay other parties' costs), that additional amount must not exceed the following sum.

(2) That sum is the likely cost to the member of the body or, as the case may be, the other person who is a party to the proceedings in which the costs order is made of the premium of an insurance policy against the risk of incurring a liability to pay the costs of other parties to the proceedings.

Collective Conditional Fee Agreements Regulations 2000, SI 2000/2988

Made 7th November 2000
Coming into force 30th November 2000

The Lord Chancellor, in exercise of the powers conferred upon him by sections 58(3)(c), 58A(3) and 119 of the Courts and Legal Services Act 1990 hereby makes the following Regulations:

Citation, commencement and interpretation

1. – (1) These regulations may be cited as the Collective Conditional Fee Agreements Regulations 2000, and shall come into force on 30th November 2000.

(2) In these Regulations, except where the context requires otherwise –

'client' means a person who will receive advocacy or litigation services to which the agreement relates;

'collective conditional fee agreement' has the meaning given in regulation 3;

'conditional fee agreement' has the same meaning as in section 58 of the Courts and Legal Services Act 1990;

'funder' means the party to a collective conditional fee agreement who, under that agreement, is liable to pay the legal representative's fees;

'legal representative' means the person providing the advocacy or litigation services to which the agreement relates.

Transitional provisions

2. These Regulations shall apply to agreements entered into on or after 30th November 2000, and agreements entered into before that date shall be treated as if these Regulations had not come into force.

Definition of 'collective conditional fee agreement'

3. – (1) Subject to paragraph (2) of this regulation, a collective conditional fee agreement is an agreement which –

(a) disregarding section 58(3)(c) of the Courts and Legal Services Act 1990, would be a conditional fee agreement; and

(b) does not refer to specific proceedings, but provides for fees to be payable on a common basis in relation to a class of proceedings, or, if it refers to more than one class of proceedings, on a common basis in relation to each class.

(2) An agreement may be a collective conditional fee agreement whether or not –

(a) the funder is a client; or

(b) any clients are named in the agreement.

Requirements for contents of collective conditional fee agreements: general

4. – (1) A collective conditional fee agreement must specify the circumstances in which the legal representative's fees and expenses, or part of them, are payable.

(2) A collective conditional fee agreement must provide that, when accepting instructions in relation to any specific proceedings the legal representative must –

(a) inform the client as to the circumstances in which the client may be liable to pay the costs of the legal representative; and

(b) if the client requires any further explanation, advice or other information about the matter referred to in sub-paragraph (a), provide such further explanation, advice or other information about it as the client may reasonably require.

(3) Paragraph (2) does not apply in the case of an agreement between a legal representative and an additional legal representative.

(4) A collective conditional fee agreement must provide that, after accepting instructions in relation to any specific proceedings, the legal representative must confirm his acceptance of instructions in writing to the client.

Requirements for contents of collective conditional fee agreements providing for success fees

5. – (1) Where a collective conditional fee agreement provides for a success fee the agreement must provide that, when accepting instructions in relation to any specific proceedings the legal representative must prepare and retain a written statement containing–

(a) his assessment of the probability of the circumstances arising in which the percentage increase will become payable in relation to those proceedings ('the risk assessment');

(b) his assessment of the amount of the percentage increase in relation to those proceedings, having regard to the risk assessment; and

(c) the reasons, by reference to the risk assessment, for setting the percentage increase at that level.

(2) If the agreement relates to court proceedings it must provide that where the success fee becomes payable as a result of those proceedings, then—

(a) if –

    (i) any fees subject to the increase are assessed, and

    (ii) the legal representative or the client is required by the court to disclose to the court or any other person the reasons for setting the percentage increase at the level assessed by the legal representative, he may do so,

(b) if –

    (i) any such fees are assessed by the court, and

    (ii) any amount in respect of the percentage increase is disallowed on the assessment on the ground that the level at which the increase was set was unreasonable in view of facts which were or should have been known to the legal representative at the time it was set

that amount ceases to be payable under the agreement, unless the court is satisfied that it should continue to be so payable, and

(c) if –

    (i) sub-paragraph (b) does not apply, and

    (ii) the legal representative agrees with any person liable as a result of the proceedings to pay fees subject to the percentage increase that a lower amount than the amount payable in accordance with the conditional fee agreement is to be paid instead,

the amount payable under the collective conditional fee agreement in respect of those fees shall be reduced accordingly, unless the court is satisfied that the full amount should continue to be payable under it.

(3) In this regulation 'percentage increase' means the percentage by which the amount of the fees which would have been payable if the agreement were not a conditional fee agreement is to be increased under the agreement.

Form and amendment of collective conditional fee agreement

6. – (1) Subject to paragraph (2), a collective conditional fee agreement must be signed by the funder, and by the legal representative.

(2) Paragraph (1) does not apply in the case of an agreement between a legal representative and an additional legal representative.

(3) Where a collective conditional fee agreement is amended, regulations 4 and 5 apply to the amended agreement as if it were a fresh agreement made at the time of the amendment.

Amendment to the Conditional Fee Agreements Regulations 2000

7. After regulation 7 of the Conditional Fee Agreements Regulations 2000 there shall be inserted the following new regulation:

'Exclusion of collective conditional fee agreements

8. These Regulations shall not apply to collective conditional fee agreements within the meaning of regulation 3 of the Collective Conditional Fee Agreements Regulations 2000.'

APPENDIX 11

Civil Procedure Rules (extracts)

PART 43: SCOPE OF COST RULES AND DEFINITIONS

Definitions and applications

43.2 (1) In Parts 44 to 48, unless the context otherwise requires –

(k) 'funding arrangement' means an arrangement where a person has –

    (i) entered into a conditional fee agreement which provides for a success fee within the meaning of section 58(2) of the Courts and Legal Services Act 1990;

    (ii) taken out an insurance policy to which section 29 of the Access to Justice Act 1999 (recovery of insurance premiums by way of costs) applies; or

    (iii) made an agreement with a membership organisation to meet his legal costs;

(l) 'percentage increase' means the percentage by which the amount of a legal representative's fee can be increased in accordance with a conditional fee agreement which provides for a success fee;

(m) 'insurance premium' means a sum of money paid or payable for insurance against the risk of incurring a costs liability in the proceedings, taken out after the event that is the subject matter of the claim;

(n) 'membership organisation' means a body prescribed for the purposes of section 30 of the Access to Justice Act 1999 (recovery where body undertakes to meet costs liabilities); and

(o) 'additional liability' means the percentage increase, the insurance premium, or the additional amount in respect of provision made by a membership organisation, as the case may be.

[The Conditional Fee Agreements Regulations 2000 and the Access to Justice (Membership Organisations) Regulations 2000 contain further provisions about conditional fee agreements and arrangements to meet costs liabilities respectively.]

PART 44: GENERAL RULES ABOUT COSTS

Costs Orders relating to funding arrangements

44.3A (1) The court will not assess any additional liability until the conclusion of the proceedings, or the part of the proceedings, to which the funding arrangement relates.

['Funding arrangement' and 'additional liability' are defined in rule 43.2.]

(2) At the conclusion of the proceedings, or the part of the proceedings, to which the funding arrangement relates the court may –

(a) make a summary assessment of all the costs, including any additional liability;

(b) make an order for detailed assessment of the additional liability but make a summary assessment of the other costs; or

(c) make an order for detailed assessment of all the costs.

[Part 47 sets out the procedure for the detailed assessment of costs.]

Limits of recovery under funding arrangements

44.3B (1) A party may not recover as an additional liability –

(a) any proportion of the percentage increase relating to the cost to the legal representative of the postponement of the payment of his fees and expenses;

(b) any provision made by a membership organisation which exceeds the likely cost to that party of the premium of an insurance policy against the risk of incurring a liability to pay the costs of other parties to the proceedings;

(c) any additional liability for any period in the proceedings during which he failed to provide information about a funding arrangement in accordance with a rule, practice direction or court order;

(d) any percentage increase where a party has failed to comply with –

(i) a requirement in the costs practice direction; or

(ii) a court order,

to disclose in any assessment proceedings the reasons for setting the percentage increase at the level stated in the conditional fee agreement.

(2) This rule does not apply in an assessment under rule 48.9 (assessment of a solicitor's bill to his client).

[Rule 3.9 sets out the circumstances the court will consider on an application for relief from a sanction for failure to comply with any rule, practice direction or court order.]

Factors to be taken into account in deciding the amount of costs

44.5 (1) The court is to have regard to all the circumstances in deciding whether costs were –

  (a) if it is assessing costs on the standard basis –

   (i)   proportionately and reasonably incurred; or

   (ii) were proportionate and reasonable in amount, or

  (b) if it is assessing costs on the indemnity basis –

   (i)   unreasonably incurred; or

   (ii) unreasonable in amount.

Procedure for assessing costs

44.7 Where the court orders a party to pay costs to another party (other than fixed costs) it may either –

  (a) make a summary assessment of the costs; or

  (b) order detailed assessment of the costs by a costs officer,

  unless any rule, practice direction or other enactment provides otherwise.

[The Costs Practice Direction sets out the factors which will affect the court's decision under this rule.]

Costs-only proceedings

44.12A (1) This rule sets out a procedure which may be followed where –

  (a) the parties to a dispute have reached an agreement on all issues (including which party is to pay the costs) which is made or confirmed in writing; but

  (b) they have failed to agree the amount of those costs; and

  (c) no proceedings have been started.

(2) Either party to the agreement may start proceedings under this rule by issuing a claim form in accordance with Part 8.

(3) The claim form must contain or be accompanied by the agreement or confirmation.

(4) In proceedings to which this rule applies the court –

(a) may

    (i)   make an order for costs; or

    (ii)   dismiss the claim; and

(b) must dismiss the claim if it is opposed.

[Rule 8.1(6) provides that a practice direction may modify the Part 8 procedure.]

Providing information about funding arrangements

44.15 (1) A party who seeks to recover an additional liability must provide information about the funding arrangement to the court and to other parties as required by a rule, practice direction or court order.

(2) Where the funding arrangement has changed, and the information a party has previously provided in accordance with paragraph (1) is no longer accurate, that party must file notice of the change and serve it on all other parties within 7 days.

(3) Where paragraph (2) applies, and a party has already filed –(a) an allocation questionnaire; or (b) a listing questionnaire, he must file and serve a new estimate of costs with the notice.

[The Costs Practice Direction sets out (a) the information to be provided when a party issues or responds to a claim form, files an allocation questionaire, a listing questionnaire, and a claim for costs; (b) the meaning of estimate of costs and the information required in it. Rule 44.3B sets out situations where a party will not recover a sum representing any additional liability.]

Adjournment where legal representative seeks to challenge disallowance of any amount of percentage increase

44.16 Where –

(a) the court disallows any amount of a legal representative's percentage increase in summary or detailed assessment proceedings; and

(b) the legal representative applies for an order that the disallowed amount should continue to be payable by his client,

the court may adjourn the hearing to allow the legally represented party to be notified of the order sought.

[Regulation 3(2)(b) of the Conditional Fee Agreements Regulations 2000 provides that a conditional fee agreement which provides for a success fee must state that any amount of a percentage increase disallowed on assessment ceases to be payable unless the court is satisfied that it should continue to be so payable.]

PART 46: FAST TRACK TRIAL COSTS

Power to award more or less than the amount of fast track trial costs

46.3   (2A) The court may in addition award a sum representing an additional liability.

[The requirements to provide information about a funding arrangement where a party wishes to recover any additional liability under a funding arrangement are set out in the costs practice direction.]

['Additional liability' is defined in rule 43.2.]

PART 48: COSTS – SPECIAL CASES

Basis of detailed assessment of solicitor and client costs

48.8   (1) This rule applies to every assessment of a solicitor's bill to his client except –

    (a) a bill which is to be paid out of the Community Legal Service Fund under the Legal Aid Act 1988 or the Access to Justice Act 1999; or

    (b) where the solicitor and his client have entered into a conditional fee agreement as defined by section 58 of the Courts and Legal Services Act 1990 whenever it was made.

Conditional fees

48.9   (1) This rule applies to every assessment (whether by the summary or detailed procedure) of a solicitor's bill to his client where the solicitor and the client have entered into a conditional fee agreement as defined in section 58 of the Courts and Legal Services Act 1990 as it was in force before 1st April 2000.

(2) In this rule –

'the base costs' means the costs other than a percentage increase;

'percentage increase' means a percentage increase pursuant to a conditional fee agreement entered into between the solicitor and his client or between counsel and the solicitor, or counsel and the client; and 'costs' includes all fees, charges, disbursements and other expenses charged by the solicitor or counsel under the conditional fee agreement in question.

(3) On an assessment to which this rule applies, the client may apply for assessment of the base costs or of a percentage increase or of both.

(4) Where the client applies for assessment of the base costs, the base costs are to be assessed in accordance with rule 48.8(2) as if the solicitor and his client had not entered into a conditional fee agreement.

(5) Where the client applies for assessment of a percentage increase, the court may reduce the percentage increase where it considers it to be disproportionate having regard to all relevant factors as they reasonably appeared to the solicitor or counsel when the conditional fee agreement was entered into.

(6) The court will not vary a percentage increase where the client is a child or patient, except in accordance with paragraph (5).

[The Costs Practice Direction specifies some of the relevant factors.]

PART 51: TRANSITIONAL ARRANGEMENTS

51   A practice direction shall make provision for the extent to which these Rules shall apply to proceedings issued before 26 April 1999.

APPENDIX 12

Practice Direction about costs (extracts)

(SUPPLEMENTING THE CIVIL PROCEDURE RULES)

Section 2 Scope of costs rules and definitions

Rule 43.2 Definitions and application

2.1   Where the court makes an order for costs and the receiving party has entered into a funding arrangement as defined in rule 43.2, the costs payable by the paying party include any additional liability (also defined in rule 43.2) unless the court orders otherwise.

2.2   In the following paragraphs –

     'funding arrangement', 'percentage increase', 'insurance premium', 'membership organisation' and 'additional liability' have the meanings given to them by rule 43.2 . A 'conditional fee agreement' is an agreement with a person providing advocacy or litigation services which provides for his fees and expenses, or part of them, to be payable only in specified circumstances, whether or not it provides for a success fee as mentioned in section 58(2)(b) of the Courts and Legal Services Act 1990.

     'base costs' means costs other than the amount of any additional liability.

2.3   Rule 44.3A(1) provides that the court will not assess any additional liability until the conclusion of the proceedings or the part of the proceedings to which the funding arrangement relates. (As to the time when detailed assessment may be carried out see paragraph 27.1 below.)

2.4   For the purposes of the following paragraphs of this practice direction and rule 44.3A proceedings are concluded when the court has finally determined the matters in issue in the claim, whether or not there is an appeal. The making of an award of provisional damages under Part 41 will also be treated as a final determination of the matters in issue.

2.5   The court may order or the parties may agree in writing that, although the proceedings are continuing, they will nevertheless be treated as concluded.

Section 3 Model forms for claims for costs

Rule 43.3 Meaning of summary assessment

3.1   Rule 43.3 defines summary assessment. When carrying out a summary assessment of costs where there is an additional liability the court may assess the base costs alone, or the base costs and the additional liability.

Rule 43.4 Meaning of detailed assessment

3.4   Rule 43.4 defines detailed assessment. When carrying out a detailed assessment of costs where there is an additional liability the court will assess both the base costs and the additional liability, or, if the base costs have already been assessed, the additional liability alone.

Section 4 Form and contents of bills of costs

4.5   The background information included in the bill of costs should set out: . . .

        (3) a brief explanation of any agreement or arrangement between the receiving party and his solicitors, which affects the costs claimed in the bill.

4.17   (1) Where a claim is made for a percentage increase in addition to an hourly rate or base fee, the amount of the increase must be shown separately, either in the appropriate arithmetic column or in the narrative column. (For an example see Precedent A or Precedent B.)

Section 6 Estimates of costs

6.1   This section sets out certain steps which parties and their legal representatives must take in order to keep the parties informed about their potential liability in respect of costs and in order to assist the court to decide what, if any, order to make about costs and about case management.

6.2   (2) A party who intends to recover an additional liability (defined in rule 43.2) need not reveal the amount of that liability in the estimate.

Section 8 Court's discretion and circumstances to be taken into account when exercising its discretion as to costs: Rule 44.3

8.3   (1) The court may make an order about costs at any stage in a case.

        (3) Rule 44.3A(1) provides that the court will not assess any additional liability until the conclusion of the proceedings or the part of the proceedings to which the funding arrangement relates. (Paragraphs 2.4 and 2.5 above explain when proceedings are concluded. As to the time when detailed assessment may be carried out see paragraphs 28.1, below.)

DIRECTIONS RELATING TO PART 44: GENERAL RULES ABOUT COSTS

Section 9 Costs orders relating to funding arrangements: Rule 44.3A

9.1   Under an order for payment of 'costs' the costs payable will include an additional liability incurred under a funding arrangement.

9.2   (1) If before the conclusion of the proceedings the court carries out a summary assessment of the base costs it may identify separately the amount allowed in respect of: solicitors' charges; counsels' fees; other disbursements; and any value added tax (VAT). (Sections 13 and 14 of this Practice Direction deal with summary assessment.)

            (2) If an order for the base costs of a previous application or hearing did not identify separately the amounts allowed for solicitor's charges, counsel's fees and other disbursements, a court which later makes an assessment of an additional liability may apportion the base costs previously ordered.

Section 10 Limits on recovery under funding arrangements: Rule 44.3B

10.1   In a case to which rule 44.3B(1)(c) or (d) applies the party in default may apply for relief from the sanction. He should do so as quickly as possible after he becomes aware of the default. An application, supported by evidence, should be made under Part 23 to a costs judge or district judge of the court which is dealing with the case. (Attention is drawn to rules 3.8 and 3.9 which deal with sanctions and relief from sanctions).

10.2   Where the amount of any percentage increase recoverable by counsel may be affected by the outcome of the application, the solicitor issuing the application must serve on counsel a copy of the application notice and notice of the hearing as soon as practicable and in any event at least 2 days before the hearing. Counsel may make written submissions or may attend and make oral submissions at the hearing. (Paragraph 1.4 contains definitions of the terms 'counsel' and 'solicitor'.)

Section 11 Factors to be taken into account in deciding the amount of costs: Rule 44.5

11.4   Where a party has entered into a funding arrangement the costs claimed may, subject to rule 44.3B include an additional liability.

11.5   In deciding whether the costs claimed are reasonable and (on a standard basis assessment) proportionate, the court will consider the amount of any additional liability separately from the base costs.

11.6   In deciding whether the base costs are reasonable and (if relevant) proportionate the court will consider the factors set out in rule 44.5.

11.7   Subject to paragraph 17.8(2), when the court is considering the factors to be taken into account in assessing an additional liability, it will have regard to the facts and circumstances as they reasonably appeared to the solicitor or counsel when the funding arrangement was entered into and at the time of any variation of the arrangement.

11.8   (1) In deciding whether a percentage increase is reasonable relevant factors to be taken into account may include:-

(a)   the risk that the circumstances in which the costs, fees or expenses would be payable might or might not occur;

(b)   the legal representative's liability for any disbursements;

(c)   what other methods of financing the costs were available to the receiving party.

(2) The court has the power, when considering whether a percentage increase is reasonable, to allow different percentages for different items of costs or for different periods during which costs were incurred.

11.9   A percentage increase will not be reduced simply on the ground that, when added to base costs which are reasonable and (where relevant) proportionate, the total appears disproportionate.

11.10   In deciding whether the cost of insurance cover is reasonable, relevant factors to be taken into account include:

(1) where the insurance cover is not purchased in support of a conditional fee agreement with a success fee, how its cost compares with the likely cost of funding the case with a conditional fee agreement with a success fee and supporting insurance cover;

(2) the level and extent of the cover provided;

(3) the availability of any pre-existing insurance cover;

(4) whether any part of the premium would be rebated in the event of early settlement;

(5) the amount of commission payable to the receiving party or his legal representatives or other agents.

11.11   Where the court is considering a provision made by a membership organisation, rule 44.3B(1) (b) provides that any such provision which exceeds the likely cost to the receiving party of the premium of an insurance policy against the risk of incurring a liability to pay the costs of other parties to the proceedings is not recoverable. In such circumstances the court will, when assessing the additional liability, have regard to the factors set out in paragraph 11.10 above, in addition to the factors set out in rule 44.5.

Section 13 Summary assessment: General provisions

13.5   (2) Each party who intends to claim costs must prepare a written statement of the costs he intends to claim showing separately in the form of a schedule: . . .

        (5) *Where the litigant is or may be entitled to claim an additional liability the statement filed and served need not reveal the amount of that liability.

13.7   If the court makes a summary assessment of costs at the conclusion of proceedings the court will specify separately

        (1) the base costs, and if appropriate, the additional liability allowed as solicitor's charges, counsel's fees, other disbursements and any VAT; and

13.8   The court awarding costs cannot make an order for a summary assessment of costs by a costs officer. If a summary assessment of costs is appropriate but the court awarding costs is unable to do so on the day, the court must give directions as to a further hearing before the same judge.

13.12   (1) Attention is drawn to rule 44.3A which prevents the court from making a summary assessment of an additional liability before the conclusion of the proceedings or the part of the proceedings to which the funding arrangement relates. Where this applies, the court should nonetheless make a summary assessment of the base costs of the hearing or application unless there is a good reason not to do so.

        (2) Where the court makes a summary assessment of the base costs all statements of costs and costs estimates put before the judge will be retained on the court file.

Section 14 Summary assessment where costs claimed include an additional liability

Orders made before the conclusion of the proceedings

14.1   The existence of a conditional fee agreement or other funding arrangement within the meaning of rule 43.2 is not by itself a sufficient reason for not carrying out a summary assessment.

14.2   Where a legal representative acting for the receiving party has entered into a conditional fee agreement the court may summarily assess all the costs (other than any additional liability).

14.3   Where costs have been summarily assessed an order for payment will not be made unless the court has been satisfied that in respect of the costs claimed, the receiving party is at the time liable to pay to his legal representative an amount equal to or greater than the costs claimed. A statement in the form of the certificate appended at the end of Form N260 may be sufficient proof of liability. The giving of information under rule 44.15 (where that rule applies) is not sufficient.

14.4   The court may direct that any costs, for which the receiving party may not in the event be liable, shall be paid into court to await the outcome of the case, or shall not be enforceable until further order, or it may postpone the receiving party's right to receive payment in some other way.

Orders made at the conclusion of the proceedings

14.5   Where there has been a trial of one or more issues separately from other issues, the court will not normally order detailed assessment of the additional liability until all issues have been tried unless the parties agree.

14.6   Rule 44.3A(2) sets out the ways in which the court may deal with the assessment of the costs where there is a funding arrangement. Where the court makes a summary assessment of the base costs:

(1) The order may state separately the base costs allowed as (a)solicitor's charges, (b) counsel's fees, (c) any other disbursements and (d) any VAT;

(2) the statements of costs upon which the judge based his summary assessment will be retained on the court file.

14.7   Where the court makes a summary assessment of an additional liability at the conclusion of proceedings, that assessment must relate to the whole of the proceedings; this will include any additional liability relating to base costs allowed by the court when making a summary assessment on a previous application or hearing.

14.8   Paragraph 13.13 applies where the parties are agreed about the total amount to be paid by way of costs, or are agreed about the amount of the base costs that will be paid. Where they disagree about the additional liability the court may summarily assess that liability or make an order for a detailed assessment.

14.9   In order to facilitate the court in making a summary assessment of any additional liability at the conclusion of the proceedings the party seeking such costs must prepare and have available for the court a bundle of documents which must include –

(1) a copy of every notice of funding arrangement (Form N251) which has been filed by him;

(2) a copy of every estimate and statement of costs filed by him;

(3) a copy of the risk assessment prepared at the time any relevant funding arrangement was entered into and on the basis of which the amount of the additional liability was fixed.

Section 17 Costs – only proceedings: Rule 44.12A

17.8   (2) In cases in which an additional liability is claimed, the costs judge or district judge should have regard to the time when and the extent to which the claim has been settled and to the fact that the claim has been settled without the need to commence proceedings.

17.9   A claim will be treated as opposed for the purposes of rule 44.12A(4)(b) if the defendant files an acknowledgement of service stating that he intends to contest the proceedings or to seek a different remedy. An order dismissing it will be made as soon as such an acknowledgement is filed. The dismissal of a claim under rule 44.12A(4) does not prevent the claimant from issuing another claim form under Part 7 or Part 8 based on the agreement or alleged agreement to which the proceedings under this rule related.

Section 19 Providing information about funding arrangements: Rule 44.15

19.1   (1) A party who wishes to claim an additional liability in respect of a funding arrangement must give any other party information about that claim if he is to recover the additional liability. There is no requirement to specify the amount of the additional liability separately nor to state how it is calculated until it falls to be assessed. That principle is reflected in rules 44.3A and 44.15, in the following paragraphs and in Sections 6, 13, 14 and 31 of this Practice Direction. Section 6 deals with estimates of costs, Sections 13 and 14 deal with summary assessment and Section 31 deals with detailed assessment.

(2) In the following paragraphs a party who has entered into a funding arrangement is treated as a person who intends to recover a sum representing an additional liability by way of costs.

(3) Attention is drawn to paragraph 57.9 of this Practice Direction which sets out time limits for the provision of information where a funding arrangement is entered into between 31 March and 2 July 2000 and proceedings relevant to that arrangement are commenced before 3 July 2000.

Method of giving information

19.2   (1) In this paragraph, 'claim form' includes petition and application notice, and the notice of funding to be filed or served is a notice containing the information set out in Form N251.

(2) (a) A claimant who has entered into a funding arrangement before starting the proceedings to which it relates must provide information to the court by filing the notice when he issues the claim form.

(b) He must provide information to every other party by serving the notice. If he serves the claim form himself he must serve the notice with the claim form. If the court is to serve the claim form, the court will also serve the notice if the claimant provides it with sufficient copies for service.

(3) A defendant who has entered into a funding arrangement before filing any document

    (a) must provide information to the court by filing notice with his first document. A 'first document' may be an acknowledgement of service, a defence, or any other document, such as an application to set aside a default judgment.

    (b) must provide information to every party by serving notice. If he serves his first document himself he must serve the notice with that document. If the court is to serve his first document the court will also serve the notice if the defendant provides it with sufficient copies for service.

(4) In all other circumstances a party must file and serve notice within 7 days of entering into the funding arrangement concerned.

(5) There is no requirement in this Practice Direction for the provision of information about funding arrangements before the commencement of proceedings. Such provision is however recommended and may be required by a pre-action protocol.

Notice of change of information

19.3   (1) Rule 44.15 imposes a duty on a party to give notice of change if the information he has previously provided is no longer accurate. To comply he must file and serve notice containing the information set out in Form N251. Rule 44.15(3) may impose other duties in relation to new estimates of costs.

    (2) Further notification need not be provided where a party has already given notice:

        (a) that he has entered into a conditional fee agreement with a legal representative and during the currency of that agreement either of them enters into another such agreement with an additional legal representative; or

        (b) of some insurance cover, unless that cover is cancelled or unless new cover is taken out with a different insurer.

    (3) Part 6 applies to the service of notices.

    (4) The notice must be signed by the party or by his legal representative.

Information which must be provided

19.4   (1) Unless the court otherwise orders, a party who is required to supply information about a funding arrangement must state whether he has –

entered into a conditional fee agreement which provides for a success fee within the meaning of section 58(2) of the Courts and Legal Services Act 1990;

taken out an insurance policy to which section 29 of the Access to Justice Act 1999 applies;

made an arrangement with a body which is prescribed for the purpose of section 30 of that Act;

or more than one of these.

(2) Where the funding arrangement is a conditional fee agreement, the party must state the date of the agreement and identify the claim or claims to which it relates (including Part 20 claims if any).

(3) Where the funding arrangement is an insurance policy the party must state the name of the insurer, the date of the policy and must identify the claim or claims to which it relates (including Part 20 claims if any).

(4) Where the funding arrangement is by way of an arrangement with a relevant body the party must state the name of the body and set out the date and terms of the undertaking it has given and must identify the claim or claims to which it relates (including Part 20 claims if any).

(5) Where a party has entered into more than one funding arrangement in respect of a claim, for example a conditional fee agreement and an insurance policy, a single notice containing the information set out in Form N251 may contain the required information about both or all of them.

19.5 Where the court makes a Group Litigation Order, the court may give directions as to the extent to which individual parties should provide information in accordance with rule 44.15. (Part 19 deals with Group Litigation Orders.)

Section 20 Procedure where legal representative wishes to recover from his client an agreed percentage increase which has been disallowed or reduced on assessment: Rule 44.16

20.1 Attention is drawn to Regulation 3(2)(b) of the Conditional Fee Agreements Regulations 2000, which provides that any amount of an agreed percentage increase, which is disallowed on assessment, ceases to be payable under that agreement unless the court is satisfied that it should continue to be so payable. Rule 44.16 allows the court to adjourn a hearing at which the legal representative acting for the receiving party applies for an order that a disallowed amount should continue to be payable under the agreement.

20.2 In the following paragraphs 'counsel' means counsel who has acted in the case under a conditional fee agreement which provides for a success fee. A reference to counsel includes a reference to any person who appeared as an advocate in the case and who is not a partner or employee of the solicitor or firm which is conducting the claim or defence (as the case may be) on behalf of the receiving party.

Procedure following Summary Assessment

20.3   (1) If the court disallows any amount of a legal representative's percentage increase, the court will, unless sub-paragraph (2) applies, give directions to enable an application to be made by the legal representative for the disallowed amount to be payable by his client, including, if appropriate, a direction that the application will be determined by a costs judge or district judge of the court dealing with the case.

(2) The court that has made the summary assessment may then and there decide the issue whether the disallowed amount should continue to be payable, if:

(a) the receiving party and all parties to the relevant agreement consent to the court doing so;

(b) the receiving party (or, if corporate, an officer) is present in court; and

(c) the court is satisfied that the issue can be fairly decided then and there.

Procedure following Detailed Assessment

20.4   (1) Where detailed assessment proceedings have been commenced, and the paying party serves points of dispute (as to which see Section 34 of this Practice Direction), which show that he is seeking a reduction in any percentage increase charged by counsel on his fees, the solicitor acting for the receiving party must within 3 days of service deliver to counsel a copy of the relevant points of dispute and the bill of costs or the relevant parts of the bill.

(2) Counsel must within 10 days thereafter inform the solicitor in writing whether or not he will accept the reduction sought or some other reduction. Counsel may state any points he wishes to have made in a reply to the points of dispute, and the solicitor must serve them on the paying party as or as part of a reply.

(3) Counsel who fails to inform the solicitor within the time limits set out above will be taken to accept the reduction unless the court otherwise orders.

20.5   Where the paying party serves points of dispute seeking a reduction in any percentage increase charged by a legal representative acting for the receiving party, and that legal representative intends, if necessary, to apply for an order that any amount of the percentage disallowed as against the paying party shall continue to be payable by his client, the solicitor acting for the receiving party must, within 14 days of service of the points of dispute, give to his client a clear written explanation of the nature of the relevant point of dispute and the effect it will have if it is upheld in whole or in part by the court, and of the client's right to attend any subsequent hearings at court when the matter is raised.

20.6   Where the solicitor acting for a receiving party files a request for a detailed assessment hearing it must if appropriate, be accompanied by a certificate signed by him stating:

    (1) that the amount of the percentage increase in respect of counsel's fees or solicitor's charges is disputed;

    (2) whether an application will be made for an order that any amount of that increase which is disallowed should continue to be payable by his client;

    (3) that he has given his client an explanation in accordance with paragraph 20.5; and,

    (4) whether his client wishes to attend court when the amount of any relevant percentage increase may be decided.

20.7   (1) The solicitor acting for the receiving party must within 7 days of receiving from the court notice of the date of the assessment hearing, notify his client, and if appropriate, counsel in writing of the date, time and place of the hearing.

    (2) Counsel may attend or be represented at the detailed assessment hearing and may make oral or written submissions.

20.8   (1) At the detailed assessment hearing, the court will deal with the assessment of the costs payable by one party to another, including the amount of the percentage increase, and give a certificate accordingly.

    (2) The court may decide the issue whether the disallowed amount should continue to be payable under the relevant conditional fee agreement without an adjournment if:

    (a) the receiving party and all parties to the relevant agreement consent to the court deciding the issue without an adjournment,

    (b) the receiving party (or, if corporate, an officer or employee who has authority to consent on behalf of the receiving party) is present in court, and

    (c) the court is satisfied that the issue can be fairly decided without an adjournment.

    (3) In any other case the court will give directions and fix a date for the hearing of the application.

Section 27 Power to award more or less than the amount of fast track trial costs: Rule 46.3

27.1 Rule 44.15 (providing information about funding arrangements) sets out the requirement to provide information about funding arrangements to the court and other parties. Section 19 of this Practice Direction sets out the information to be provided and when this is to be done.

27.2 Section 11, of this Practice Direction explains how the court will approach the question of what sum to allow in respect of additional liability.

27.3 The court has the power, when considering whether a percentage increase is reasonable, to allow different percentages for different items of costs or for different periods during which costs were incurred.

DIRECTIONS RELATING TO PART 47: PROCEDURE FOR DETAILED ASSESSMENT OF COSTS AND DEFAULT PROVISIONS

Section 32 Commencement of detailed assessment proceedings: Rule 47.6

32.2 A detailed assessment may be in respect of:

(1) base costs, where a claim for additional liability has not been made or has been agreed;

(2) a claim for additional liability only, base costs having been summarily assessed or agreed;

or

(3) both base costs and additional liability.

32.4 If the detailed assessment is in respect of an additional liability only, the receiving party must serve on the paying party and all other relevant persons the following documents:

(a) a notice of commencement;

(b) a copy of the bill of costs;

(c) the relevant details of the additional liability;

(d) a statement giving the name and address of any person upon whom the receiving party intends to serve the notice of commencement.

32.5 The relevant details of an additional liability are as follows:

(1) In the case of a conditional fee agreement with a success fee:

(a) a statement showing the amount of costs which have been summarily assessed or agreed, and the percentage increase which has been claimed in respect of those costs;

> (b) a statement of the reasons for the percentage increase given in accordance with Regulation 3 of the Conditional Fee Agreement Regulations 2000.
>
> (2) If the additional liability is an insurance premium: a copy of the insurance certificate showing whether the policy covers the receiving party's own costs; his opponent's costs; or his own costs and his opponent's costs; and the maximum extent of that cover, and the amount of the premium paid or payable.
>
> (3) If the receiving party claims an additional amount under Section 30 of the Access of Justice Act 1999: a statement setting out the basis upon which the receiving party's liability for the additional amount is calculated.

32.6   Attention is drawn to the fact that the additional amount recoverable pursuant to section 30 of the Access to Justice Act 1999 in respect of a membership organisation must not exceed the likely cost of the premium of an insurance policy against the risk of incurring a liability to pay the costs of other parties to the proceedings as provided by the Access to Justice (Membership Organisation) Regulations 2000 Regulation 4.

32.7   If a detailed assessment is in respect of both base costs and an additional liability, the receiving party must serve on the paying party and all other relevant persons the documents listed in paragraph 32.3 and the documents giving relevant details of an additional liability listed in paragraph 32.5.

Section 35 Points of dispute and consequences of not serving: Rule 47.9

35.7   (1) Where the receiving party claims an additional liability, a party who serves points of dispute on the receiving party may include a request for information about other methods of financing costs which were available to the receiving party.

(2) Part 18 (further information) and the Practice Direction Supplementing that part apply to such a request.

Section 40 Detailed assessment hearing: Rule 47.14

40.2   The request for a detailed assessment hearing must be in Form N258. The request must be accompanied by:

(i) where there is a dispute as to the receiving party's liability to pay costs to the solicitors who acted for the receiving party, any agreement, letter or other written information provided by the solicitor to his client explaining how the solicitor's charges are to be calculated;

40.3   (1) This paragraph applies to any document described in paragraph 40.2(i) above which the receiving party has filed in the appropriate office. The document must be the latest relevant version and in any event have been filed not more than 2 years before filing the request for a detailed assessment hearing.

(2) In respect of any documents to which this paragraph applies, the receiving party may, instead of filing a copy of it, specify in the request for a detailed assessment hearing the case number under which a copy of the document was previously filed.

40.11 Unless the court directs otherwise the receiving party must file with the court the papers in support of the bill not less than 7 days before the date for the detailed assessment hearing and not more than 14 days before that date.

40.12 The following provisions apply in respect of the papers to be filed in support of the bill;

(a) If the claim is for costs only without any additional liability the papers to be filed, and the order in which they are to be arranged are as follows:

(i) instructions and briefs to counsel arranged in chronological order together with all advices, opinions and drafts received and response to such instructions;

(ii) reports and opinions of medical and other experts;

(iii) any other relevant papers;

(iv) a full set of any relevant pleadings to the extent that they have not already been filed in court.

(v) correspondence, files and attendance notes;

(b) where the claim is in respect of an additional liability only, such of the papers listed at (a) above, as are relevant to the issues raised by the claim for additional liability;

(c) where the claim is for both base costs and an additional liability, the papers listed at (a) above, together with any papers relevant to the issues raised by the claim for additional liability.

40.13 The provisions set out in Section 20 of this Practice Direction apply where the court disallows any amount of a legal representative's percentage increase, and the legal representative applies for an order that the disallowed amount should continue to be payable by the client in accordance with Rule 44.16.

40.14 The court may direct the receiving party to produce any document which in the opinion of the court is necessary to enable it to reach its decision. These documents will in the first instance be produced to the court, but the court may ask the receiving party to elect whether to disclose the particular document to the paying party in order to rely on the contents of the document, or whether to decline disclosure and instead rely on other evidence.

40.15 Costs assessed at a detailed assessment at the conclusion of proceedings may include an assessment of any additional liability in respect of the costs of a previous application or hearing.

DIRECTIONS RELATING TO PART 48: COSTS – SPECIAL CASES

Section 55 Conditional fees: Rule 48.9

55.1   (1) Attention is drawn to rule 48.9(1) as amended by the Civil Procedure (Amendment No.3) Rules 2000 (SI 2000/1317) with effect from 3 July 2000. Rule 48.9 applies only where the solicitor and the client have entered into a conditional fee agreement as defined in section 58 of the Courts and Legal Services Act 1990 as it was in force before 1 April 2000. A client who has entered into a conditional fee agreement with a solicitor may apply for assessment of the base costs (which is carried out in accordance with rule 48.8(2) as if there were no conditional fee agreement) or for assessment of the percentage increase (success fee) or both.

        (2) Where the court is to assess the percentage increase the court will have regard to all the relevant factors as they appeared to the solicitor or counsel when the conditional fee agreement was entered into.

55.2   Where the client applies to the court to reduce the percentage increase which the solicitor has charged the client under the conditional fee agreement, the client must set out in his application notice:

        (a) the reasons why the percentage increase should be reduced; and

        (b) what the percentage increase should be.

55.3   The factors relevant to assessing the percentage increase include –

        (a) the risk that the circumstances in which the fees or expenses would be payable might not occur;

        (b) the disadvantages relating to the absence of payment on account;

        (c) whether the amount which might be payable under the conditional fee agreement is limited to a certain proportion of any damages recovered by the client;

        (d) whether there is a conditional fee agreement between the solicitor and counsel;

        (e) the solicitor's liability for any disbursements.

55.4   When the court is considering the factors to be taken into account, it will have regard to the circumstances as they reasonably appeared to the solicitor or counsel when the conditional fee agreement was entered into.

Section 57 Transitional arrangements

57.1   In this section 'the previous rules' means the Rules of the Supreme Court 1965 ('RSC') or County Court Rules 1981 ('CCR'), as appropriate.

General Scheme of Transitional Arrangements concerning Costs Proceedings

57.2   (1) Paragraph 18 of the Practice Direction which supplements Part 51 (Transitional Arrangements) provides that the CPR govern any assessments of costs which take place on or after 26 April 1999 and states a presumption to be applied in respect of costs for work undertaken before 26 April 1999.

      (2) The following paragraphs provide five further transitional arrangements:

         (a) to provide an additional presumption to be applied when assessing costs which were awarded by an order made in a county court before 26 April 1999 which allowed costs 'on Scale 1' to be determined in accordance with CCR Appendix A, or 'on the lower scale' to be determined in accordance with CCR Appendix C. . . .

         (e) to deal with funding arrangements made before 3 July 2000.

Transitional provisions concerning the Access to Justice Act 1999 sections 28 to 31

57.8   (1) Sections 28 to 31 of the Access to Justice Act 1999, the Conditional Fee Agreements Regulations 2000, the Access to Justice (Membership Organisations) Regulations 2000, and the Access to Justice Act 1999 (Transitional Provisions) Order 2000 came into force on 1 April 2000. The Civil Procedure (Amendment No.3) Rules come into force on 3 July 2000.

      (2) The Access to Justice Act 1999 (Transitional Provisions) Order 2000 provides that no conditional fee agreement or other arrangement about costs entered into before 1 April 2000 can be a funding arrangement, as defined in rule 43.2 The order also has the effect that where an conditional fee agreement or other funding arrangement has been entered into before 1 April 2000 and a second or subsequent funding arrangement is entered into on or after 1 April 2000, the second or subsequent funding arrangement does not give rise to an additional liability which is recoverable from a paying party.

57.9   (1) Rule 39 of the Civil Procedure (Amendment No 3) Rules 2000 [see note at end] applies where between 1 April and 2 July 2000 (including both dates) –

      a funding arrangement is entered into, and

      proceedings are started in respect of a claim which is the subject of that agreement.

      (2) Attention is drawn to the need to act promptly so as to comply with the requirements of the Rules and the Practice Directions by 31 July 2000 (i.e. within the 28 days from 3 July 2000 permitted by Rule 39) if that

compliance is to be treated as compliance with the relevant provision. Attention is drawn in particular to Rule 44.15 (Providing Information about Funding Arrangements) and Section 19 of this Practice Direction.

(3) Nothing in the legislation referred to above makes provision for a party who has entered into a funding arrangement to recover from another party any amount of an additional liability which relates to anything done or any costs incurred before the arrangement was entered into.

PRACTICE DIRECTION – TRANSITIONAL ARRANGEMENTS

This Practice Direction supplements CPR Part 51

Contents of this Practice Direction

1   (1) This Practice Direction deals with the application of the Civil Procedure Rules ('CPR') to proceedings issued before 26 April 1999 ('existing proceedings').

Costs

18   (1) Any assessment of costs that takes place on or after 26 April 1999 will be in accordance with CPR Parts 43 to 48.

(2) However, the general presumption is that no costs for work undertaken before 26 April 1999 will be disallowed if those costs would have been allowed in a costs taxation before 26 April 1999.

(3) The decision as to whether to allow costs for work undertaken on or after 26 April will generally be taken in accordance with CPR Parts 43 to 48.

[The Costs Practice Direction contains more information on the operation of the transitional arrangements in relation to costs.]

(4) For the purposes of this paragraph proceedings will not be 'existing proceedings' once final judgment has been given.

CIVIL PROCEDURE (AMENDMENT NO. 3) RULES 2000, SI 2000/1317, RULE 39

(See 57.9(1) above)

Transitional provisions

39. – (1) This rule applies where a person has –

(a) entered into a funding arrangement, and

(b) started proceedings in respect of a claim the subject of that funding arrangement,

before the date on which these Rules come into force.

(2) Any requirement imposed –

(a) by any provision of the Civil Procedure Rules 1998 amended by these Rules, or

(b) by a practice direction

in respect of that funding arrangement may be complied with within 28 days of the coming into force of these Rules, and that compliance shall be treated as compliance with the relevant rule or practice direction.

(3) For the purpose of this rule, 'funding arrangement' means an arrangement where a person has–

(a) entered into a conditional fee agreement which provides for a success fee within the meaning of section 58(2) of the Courts and Legal Services Act 1990;

(b) taken out an insurance policy to which section 29 of the Access to Justice Act 1999 (recovery of insurance premiums by way of costs) applies; or

(c) made an agreement with a membership organisation prescribed for the purpose of section 30 of the Access to Justice Act 1999 (recovery where body undertakes to meet cost liabilities) to meet his legal costs.

APPENDIX 13

Notice of Funding of Case or Claim 📝

In the	
Claim No.	
Claimant (include Ref.)	
Defendant (include Ref.)	

Notice of funding by means of a conditional fee agreement, insurance policy or undertaking given by a prescribed body should be given to the court and all other parties to the case:
- on commencement of proceedings
- on filing an acknowledgment of service, defence or other first document; and
- at any later time that such an arrangement is entered into, changed or terminated

Take notice that in respect of [all claims herein][the following claims . . . .]
the case of . . . . *(specify name of party)*

[is now][was] being funded by:
(Please tick those boxes which apply)

☐ a conditional fee agreement dated . . . . which provides for a success fee;

☐ an insurance policy issued on *(date)* . . . . . by *(name of insurers)* . . . . ;

☐ an undertaking given on *(date)* . . . . . by *(name of prescribed body)* . . . . in the
following terms . . . .

The funding of the case has now changed:

☐ the above funding has now ceased

☐ the conditional fee agreement has been terminated

☐ a conditional agreement dated . . . . which provides for a success fee has been entered into

☐ the insurance policy dated . . . . has been cancelled

☐ an insurance policy has been issued by *(name of insurer)* . . . .
on *(date)* . . . .

☐ the undertaking given on *(date)* . . . . has been terminated

☐ an undertaking has been given on *(date)* . . . . by *(name of prescribed body)* . . . .
in the following terms . . . .

📝

Signed . . . . **Date** . . . .
Solicitor for the (claimant) (defendant) (Part 20 defendant)
(respondent)(appellant)

The court office at

is open between 10 am and 4 pm Monday to Friday. When corresponding with the court, please address forms or letters to the Court Manager and quote the claim number
N251 Notice of funding of case or claim (7.00)   *The Court Service Publications Unit*

203

Solicitors' Practice Rules (extracts)

Practice Rule 1 (Basic principles)

A solicitor shall not do anything in the course of practising as a solicitor, or permit another person to do anything on his or her behalf, which compromises or impairs or is likely to compromise or impair any of the following:

(a) the solicitor's independence or integrity;

(b) a person's freedom to instruct a solicitor of his or her choice;

(c) the solicitor's duty to act in the best interests of the client;

(d) the good repute of the solicitor or of the solicitors' profession;

(e) the solicitor's proper standard of work;

(f) the solicitor's duty to the Court.

Practice Rule 8 (Contingency fees)

(1) A solicitor who is retained or employed to prosecute or defend any action, suit or other contentious proceeding shall not enter into any arrangement to receive a contingency fee in respect of that proceeding, save one permitted under statute or by the common law.

(2) Paragraph (1) of this rule shall not apply to an arrangement in respect of an action, suit or other contentious proceeding in any country other than England and Wales to the extent that a local lawyer would be permitted to receive a contingency fee in respect of that proceeding.

Practice Rule 15 (Costs information and client care)

Solicitors shall:

(a) give information about costs and other matters, and

(b) operate a complaints handling procedure,

in accordance with a Solicitors' Costs Information and Client Care Code made from time to time by the Council of the Law Society with the concurrence of the Master of the Rolls, but subject to the notes.

Notes

i.   *A serious breach of the code, or persistent breaches of a material nature, will be a breach of the rule, and may also be evidence of inadequate professional services under section 37A of the Solicitors Act 1974.*

ii.   *Material breaches of the code which are not serious or persistent will not be a breach of the rule, but may be evidence of inadequate professional services under section 37A.*

iii.   *The powers of the Office for the Supervision of Solicitors on a finding of inadequate professional services include:*

(a)   *disallowing all or part of the solicitor's costs; and*

(b)   *directing the solicitor to pay compensation to the client up to a limit of £1,000.*

iv.   *Non-material breaches of the code will not be a breach of the rule, and will not be evidence of inadequate professional services under section 37A.*

v.   *Registered foreign lawyers, although subject to Rule 15 as a matter of professional conduct, are not subject to section 37A. However, solicitor partners in a multi-national partnership are subject to section 37A for professional services provided by the firm.*

Practice Rule 18 (Definitions)

(2) (C) . . .

'contingency fee' means any sum (whether fixed, or calculated either as a percentage of the proceeds or otherwise howsoever) payable only in the event of success in the prosecution or defence of any action, suit or other contentious proceeding.

APPENDIX 15

Solicitors' Costs Information and Client Care Code

1. INTRODUCTION

(a) This code replaces the written professional standards on costs information for clients (see paragraphs 3–6) and the detail previously contained in Practice Rule 15 (client care) (see paragraph 7).

(b) The main object of the code is to make sure that clients are given the information they need to understand what is happening generally and in particular on:

    (i)   the cost of legal services both at the outset and as a matter progresses; and

    (ii) responsibility for clients' matters.

(c) The code also requires firms to operate a complaints handling procedure.

(d) It is good practice to record in writing:

    (i)   all information required to be given by the code including all decisions relating to costs and the arrangements for updating costs information; and

    (ii) the reasons why the information required by the code has not been given in a particular case.

(e) References to costs, where appropriate, include fees, VAT and disbursements.

2. APPLICATION

(a) The code is of general application, and it applies to registered foreign lawyers as well as to solicitors. However, as set out in paragraph 2(b), parts of the code may not be appropriate in every case, and solicitors should consider the interests of each client in deciding which parts not to apply in the particular circumstances.

(b) The full information required by the code may be inappropriate, for example:

    (i)   in every case, for a regular client for whom repetitive work is done, where the client has already been provided with the relevant information, although such a client should be informed of changes; and

(ii) if compliance with the code may at the time be insensitive or impractical. In such a case relevant information should be given as soon as reasonably practicable.

(c) Employed solicitors should have regard to paragraphs 3–6 of the code where appropriate, e.g. when acting for clients other than their employer. Paragraph 7 does not apply to employed solicitors.

(d) Solicitors should comply with paragraphs 3–6 of the code even where a client is legally aided if the client may have a financial interest in the costs because contributions are payable or the statutory charge may apply or they may become liable for the costs of another party.

(e) The code also applies to contingency fee and conditional fee arrangements and to arrangements with a client for the solicitor to retain commissions received from third parties.

3. INFORMING THE CLIENT ABOUT COSTS

(a) Costs information must not be inaccurate or misleading.

(b) Any costs information required to be given by the code must be given clearly, in a way and at a level which is appropriate to the particular client. Any terms with which the client may be unfamiliar, for example 'disbursement', should be explained.

(c) The information required by paragraphs 4 and 5 of the code should be given to a client at the outset of, and at appropriate stages throughout, the matter. All information given orally should be confirmed in writing to the client as soon as possible.

4. ADVANCE COSTS INFORMATION – GENERAL

The overall costs

(a) The solicitor should give the client the best information possible about the likely overall costs, including a breakdown between fees, VAT and disbursements.

(b) The solicitor should explain clearly to the client the time likely to be spent in dealing with a matter, if time spent is a factor in the calculation of the fees.

(c) Giving 'the best information possible' includes:

(i) agreeing a fixed fee; or

(ii) giving a realistic estimate; or

(iii) giving a forecast within a possible range of costs; or

(iv) explaining to the client the reasons why it is not possible to fix, or give a realistic estimate or forecast of, the overall costs, and giving instead the best information possible about the cost of the next stage of the matter.

(d) The solicitor should, in an appropriate case, explain to a privately paying client that the client may set an upper limit on the firm's costs for which the client may be liable without further authority. Solicitors should not exceed an agreed limit without first obtaining the client's consent.

(e) The solicitor should make it clear at the outset if an estimate, quotation or other indication of cost is not intended to be fixed.

Basis of firm's charges

(f) The solicitor should also explain to the client how the firm's fees are calculated except where the overall costs are fixed or clear. If the basis of charging is an hourly charging rate, that must be made clear.

(g) The client should be told if charging rates may be increased.

Further information

(h) The solicitor should explain what reasonably foreseeable payments a client may have to make either to the solicitor or to a third party and when those payments are likely to be needed.

(i) The solicitor should explain to the client the arrangements for updating the costs information as set out in paragraph 6.

Client's ability to pay

(j) The solicitor should discuss with the client how **and when** any costs are to be met, and consider:

(i) whether the client may be eligible and should apply for legal aid (including advice and assistance);

(ii) whether the client's liability for their own costs may be covered by insurance;

(iii) whether the client's liability for another party's costs may be covered by pre-purchased insurance and, if not, whether it would be advisable for the client's liability for another party's costs to be covered by after the event insurance (including in every case where a conditional fee or contingency fee arrangement is proposed); and

(iv) whether the client's liability for costs (including the costs of another party) may be paid by another person e.g. an employer or trade union.

Cost-benefit and risk

(k) The solicitor should discuss with the client whether the likely outcome in a matter will justify the expense or risk involved including, if relevant, the risk of having to bear an opponent's costs.

5. ADDITIONAL INFORMATION FOR PARTICULAR CLIENTS

Legally aided clients

(a) The solicitor should explain to a legally aided client the client's potential liability for the client's own costs and those of any other party, including:

(i) the effect of the statutory charge and its likely amount;

(ii) the client's obligation to pay any contribution assessed and the consequences of failing to do so;

(iii) the fact that the client may still be ordered by the court to contribute to the opponent's costs if the case is lost even though the client's own costs are covered by legal aid; and

(iv) the fact that even if the client wins, the opponent may not be ordered to pay or be capable of paying the full amount of the client's costs.

Privately paying clients in contentious matters (and potentially contentious matters)

(b) The solicitor should explain to the client the client's potential liability for the client's own costs and for those of any other party, including:

(i) the fact that the client will be responsible for paying the firm's bill in full regardless of any order for costs made against an opponent;

(ii) the probability that the client will have to pay the opponent's costs as well as the client's own costs if the case is lost;

(iii) the fact that even if the client wins, the opponent may not be ordered to pay or be capable of paying the full amount of the client's costs; and

(iv) the fact that if the opponent is legally aided the client may not recover costs, even if successful.

Liability for third party costs in non-contentious matters

(c) The solicitor should explain to the client any liability the client may have for the payment of the costs of a third party. When appropriate, solicitors are advised to obtain a firm figure for or agree a cap to a third party's costs.

6. UPDATING COSTS INFORMATION

The solicitor should keep the client properly informed about costs as a matter progresses. In particular, the solicitor should:

(a) tell the client, unless otherwise agreed, how much the costs are at regular intervals (at least every six months) and in appropriate cases deliver interim bills at agreed intervals;

(b) explain to the client (and confirm in writing) any changed circumstances which will, or which are likely to, affect the amount of costs, the degree of risk involved, or the cost-benefit to the client of continuing with the matter;

(c) inform the client in writing as soon as it appears that a costs estimate or agreed upper limit may or will be exceeded; and

(d) consider the client's eligibility for legal aid if a material change in the client's means comes to the solicitor's attention.

7. CLIENT CARE AND COMPLAINTS HANDLING

Information for clients

(a) Every solicitor in private practice must ensure that the client:

(i) is given a clear explanation of the issues raised in a matter and is kept properly informed about its progress (including the likely timescale);

(ii) is given the name and status of the person dealing with the matter and the name of the principal responsible for its overall supervision;

(iii) is told whom to contact about any problem with the service provided; and

(iv) is given details of any changes in the information required to be given by this paragraph.

Complaints handling

(b) Every principal in private practice must:

(i) ensure the client is told the name of the person in the firm to contact about any problem with the service provided;

(ii) have a written complaints procedure and ensure that complaints are handled in accordance with it; and

(iii) ensure that the client is given a copy of the complaints procedure on request.

211

Solicitors' Publicity Code 1990

(with consolidated amendments to 3rd March 1999)

Code dated 18th July 1990 promulgated by the Council of the Law Society with the concurrence of the Master of the Rolls under Rule 2 of the Solicitors' Practice Rules 1990, regulating the publicity of solicitors and recognised bodies in England and Wales or overseas, and the publicity of registered foreign lawyers practising in England and Wales.

1. GENERAL PRINCIPLES

(a) Compliance with professional obligations

Nothing in this code shall be construed as authorising any breach of the Solicitors' Practice Rules, and in particular Rule 1 thereof, or any other professional obligation or requirement.

(b) Publicity in bad taste

Solicitors shall not publicise their practices in any manner which may reasonably be regarded as being in bad taste.

(c) Misleading or inaccurate publicity

Publicity must not be inaccurate or misleading in any way.

(d) Statutory requirements

As a matter of professional conduct the publicity of a solicitor must comply with the general law. Solicitors are reminded, *inter alia*, of the requirements of:

(i) any regulations made under the Consumer Credit Act 1974 concerning the content of advertisements;

(ia) sections 20 and 21 of the Consumer Protection Act 1987 concerning misleading price indications;

(ii) the Business Names Act 1985 concerning lists of partners and an address for service on stationery, etc.; and

(iii) Chapter 1 of Part XI of the Companies Act 1985 concerning the appearance of the company name and other particulars on stationery, etc.

(e) [repealed]

(f) Solicitors' responsibility for publicity

It is the responsibility of solicitors to ensure that all their publicity, and all publicity for their services which is conducted by other persons, complies with the provisions of this code. The responsibility cannot be delegated. Where solicitors become aware of any impropriety in any publicity appearing on their behalf, they must use their best endeavours to have the publicity rectified or withdrawn as appropriate.

2. CONTENTS OF PUBLICITY – GENERAL

(a) Solicitor to be identified

Every advertisement by a solicitor must bear the solicitor's name or firm name (subject to paragraph 10 below on flag advertising).

(b) Claims to specialisation or particular expertise

It is not improper for a claim to be made that a solicitor (or a registered foreign lawyer) is a specialist, or an expert, in a particular field provided that such a claim can be justified.

(c) Success rate

No publicity may refer to a solicitor's success rate (or that of a registered foreign lawyer practising with the solicitor).

(d) Comparisons and criticisms

No publicity may make direct comparison or criticism in relation to the charges or quality of service of any other identifiable solicitor. However, a solicitor may participate in the preparation of a bona fide survey of legal services conducted by a third party which may make comparisons between the charges of or quality of service provided by different solicitors.

(e) The Law Society's coat of arms

The armorial bearings of the Law Society may not appear in a solicitor's publicity.

(f) Legal aid logo

Solicitors willing to undertake legal aid cases may use the legal aid logo in their publicity, but the logo must not be altered in any way. (Photographic copies of the logo can be obtained from the Legal Aid Board.)

3. UNSOLICITED VISITS AND TELEPHONE CALLS

Solicitors may not publicise their practices or properties for sale or to let by means of unsolicited visits or telephone calls except:

(i)   by means of a telephone call to a current or former client; or

(ii) by means of a visit or telephone call to another solicitor or to an existing or potential professional connection; or

(iii) by means of a visit or telephone call made to publicise a specific commercial property or properties the solicitor has for sale or to let.

4. NAMING CLIENTS

Solicitors may name or identify their clients in advertisements for their practices or in the public media, or supply information about their clients to publishers of directories, provided that:

(i)   the client gives consent which, in the case of advertisements and directories, shall be in writing; and

(ii) any such naming or identification of a client is not likely to prejudice the client's interests.

5. STATEMENTS AS TO CHARGES

(a) Clarity

Any publicity as to charges or a basis of charging must be clearly expressed. It must be stated what services will be provided for those charges or on that basis of charging. Any circumstances in which the charges may be increased or the basis altered must be stated. It must be clear whether disbursements and VAT are included.

(b) Fee from or upwards of a figure

It is prohibited to state a fee as being from or upwards of a certain figure.

(c) Service free of charge

Publicity may state that a particular service of a solicitor is free of charge, but this must not be conditional on the solicitor or any other person being given any other instructions, or receiving any commission or other benefit, in connection with that or any other matter.

(d) Composite fees

Solicitors may quote a composite fee for two or more separate services offered, but

(i)   the solicitor must if required quote separate fees for the individual services; and

(ii) the solicitor must if required carry out any one only of those services on the basis of the separate fee quoted; and

(iii) except in relation to a composite fee for property selling and conveyancing services, the separate fees quoted may not total more than the composite fee.

(e) Commissions from third parties

In publicity for conveyancing or other services of a solicitor, fees must not be quoted which are intended to be net fees, i.e. fees which are reduced by the availability of any commission (such as that on an endowment policy). Any fee quoted in such circumstances must be the gross fee, although there is no objection to mentioning that the availability for the benefit of the client of a commission may reduce the net cost of the transaction to the client; provided that, where such mention is made in connection with mortgages, there must be no implication that endowment mortgages are appropriate in all circumstances, and there must be included an indication of the solicitor's willingness to advise as to the appropriate type of mortgage for the client's circumstances.

(f) Fees for conveyancing services

In publicity which includes references to charges for conveyancing services, regard must be had to paragraph 1(c) above (misleading or inaccurate publicity) and paragraph 5(a) above (clarity in statements as to charges).

The following are examples of publicity which would breach these provisions:

(i)   publicity which includes an estimated fee pitched at an unrealistically low level, if the solicitor then charges higher or additional fees;

(ii) publicity which refers to an estimated or fixed fee plus disbursements, if the solicitor then charges as disbursements expenses which are in the nature of overheads such as normal postage and telephone calls, *unless* the publicity explicitly states that such charges will be made;

(iii) publicity which includes an estimated or fixed fee for conveyancing services, if the solicitor then makes an additional charge for work on a related mortgage loan or repayment, including work done for a lender, *unless* the publicity makes it clear that any such additional charge may be payable (e.g. by use of a formula like 'excluding VAT, disbursements, mortgage related charges and fees for work done for a lender').

6. DESCRIPTION OF A MULTI-NATIONAL PRACTICE

In the case of a practice which has at least one registered foreign lawyer as a partner (or director, registered member or beneficial shareowner), a description of the firm appearing on any letterhead (or fax heading, or heading used for bills) of an English or Welsh office of the practice must, if the description includes the word 'solicitor(s)', also include:

(i) words denoting the countries or jurisdictions of qualification of the foreign lawyer partners (or directors, registered members and beneficial owners) and their professional qualifications; or

(ii) the words 'registered foreign lawyer(s)';

and the categories of lawyer must appear in order, with the largest group of partners (or directors, registered members and beneficial shareowners) placed first. There must be no breach of paragraph 14(b) below on the use of the word 'lawyer(s)'.

7. NAMING AND DESCRIBING PARTNERS AND STAFF

(a) Provisions applying to all practices

(i) A member of staff (including a partner or director) other than a solicitor who holds a current practising certificate may only be named in a practitioner's publicity, including stationery, if the status of that person is unambiguously stated.

(ii) The term 'legal executive' may only be used in a practitioner's publicity, including stationery, to refer to a Fellow of the Institute of Legal Executives; and 'trainee solicitor' to refer to a person training as a solicitor under a training contract registered with the Law Society.

(iii) Practitioners are reminded of the danger of inadvertently holding out persons as partners in a firm by inclusion of both partners' and non-partners'

217

names in a list. The status of non-partners must be indicated for avoidance of doubt whenever a situation of inadvertent holding out might otherwise arise.

(iv) The following terms, used alone or in combination, will be deemed to indicate that a person is a solicitor holding a current practising certificate, unless it is made clear that the person is not so qualified:

(A) associate;

(B) assistant;

(C) consultant.

(v) The following terms, used alone or in combination, will be deemed to indicate that a person is not a solicitor holding a current practising certificate, unless a contrary indication appears:

(A) executive;

(B) clerk;

(C) manager;

(D) secretary;

(E) paralegal.

(vi) The appearance against a person's name of an indication that he or she is qualified in a jurisdiction other than England and Wales, or the title licensed conveyancer, or registered foreign lawyer, or the title of any other profession, will be deemed to indicate that the person is not a solicitor holding a current practising certificate, unless a contrary indication appears. (See also paragraph 14(b) below on the use of the word 'lawyer(s)'.)

(b) Additional provisions applying to multi-national practices

(i) In the case of a practice which has at least one registered foreign lawyer as a partner, director, registered member or beneficial owner of a share, the notepaper of an English or Welsh office of the practice must contain either:

(A) a list of the partners or directors; or

(B) a statement that a list of the partners or directors and their professional qualifications is open to inspection at that office (see also paragraph 1(d)(ii) above, the Business Names Act 1985 and Rule 23 of the Solicitors' Incorporated Practice Rules).

(ii) Any such list, as well as a list of the partners or directors in any other publicity conducted in England and Wales, must indicate the countries or jurisdictions of qualification of the partners or directors and their professional qualifications.

(iii) Any letterhead (or fax heading, or heading used for bills) of an English or Welsh office of the practice must bear either:

(A) a description of the firm which includes the word 'solicitor(s)' and complies with paragraph 6 above; or

    (B) a firm name which includes the word 'Solicitor(s)' and complies with note (iv) to Practice Rule 11 (names used by a firm); or

    (C) a list of the partners (or directors) which indicates their countries or jurisdictions of qualification and their professional qualifications as required by sub-paragraph (b)(ii) above; or

    (D) a statement that the partners (or directors) are solicitors and others, described in a way, and in an order, which would comply with paragraph 6 above.

  (iv) For the purpose of sub-paragraphs (b)(ii) and (iii) above:

    (A) there must be no breach of the principle set out in paragraph 14(b) below on the use of the word 'lawyer(s)'; and

    (B) the word 'solicitor(s)' is sufficient in itself to indicate that a solicitor's jurisdiction of qualification is England and Wales.

8. DIRECTORY HEADINGS

A firm may have an entry or advertisement in a directory or listing under any appropriate heading provided that either:

  (i) the word 'solicitor(s)'; or

  (ii) as an additional option in the case of a directory referring wholly or mainly to practise outside England and Wales, the word 'lawyer(s)' (but see paragraph 14(b) below);

appears either in the heading of the directory or listing or in a name or description of the practice appearing in the entry or advertisement itself.

9. SUBSIDIARY PRACTISING STYLE

[Repealed]

10. FLAG ADVERTISING

  (a) For the purpose of this paragraph, 'flag advertising' means advertising conducted by or on behalf of solicitors under the logo of or in the name of a grouping or association including one or more firms of solicitors (or recognised bodies or multi-national partnerships) but without naming the firm or firms whose services are being advertised.

  (b) Any flag advertising must include the word 'solicitor(s)' (or, as an additional option in the case of publicity conducted outside England and

Wales, the word 'lawyer(s)') and an address at which the names of all the firms involved are available. For the use of the word 'lawyer(s)' see paragraph 14(b) below.

(c) Notwithstanding anything in this paragraph, notepaper used on legal professional business must include the name of the firm concerned and not merely the name of a grouping or association.

11. ADDRESSES TO THE COURT

It is not proper for solicitors to distribute to the press, radio or television copies of a speech or address to any court, tribunal or inquiry, except at the time and place of the hearing to persons attending the hearing to report the proceedings.

12. PROFESSIONAL STATIONERY

(a) Application of the code to stationery

The provisions of this code apply to a solicitor's letterhead and matter similarly forming part of a solicitor's professional stationery.

(b) Practising address on stationery

Any stationery used by solicitors for their professional work must include a practising address and not merely a box number. Where a facsimile transmission is being sent, the frontsheet should contain the solicitor's address if this is not contained in some other part of the transmission.

(c) Use of client's or employer's stationery and client's or employer's name on solicitor's stationery

Solicitors may use for their professional work the stationery of, or stationery including the name of, a client or non-solicitor employer, provided that:

(i) either the letterhead or the signature makes it clear that the stationery is being used by a solicitor on legal professional business and that the solicitor is responsible for the contents of the letter; and

(ii) the stationery is being used for the business of that client or non-solicitor employer or for third parties in circumstances permitted by Practice Rule 4.

(d) Stationery of a recognised body

The professional stationery of a recognised body and of a partnership which includes a recognised body as a partner must comply with the Solicitors' Incorporated Practice Rules from time to time in force.

13. PROFESSIONAL ANNOUNCEMENTS, ADVERTISEMENTS FOR STAFF, ETC.

Any professional announcement, advertisement for staff, advertisement offering agency services, or any other like advertisement by a solicitor (including any advertisement in the Law Society's Gazette) must comply with the provisions of this code.

14. INTERNATIONAL ASPECTS OF PUBLICITY

(a) No publicity for a solicitor's practice may be conducted in a jurisdiction other than England and Wales in any manner that would contravene either (i) the provisions of this code or (ii) any restrictions in force in that other jurisdiction concerning lawyers' publicity. For the purposes of this paragraph publicity shall be deemed to be conducted in the jurisdiction in which it is received. However, publicity shall not be regarded as being conducted in a jurisdiction in which such publicity would be improper if it is conducted for the purpose of reaching persons in a jurisdiction or jurisdictions where such publicity is permitted and its receipt in the former jurisdiction is incidental.

(b) Whether in England and Wales or in any other jurisdiction, a solicitor's advertising (including stationery – see paragraph 16(ii) below) must not, except in the expression 'registered foreign lawyer(s)', use the word 'lawyer(s)' to refer to a person's qualification in a member state of the European Community unless the qualification is that of a 'lawyer' as defined in the 1977 Lawyers' Services Directive as from time to time amended.

15. INSTITUTIONAL PUBLICITY

(a) Institutional publicity by the Law Society

This code does not apply to publicity by the Law Society, or any body established under the control of the Law Society, concerning the services of solicitors in general or any class or group of solicitors.

221

(b) Institutional publicity by local law societies

This code does not apply to publicity by a local law society concerning the services of solicitors in general.

(c) Publicity naming solicitors

Where any publicity referred to in (a) and (b) above names individual solicitors or firms, such publicity must comply with this code as if the publication were by individual solicitors.

16. INTERPRETATION

In this code:

(i) all references to individual practice rules are references to the Solicitors' Practice Rules 1990 and all words have the meanings assigned to them in Rule 18 of those rules; and

(ii) 'advertisement' and 'advertising', except where the context otherwise requires, refer to any form of advertisement and include *inter alia* brochures, directory entries, stationery, and press releases promoting a solicitor's practice; but exclude press releases prepared on behalf of a client.

17. COMMENCEMENT

This code will come into force on 1st September 1990.

NOTE: BREACHES OF THE PUBLICITY CODE

Where contravention of this code is not serious, the Council encourages local law societies to bring breaches to the attention of the solicitors concerned. Serious or persistent cases should be reported to the Office for the Supervision of Solicitors.

Solicitors' Introduction and Referral Code 1990

(with consolidated amendments to 29 March 1999)

Code dated 18th July 1990 promulgated by the Council of the Law Society with the concurrence of the Master of the Rolls under Rule 3 of the Solicitors' Practice Rules 1990, regulating the introduction of clients to and by solicitors, registered foreign lawyers and recognised bodies practising in England and Wales.

Introduction

(1) This code states the principles to be observed in relation to the introduction of clients by third parties to solicitors or by solicitors to third parties.

(2) The code does not apply to introductions and referrals between solicitors, between solicitors and barristers or between solicitors and lawyers of other jurisdictions.

(3) Non-compliance, evasion or disregard of the code could represent not only a breach of Practice Rule 3 (introductions and referrals) but also a breach of Practice Rule 1 (basic principles) or one of the other practice rules, and conduct unbefitting a solicitor.

(4) Those wishing to advertise the services of solicitors to whom they refer work should be encouraged to publicise their adherence to the code by means of a notice on the following lines:

'We comply with the Solicitors' Introduction and Referral Code published by the Law Society, and any solicitor to whom we may refer you is an independent professional from whom you will receive impartial and confidential advice. You are free to choose another solicitor.'

(5) In this code all references to individual practice rules are references to the Solicitors' Practice Rules 1990 and all words have the meanings assigned to them in Rule 18 of those rules.

(6) The code will come into force on 1st September 1990.

Section 1: The basic principles

(1) Solicitors must always retain their professional independence and their ability to advise their clients fearlessly and objectively. Solicitors should never permit the requirements of an introducer to undermine this independence.

(2) In making or accepting introductions or referrals, solicitors must do nothing which would be likely to compromise or impair any of the principles set out in Practice Rule 1:

    (a) the solicitor's independence or integrity;

    (b) a person's freedom to instruct a solicitor of his or her choice;

    (c) the solicitor's duty to act in the best interests of the client;

    (d) the good repute of the solicitor or the solicitors' profession;

    (e) the solicitor's proper standard of work;

    (f) the solicitor's duty to the Court.

(3) Practice Rule 9 prevents a solicitor from entering into any arrangement with a claims assessor for the introduction of personal injury clients to the solicitor.

(4) Practice Rule 12 makes provision in respect of introductions and referrals in the field of investment business. In particular the rule prevents a solicitor from acting as an appointed representative as defined in the Financial Services Act 1986 other than by having a separate business which is the appointed representative of an independent financial adviser.

Note

An independent financial adviser is a financial adviser authorised under the Financial Services Act 1986, or subsequent relevant legislation, who is not constrained to recommend to clients or effect for them transactions in some investments but not others, with some persons but not others; or to refrain from doing so.

Section 2: Introduction or referral of business to solicitors

(1) Solicitors may discuss and make known to potential introducers the basis on which they would be prepared to accept instructions and the fees they would charge to clients referred.

(2) Solicitors should draw the attention of potential introducers to the provisions of this code and the relevant provisions of the Solicitors' Publicity Code.

(3) Solicitors must not reward introducers by the payment of commission or otherwise. However, this does not prevent normal hospitality. A solicitor may refer clients to an introducer provided the solicitor complies with Section 4 below.

(4) Solicitors should not allow themselves to become so reliant on a limited number of sources of referrals that the interests of an introducer affect the advice given by the solicitor to clients.

(5) Solicitors should be particularly conscious of the need to advise impartially and independently clients referred by introducers. They should ensure that the wish to avoid offending the introducer does not colour the advice given to such clients.

(6) Where a tied agent refers to a solicitor a client who is proposing to take out a company life policy, the solicitor should, where necessary, have regard to the suitability of that policy in each particular case.

(7) Solicitors must ensure that they alone are responsible for any decisions taken in relation to the nature, style or extent of their practices.

(8) This code does not affect the need for the solicitor to communicate directly with the client to obtain or confirm instructions, in the process of providing advice and at all appropriate stages of the transaction.

(9) Each firm should keep a record of agreements for the introduction of work.

(10) Each firm should conduct a review at six-monthly intervals, which should check:

    (a)   that the provisions of this code have been complied with;

    (b)   that referred clients have received impartial advice which has not been tainted by the relationship between the firm and the introducer; and

    (c)   the income arising from each agreement for the introduction of business.

(11) Where, so far as can be reasonably ascertained, more than 20 per cent of a firm's income during the period under review arises from a single source of introduction of business, the firm should consider whether steps should be taken to reduce that proportion.

(12) Factors to be taken into account in considering whether to reduce the proportion include:

    (a)   the percentage of income deriving from that source;

    (b)   the number of clients introduced by that source;

    (c)   the nature of the clients and the nature of the work; and

    (d)   whether the introducer could be affected by the advice given by the solicitor to the client.

Section 3: Solicitor agreeing to be paid by a third party to do work for the third party's customers other than conveyancing work

(1) In addition to the other provisions of this code the following requirements should be observed in relation to agreements for the introduction of clients/business to solicitors under which the solicitor agrees with the introducer to be paid by the introducer to do work other than conveyancing work for the introducer's customers.

(2) The terms of the agreement should be set out in writing and a copy available for inspection by the Law Society or the Solicitors Complaints Bureau *[now the Office for the Supervision of Solicitors]*.

(3) The solicitor may agree to be remunerated by the introducer either on a case by case basis or on a hourly, monthly or any other appropriate basis.

(4) The solicitor should ensure that any agreement between the introducer and customer for the provision of services under this section includes:

    (a) express mention of the independence of the solicitor's professional advice;

    (b) a provision that control of the professional work should remain in the hands of the solicitor subject to the instructions of the client; and

    (c) a provision that information disclosed by the client to the solicitor should not be disclosed to the introducer unless the client consents.

Section 3A: Contractual referrals for conveyancing

(1) In addition to the other provisions of this code the following requirements must be observed in relation to agreements for the introduction of clients/business to solicitors under which the solicitor agrees with the introducer to be paid by the introducer to provide conveyancing services for the introducer's customers.

Agreements for referrals

(2) Solicitors may enter into agreements under this section for referrals for conveyancing services only with introducers who undertake in such agreements to comply with the terms of this code.

(3) Referrals under this section must not be made where the introducer is a seller or seller's agent and the conveyancing services are to be provided to the buyer.

(4) The agreement between the solicitor and the introducer must be set out in writing. A copy of the agreement and of records of the six-monthly reviews carried out under paragraph 10 of Section 2 of this code in relation to transactions under the agreement must be retained by the solicitor for production on request to the Law Society or the Solicitors Complaints Bureau *[now the Office for the Supervision of Solicitors]*.

(5) If the solicitor has reason to believe that the introducer is breaching terms of the agreement required by this section the solicitor must take all reasonable steps to procure that the breach is remedied. If the introducer persists in breaches the solicitor must terminate the agreement in respect of future referrals.

(6) The agreement between the introducer and the solicitor must not include any provisions which would:

    (a) compromise, infringe or impair any of the principles set out in Rule 1 of the Solicitors' Practice Rules or any duties owed by the solicitor to the introducer's customer by virtue of the solicitor/client relationship and/or the requirements of professional conduct; or

(b) restrict the scope of the duties which the solicitor owes to the customer in relation to the services agreed to be provided by virtue of the professional relationship between solicitor and client; or

(c) interfere with or inhibit the solicitor's responsibility for the control of the professional work.

Publicity as to conveyancing services

(7) Publicity material of the introducer which includes reference to any service that may be provided by the solicitor must comply with the following:

(a) Any reference to the charge for the conveyancing service must be clearly expressed separately from charges for other services. Any circumstances in which the charges may be increased must be stated. It must be made clear whether disbursements and VAT are or are not included.

(b) The publicity must not suggest that the service is free, nor that different charges for the conveyancing services would be made according to whether the customer takes other products or services offered by the introducer or not.

(c) Charges must not be stated as being from or upwards of a certain figure.

(d) The publicity must not suggest that the availability or price of other services offered by the introducer are conditional on the customer instructing the solicitor.

Notice to customer

(8) Before making a referral the introducer must give the customer in writing:

(a) details of the conveyancing service to be provided under the terms of the referral;

(b) notification of:

(i) the charge payable by the customer to the introducer for the conveyancing services;

(ii) the liability for VAT and disbursements and how these are to be discharged; and

(iii) what charge if any is to be made if the transaction does not proceed to completion or if the solicitor is unable to continue to act;

(c) notification of the amount the introducer will be paying to the solicitor for the provision of conveyancing services relating to the customer's transaction;

(d) a statement to the effect that the charge for conveyancing services will not be affected whether or not the customer takes other products or services offered by the introducer, and that the availability and price of other services will not be affected whether the customer chooses to instruct a solicitor under the referral or decides to instruct another solicitor or conveyancer; and

(e) a statement to the effect that the advice and service of the solicitor to whom the customer is to be referred will remain independent and subject to the instructions of the customer.

Solicitor's terms of business

(9) Where a solicitor accepts instructions on referral under this section the solicitor must provide the client with written terms of business which must include:

(a) details of the conveyancing service to be provided under the referral and if appropriate any other services the solicitor is to provide and on what terms;

(b) a statement that any advice given by the solicitor will be independent and that the client is free to raise questions on all aspects of the transaction;

(c) confirmation that information disclosed by the client to the solicitor will not be disclosed to the introducer unless the client consents; but that where the solicitor is also acting for the introducer in the same matter and a conflict of interest arises, the solicitor might be obliged to cease acting.

Definition

(10) In this section references to a conveyancing service or services include services to be provided to the introducer if the solicitor is also to be instructed to act for the introducer.

Section 4: Referral of clients by solicitors

(1) If a solicitor recommends that a client use a particular firm, agency or business, the solicitor must do so in good faith, judging what is in the client's best interest. A solicitor should not enter into any agreement or association which would restrict the solicitor's freedom to recommend any particular firm, agency or business.

(2) The referral to a tied agent of a client requiring life insurance would not discharge the solicitor's duty to give his/her client independent advice. In such circumstances, any referral should be to an independent intermediary.

(3) If the best interests of the client require it, a solicitor may refer a client requiring a mortgage to a tied agent, provided that the client is informed that the agent offers products from only one company.

(4) In relation to commission received for the introduction of clients' business to third parties, Practice Rule 10 applies.

APPENDIX 18

Examples of contentious and non-contentious business

CONTENTIOUS

1. Proceedings actually begun in the county courts, High Court, magistrates' courts (including licensing), Crown Court, and the Court of Protection.

2. Proceedings actually begun before the Lands Tribunal and the Employment Appeals Tribunal.

3. Contentious probate proceedings actually begun.

4. Proceedings on appeal to the Court of Appeal, Privy Council and House of Lords.

5. Proceedings in an arbitration.

6. Work done preliminary to proceedings covered by 1–5 above including advice, preparation and negotiations provided the proceedings are subsequently begun.

NON-CONTENTIOUS

1. Proceedings before all tribunals other than the Lands Tribunal and the Employment Appeals Tribunal.

2. Planning and other public inquiries.

3. Non-contentious or common form probate business.

4. Conveyancing, company acquisitions and mergers, the administration of estates and trusts out of court, the preparation of wills, statements and contracts, and any other work not included in the 'contentious' column.

5. Work done preliminary to the proceedings included in the 'contentious' column if such proceedings are *not* subsequently begun.

APPENDIX 19

Ready reckoner for mathematical calculation of the success fee

Prospect of success %	Success fee %	Prospect of success %	Success fee %	Prospect of success %	Success fee %
100	0	70	43	40	150
99	1	69	45	39	156
98	2	68	47	38	163
97	3	67	49	37	170
96	4	66	52	36	178
95	5	65	54	35	186
94	6	64	56	34	194
93	8	63	59	33	203
92	9	62	61	32	213
91	10	61	64	31	223
90	11	60	67	30	233
89	12	59	69	29	245
88	14	58	72	28	257
87	15	57	75	27	270
86	16	56	79	26	285
85	18	55	82	25	300
84	19	54	85	24	317
83	20	53	89	23	335
82	22	52	92	22	355
81	23	51	96	21	376
80	25	50	100	20	400
79	27	49	104	19	426
78	28	48	108	18	456
77	30	47	113	17	488
76	32	46	177	16	525
75	33	45	144	15	567
74	35	44	127	14	614
73	37	43	133	13	669
72	39	42	138	12	733
71	41	41	144	11	809

Locate success rate and read off the required uplift from the adjacent column.

Law Society model CFA

CONDITIONAL FEE AGREEMENT

For use in personal injury cases, but not clinical negligence.

This agreement is a binding legal contract between you and your solicitor/s.

Before you sign, please read everything carefully.

Words like 'our disbursements', 'basic charges', 'win' and 'lose' are explained in condition 3 of the Law Society Conditions which you should also read carefully.

Agreement date

```
┌─────────────────────────────┐
│                             │
└─────────────────────────────┘
```

I/We, the solicitor/s

```
┌──────────────────────────────────────────────────────────┐
│                                                          │
│                                                          │
│                                                          │
│                                                          │
│                                                          │
│                                                          │
└──────────────────────────────────────────────────────────┘
```

You, the client

```
┌──────────────────────────────────────────────────────────┐
│                                                          │
│                                                          │
│                                                          │
│                                                          │
│                                                          │
└──────────────────────────────────────────────────────────┘
```

What is covered by this agreement

- Your claim against [1] [   ]
  for damages [2] for personal injury suffered on [3] [   ].
- Any appeal by your opponent.
- Any appeal you make against an interim order during the proceedings.
- Any proceedings you take to enforce a judgment, order or agreement.

[4] What is not covered by this agreement

- Any counterclaim against you.
- [5] Any appeal you make against the final judgment order.

[6] Paying us

If you win your claim, you pay our basic charges, our disbursements and a success fee. The amount of these is not based on or limited by the damages. [7] [8] You are entitled to seek recovery from your opponent of part or all of our basic charges, our disbursements, a success fee and insurance premium. Please also see conditions 4 and 6.

[9] It may be that your opponent makes a Part 36 offer or payment which you reject and, on our advice, your claim for damages goes ahead to trial where you recover damages that are less than that offer or payment. We will not add our success fee to the basic charges for the work done after we received notice of the offer or payment.

[10] If you receive interim damages, we may require you to pay our disbursements at that point and a reasonable amount for our future disbursements.

[11] If you receive provisional damages, we are entitled to payment of our basic charges our disbursements and success fee at that point.

[12] If you win but on the way lose an interim hearing, you may be required to pay your opponent's charges of that hearing. Please see conditions 3(h) and 5.

[13] If on the way to winning or losing you win an interim hearing, then we are entitled to payment of our basic charges and disbursements related to that hearing together with a success fee on those charges if you win overall.

[14] If you lose, you pay your opponent's charges and disbursements. You may be able to take out an insurance policy against this risk. Please also see conditions 3(j) and 5. If you lose, you do not pay our charges but we may require you to pay our disbursements.

[15] If you end this agreement before you win or lose, you pay our basic charges. If you go on to win, you pay a success fee. Please also see condition 7(a).

We may end this agreement before you win or lose. Please also see condition 7(b) for details.

[16] Basic charges

These are for work done from now until this agreement ends.

How we calculate our basic charges

These are calculated for each hour engaged on your matter [from now until the review date on ⬚]. Routine letters and telephone calls will be charged as units of one tenth of an hour. Other letters and telephone calls will be charged on a time basis. The hourly rates are:

- Solicitors with over four years' experience after qualification

  £ ⬚

- Other solicitors and legal executives and other staff of equivalent experience

  £ ⬚

- Trainee solicitors and other staff of equivalent experience

  £ ⬚

[17] [We will review the hourly rate on the review date and on each anniversary of the review date. We will not increase the rate by more than the rise in the Retail Prices Index and will notify you of the increased rate in writing.]

[18] Success fee

[19] This is ⬚ % of our basic charges.

The reasons for calculating the success fee at this level are set out in Schedule 1 to this agreement.

You cannot recover from your opponent the part of the success fee that relates to the cost to us of postponing receipt of our charges and disbursements (as set out at paragraphs (a) and (b) at Schedule 1). This part of the success fee remains payable by you.

[20] Value added tax (VAT)

We add VAT, at the rate (now ⬚ %) that applies when the work is done, to the total of the basic charges and success fee.

[21] Law Society Conditions

The Law Society Conditions are attached because they are part of this agreement. Any amendments or additions to them will apply to you. You should read the conditions carefully and ask us about anything you find unclear.

Other points

[22] **Immediately before you signed this agreement, we verbally explained to you the effect of this agreement and in particular the following:**

(a) [23] the circumstances in which you may be liable to pay our disbursements and charges;

(b) [24] the circumstances in which you may seek assessment of our charges and disbursements and the procedure for doing so;

(c) [25] whether we consider that your risk of becoming liable for any costs in these proceedings is insured under an existing contract of insurance;

(d) [26] other methods of financing those costs, including private funding, Community Legal Service funding, legal expenses insurance, trade union funding;

(e) [27] (i) In all the circumstances, on the information currently available to us, we believe that a contract of insurance with ☐ is appropriate. Detailed reasons for this are set out in Schedule 2.

(ii) In any event, we believe it is desirable for you to insure your opponent's charges and disbursements in case you lose.

(iii) We confirm that we do not have an interest in recommending this particular insurance agreement.

[28] Signatures   **Signed for the solicitor/s**

_____

Signed by the client

_____

[29] I confirm that my solicitor has verbally explained to me the matters in paragraphs (a) to (e) under 'Other points' above.

Signed

_____ **(Client)**

I specifically confirm that I verbally explained to the client the matters in paragraphs (a) to (e) under 'Other points' and confirm the matters at (e) in writing in Schedule 2.

Signed

_____ **(Solicitors)**

This agreement complies with the Conditional Fee Agreements Regulations 2000 (S.I. 2000 No. 692).

[30] SCHEDULE 1 The success fee

[31] The success fee is set at [   ] % of basic charges and cannot be more than 100% of the basic charges.

The percentage reflects the following:

(a) the fact that if you win we will not be paid our basic charges until the end of the claim;

(b) our arrangements with you about paying disbursements;

(c) the fact that if you lose, we will not earn anything;

(d) our assessment of the risks of your case. These include the following:

(e) any other appropriate matters.

[32] The matters set out at paragraphs (a) and (b) above together make up [   ] % of the increase on basic charges. The matters at paragraphs (c), (d) [and (e)] make up [   ] % of the increase on basic charges. So the total success fee is [   ] % as stated above.

[33] SCHEDULE 2 The insurance policy

In all the circumstances and on the information currently available to us, we believe, that a contract of insurance with [   ] is appropriate to cover your opponent's charges and disbursements in case you lose.

This is because

[34] We are not, however, insurance brokers and cannot give advice on all products which may be available.

LAW SOCIETY CONDITIONS

1. [35] Our responsibilities

We must:

- always act in your best interests, subject to our duty to the court;
- explain to you the risks and benefits of taking legal action;
- give you our best advice about whether to accept any offer of settlement;
- give you the best information possible about the likely costs of your claim for damages.

2. [36] Your responsibilities

You must:

- give us instructions that allow us to do our work properly;
- not ask us to work in an improper or unreasonable way;
- not deliberately mislead us;
- co-operate with us;
- go to any medical or expert examination or court hearing.

3. [37] Explanation of words used

(a) [38] Advocacy

Appearing for you at court hearings.

(b) [39] Basic charges

Our charges for the legal work we do on your claim for damages.

(c) Claim

Your demand for damages for personal injury whether or not court proceedings are issued.

(d) Counterclaim

A claim that your opponent makes against you in response to your claim.

(e) Damages

Money that you win whether by a court decision or settlement.

(f) [40] Our disbursements

Payment we make on your behalf such as:

- court fees;
- experts' fees;
- accident report fees;
- travelling expenses.

(g) [41] Interim damages

Money that a court says your opponent must pay or your opponent agrees to pay while waiting for a settlement or the court's final decision.

(h) [42] Interim hearing

A court hearing that is not final.

(i) [43] Lien

Our right to keep all papers, documents, money or other property held on your behalf until all money due to us is paid. A lien may be applied after this agreement ends.

(j) [44] Lose

The court has dismissed your claim or you have stopped it on our advice.

(k) [45] Part 36 offers or payments

An offer to settle your claim made in accordance with Part 36 of the Civil Procedure Rules.

(l) [46] Provisional damages

Money that a court says your opponent must pay or your opponent agrees to pay, on the basis that you will be able to go back to court at a future date for further damages if:

- you develop a serious disease; or
- your condition deteriorates in a way that has been proved or admitted to be linked to your personal injury claim.

(m) [47] Success fee

The percentage of basic charges that we add to your bill if you win your claim for damages and that we will seek to recover from your opponent.

(n) [48] Win

Your claim for damages is finally decided in your favour, whether by a court decision or an agreement to pay you damages. 'Finally' means that your opponent:

- is not allowed to appeal against the court decision; or
- has not appealed in time; or
- has lost any appeal.

4. [49] What happens if you win?

If you win:

- [50] You are then liable to pay all our basic charges, our disbursements and success fee – please see condition 3(n).
- [51] Normally, you will be entitled to recover part or all of our basic charges, our disbursements and success fee from your opponent.
- [52] If you and your opponent cannot agree the amount, the court will decide how much you can recover. If the amount agreed or allowed by the court does not cover all our basic charges and our disbursements, then you pay the difference.
- [53] You will not be entitled to recover from your opponent the part of the success fee that relates to the cost to us of postponing receipt of our charges and our disbursements. This remains payable by you.
- [54] You agree that after winning, the reasons for setting the success fee at the amount stated may be disclosed:
  (i) to the court and any other person required by the court;
  (ii) to your opponent in order to gain his or her agreement to pay the success fee.
- [55] If the court carries out an assessment and disallows any of the success fee percentage because it is unreasonable in view of what we knew or should have known when it was agreed, then that amount ceases to be payable unless the court is satisfied that it should continue to be payable.
- [56] If we agree with your opponent that the success fee is to be paid at a

lower percentage than is set out in this agreement, then the success fee percentage will be reduced accordingly unless the court is satisfied that the full amount is payable.

- [57] It may happen that your opponent makes an offer that includes payment of our basic charges and a success fee. If so, unless we consent, you agree not to tell us to accept the offer if it includes payment of the success fee at a lower rate than is set out in this agreement.

- [58] If your opponent is receiving Community Legal Service funding, we are unlikely to get any money from him or her. So if this happens, you have to pay us our basic charges, disbursements and success fee.

[59] You remain ultimately responsible for paying our success fee.

[60] You agree to pay into a designated account any cheque received by you or by us from your opponent and made payable to you. Out of the money, you agree to let us take the balance of the basic charges; success fee; insurance premium; our remaining disbursements; and VAT. You take the rest.

[61] We are allowed to keep any interest your opponent pays on the charges.

[62] Payment for advocacy is explained in condition 6.

If your opponent fails to pay

[63] If your opponent does not pay any damages or charges owed to you, we have the right to take recovery action in your name to enforce a judgment, order or agreement. The charges of this action become part of the basic charges.

5. [64] What happens if you lose?

[65] If you lose, you do not have to pay any of our basic charges or success fee. You do have to pay:

- [66] us for our disbursements;
- [67] your opponent's legal charges and disbursements.

[68] If you are insured against payment of these amounts by your insurance policy, we will make a claim on your behalf and receive any resulting payment in your name. We will give you a statement of account for all money received and paid out.

[69] If your opponent pays the charges of any hearing, they belong to us.

Payment for advocacy is dealt with in condition 6.

6. [70] Payment for advocacy

The cost of advocacy and any other work by us, or by any solicitor agent on our behalf, forms part of our basic charges.

[71] We shall discuss with you the identity of any barrister instructed, and the arrangements made for payment.

[72] Barristers who have a conditional fee agreement with us

If you win, you are normally entitled to recover their fee and success fee from your opponent. The barrister's success fee is shown in the separate conditional fee agreement we make with the barrister. We will discuss the barrister's success fee with you before we instruct him or her. If you lose, you pay the barrister nothing.

[73] Barristers who do not have a conditional fee agreement with us

If you win, then you will normally be entitled to recover all or part of their fee from your opponent. If you lose, then you must pay their fee.

7. [74] What happens when this agreement ends before your claim for damages ends?

(a) [75] Paying us if you end this agreement

You can end the agreement at any time. We then have the right to decide whether you must:

- pay our basic charges and our disbursements including barristers' fees when we ask for them; or
- pay our basic charges, and our disbursements including barristers' fees and success fees if you go on to win your claim for damages.

(b) [76] Paying us if we end this agreement

- (i) We can end this agreement if you do not keep to your responsibilities in condition 2. We then have the right to decide whether you must:
- pay our basic charges and our disbursements including barristers' fees when we ask for them; or
- pay our basic charges and our disbursements including barristers' fees and success fees if you go on to win your claim for damages.

(ii) [77] We can end this agreement if we believe you are unlikely to win. If this happens, you will only have to pay our disbursements. These will include barristers' fees if the barrister does not have a conditional fee agreement with us.

(iii) [78] We can end this agreement if you reject our opinion about making a settlement with your opponent. You must then:

- pay the basic charges and our disbursements, including barristers' fees;
- pay the success fee if you go on to win your claim for damages.

If you ask us to get a second opinion from a specialist solicitor outside our firm, we will do so. You pay the cost of a second opinion.

(iv) We can end this agreement if you do not pay your insurance premium when asked to do so.

(c) [79] Death

This agreement automatically ends if you die before your claim for damages is concluded. We will be entitled to recover our basic charges up to the date of your death from your estate.

If your personal representatives wish to continue your claim for damages, we may offer them a new conditional fee agreement, as long as they agree to pay the success fee on our basic charges from the beginning of the agreement with you.

8. [80] What happens after this agreement ends

After this agreement ends, we will apply to have our name removed from the record of any court proceedings in which we are acting unless you have another form of funding and ask us to work for you.

We have the right to preserve our lien unless another solicitor working for you undertakes to pay us what we are owed including a success fee if you win.

© The Law Society, July 2000.

SOLICITOR'S CHECKLIST

For use with the Law Society's Model Conditional Fee Agreement

The following is a non-exhaustive list of issues which should be considered *before* signing the conditional fee agreement.

HAVE YOU . . .

1. TAKEN into account the overriding objective and proportionality in considering the potential net benefit of the case to your client?

2. CONSIDERED whether the case could be allocated to the Small Claims Track and the costs implications if that occurred?

3. CHECKED that you have the correct model agreement for this type of case?

4. UNDERTAKEN a thorough risk assessment?

5. APPLIED your risk assessment to your success fee, taking account of:

    - the prospects of success/failure;
    - payments on account/financial subsidy;
    - the risk that losing cases often have higher costs than winning ones?

    and when setting your success fee,

    - considered the element of the success fee relating to financial subsidy separately;
    - recorded your reasons in writing and provided a copy to your client?

6. CONSIDERED the possibility of achieving success on liability but failure on enforceability?

7. DISCUSSED with your client whether a barrister will be used? If so, have you discussed:

    - whether the barrister will be instructed on a conditional fee agreement;
    - whether the conditional fee agreement with the barrister will be on the same terms as the conditional fee agreement with the client, e.g. success fee?

8. EXPLAINED to your client the information required by the Conditional Fee Regulations:

    - the circumstances which will make them liable to pay your costs or disbursements and discussed how the client will fund these amounts;
    - when they can seek assessment of your costs and the procedure for doing so;
    - the circumstances which will make them liable to pay the costs of any other party;
    - whether their risk of becoming liable for costs is insured under an existing contract of insurance;
    - other methods of financing costs;
    - whether you believe a particular contract of insurance is appropriate (this should be confirmed in writing);
    - the requirement of their consent to disclose to the court or opponent at the end of the case the reasons for setting the success fee?

9. CHECKED whether your client's proposed insurance will meet the other side's costs, if a Part 36 offer or payment is not beaten?

10. THOUGHT through the different clauses which can be used regarding Part 36 offers and payments? (There are two possible options if ALP insurance is used. Other insurers may have different approaches. Check the requirements of your AEI – they may specify the approach you must take.)

11. EXPLAINED to your client the information on costs required by the Solicitors' Costs Information and Client Care Code 1999?

    Remember the Code imposes a duty on you to:

    - give to your client the best costs information possible – paragraphs 4 (a) and (c);
    - keep your client updated about costs as the matter progresses – paragraph 6.

12. EXPLAINED to your client that the agreement prevents the client from instructing you to accept an offer to settle which does not provide for your full success fee?

13. MADE SURE the agreement:-

    - specifies the proceedings to which it relates;
    - will be signed by you and your client;
    - specifies the reasons for setting the success fee, and specifies how much of the success fee, if any, relates to the cost of financial subsidy;
    - deals with appropriate funding methods and the insurance position?

[81] NOTES for Accident Line Protect cases

- For Accident Line Protect cases, you need to annex the following clause to the agreement

'Accident Line Protect insurance (ALP)

Accident Line Protect is an insurance policy only made available to you by solicitors who have joined the Accident Line Protect scheme.

You agree to pay a premium of £ ☐ for Accident Line Protect Insurance when you sign this agreement. We undertake to send this to the broker on your behalf. If you lose after proceedings have been issued, Accident Line Protect will cover our disbursements and your opponent's charges and disbursements. It will not cover fees to your barristers or advocates. The maximum cover is £100,000.

If this agreement ends before your claim for damages ends, Accident Line Protect ends automatically at the same time.'

Bar Council CFA Guidance: General introduction

It will be apparent to anyone reading this Guidance that conditional fees and the legislation governing them are complex, that they raise novel practical problems, and that they have significant potential pitfalls for the Bar, whose risk profile is different to that of solicitors. The reforms of 2000, which primarily permitted the recovery of success fees from losing parties, have served to increase the complexity.

Therefore any barrister who carries out, or who is considering carrying out, CFA work, must be fully conversant with the relevant source materials governing practice under CFAs, which are:

1. Statute

2. Statutory instruments

3. The CPR, Pre-action Protocols, and the Costs Practice Direction

4. Case law

5. The Code of Conduct and the Ethical Guidance contained in this Guidance

6. Any chambers protocols

7. The requirements of the BMIF

8. Relevant Specialist Bar Association model agreements and guidelines

9. Barmark requirements (where applicable)

Equally, no barrister should carry out CFA work unless his/her chambers have established systems for handling CFA cases that are compliant with these guidelines. This is important not only to ensure the efficient handling of cases, but also to permit the overall monitoring of CFA work.

This Guidance is an attempt to give the Bar the best advice currently available, but we welcome any suggestions from practitioners for improvements.

John Grace QC
Chairman, Bar Council CFA panel
January 2001

Bar Council CFA Guidance: Part 1 – Ethical guidance

1. Introduction

This Part is intended to provide guidance only on the ethical problems which may arise from the operation of Conditional Fee Agreements ('CFAs'). It does not form part of the Bar's Code of Conduct. However, it is strongly advised that barristers should follow the advice set out here, which is intended to ensure compliance with the Code of Conduct. The Practical Guidance section of the Bar Council's CFA Guidance should be referred to for guidance on practical matters.

2. General

Paragraph 405 of the Code of Conduct permits a barrister in independent practice to charge for any work undertaken by her/him (whether or not it involves an appearance in court) on any basis or by any method s/he thinks fit provided that such basis or method is permitted by law; and does not involve the payment of a wage or salary. It is the responsibility of any member of the Bar who enters into a CFA to ensure that:

1.2.1 he or she is familiar with the statutory provisions and regulations and orders made thereunder (see paragraphs 3 to 5 of Practical Guidance, and note in particular the distinction between 'old' and 'new' CFAs, and the different legislative regimes applicable thereto);

1.2.2 he or she at all times acts in accordance with the Code of Conduct (relevant extracts of which are included in part 3 of the Guidance). For example, the barrister, before entering a CFA, must bear in mind the provisions of paragraph 603 of the Code, namely, that 'A practising barrister must not accept any brief or instructions if to do so would cause him to be professionally embarrassed', and the subsequent sub paragraphs of the Code defining circumstances in which such professional embarrassment may arise;

1.2.3 the terms of the CFA comply with the requirements of the law and the Code. Compliance with the Code will be ensured if a Bar Council approved CFA is used.

3. The 'cab rank' rule

The 'cab rank' rule does not apply to CFAs. In other words, counsel cannot be compelled to accept instructions upon a CFA basis. See § 604(c) of the Code.

4. Internal agreements and arrangements between barristers

Some barristers and some chambers will find it appropriate to enter into standing agreements with each other or to establish practices whereby they will work under CFAs as a chambers or in groups. However, there are many barristers and sets of chambers who will not consider it appropriate to work under CFAs at all, or who will only consider it appropriate to work under them on a one off basis agreed for each particular CFA. The considerations to be taken into account when considering such internal arrangements are as follows:

1.4.1 It is important to ensure that no arrangement or agreement is entered into which compromises or appears to compromise a barrister's integrity or independence, which creates or may create a partnership, or which creates or appears to create a conflict of interest (see Code §§ 104(a)(i), 301, 303, 306, 307(a), 603(e)). The Professional Standards Committee are presently considering whether any form of fee or profit sharing arrangements within a CFA team are or should be permitted under the Code of Conduct. Even if any such arrangement is or will be permitted, counsel who has such an arrangement with another counsel could not appear in front of that other counsel (acting as a judge or arbitrator) and could not act against that other counsel, in any action to which the fee or profit sharing arrangement applies: to do so would give rise to irresolvable conflicts of interest.

1.4.2 However, leaving aside the position of the Bar Council, there remains a likelihood that a court or arbitral institution would conclude that such an arrangement created a conflict of interest or the appearance of such a conflict, such that counsel involved should not be permitted to act against each other or as judge or arbitrator in any case. Pending guidance from the Professional Standards Committee, the Bar Council CFA Panel advises against any fee- or profit-sharing agreement, or any agreement which provides for a subsidy to be paid by chambers or a CFA group to members in respect of lost CFA cases. In our view, the better policy is to reduce the financial risks of CFAs by proper risk assessment and screening procedures (see Practical Guidance).

1.4.3 The Professional Standards Committee are also considering the implications of arrangements between counsel whereby they agree to accept each others' return CFA briefs and whether, in those circumstances, they would be precluded from acting against each other in any action to which such arrangements applied or from appearing in front of a counsel who was a party to such arrangements (acting as a judge or arbitrator).

5. Screening

If chambers operate a form of screening of CFA cases whereby one or more members of chambers read the papers in a case sent to another member with a view to deciding whether or not that case should be accepted on a CFA basis, the screener could not, in future, act on the other side, or as judge or arbitrator, in that case. Barristers acting as screeners should therefore keep records of the cases they have screened, and a record must be kept in each case of the identity of the screener. If screening would involve the disclosure of confidential information to the screener, consent to screening should be obtained in advance of the screening.

6. Forms of CFAs

There is no form of CFA prescribed by the Bar Council or any other body or specialist association; but see the guidance relating to insurance and the BMIF in paragraph 1.7 below. There is an approved form of CFA for use in personal injury and clinical negligence cases, and in chancery cases; draft model forms of agreement are under preparation for employment cases and commercial cases. These forms of CFA have been approved by, or are being prepared by, the relevant specialist bar associations, and barristers and their clerks would be well advised to make use of these forms. It is for the barrister entering into a CFA to be satisfied that the form of agreement used is appropriate and lawful. In any case where a barrister proposes or is asked to enter into a CFA with a solicitor upon terms which materially depart from any form of agreement approved by a specialist bar association, the barrister should ensure that such departure is lawful, fair to the lay client and reasonable in the particular circumstances of the case before agreeing to act on such terms. In particular, the barrister should ensure that no term increases or tends to increase inappropriate pressure on the lay client to reach a settlement. Although currently most CFAs are expressed not to intend the creation of legal relations, there is no objection to barristers entering into contractually binding agreements. If a barrister proposes or is asked to enter a CFA which is intended to be a binding legal agreement, the barrister should ensure that the agreement does not contain any clause inconsistent with the Code.

7. Insurance

Under §§ 204(b) and 402.1 of the Code, every barrister must be covered by insurance against claims for professional negligence, and be entered as a member with BMIF. Many standard form CFAs, including the APIL/PIBA model, provide for an indemnity in favour of the solicitor in the event that counsel's breach of duty causes the solicitor to suffer a loss of fees. The BMIF has agreed (subject to financial limits) to indemnify barristers against this type of claim, provided it has approved the form of the relevant agreement. A barrister will therefore not be insured against such a claim by the solicitor if he/she has entered into an agreement on a form not approved by the BMIF.

8. Inducements

The payment by barristers or their chambers of commissions or inducements is strictly prohibited by the Code: see §§ 307(d) and (e). Thus, for example, the payment of 'introduction' or 'administration' fees to an insurer or claims organisation is not permissible. Barristers may also be invited to enter into a CFA upon the basis that a concession will be given by the barrister in relation to fee levels on that CFA in the expectation of receiving further CFA instructions in other cases in the future. The request for the concession is likely to originate from the insurer of the lay client's costs exposure. Such arrangements are objectionable as they undermine the barrister's independence of judgment (both apparent and real) in assessing and dealing with the inevitable conflicts of interest that arise in relation to CFAs

9. Impartiality / conflicts of interest

Having accepted instructions to act under a CFA, a barrister shall thereafter give impartial advice to the lay client at all times and take all reasonable steps to identify and declare to the lay client and to the instructing solicitor any actual or apparent conflict of interest between the barrister and the lay client.

10. Advice and interests of lay client

During the currency of a CFA, the barrister should use his/her best endeavours to ensure that:

(a) any advice given by the barrister in relation to the case is communicated and fully explained to the lay client;

(b) any offer of settlement is communicated to the lay client forthwith;

(c) the consequences of particular clauses in the solicitor/lay client agreement and the solicitor/barrister agreement are explained to the client as and when they become relevant, particularly after an offer of settlement has been made.

This last obligation applies in particular to the financial consequences which may arise from the making of an offer to settle the case including consideration of (1) any increase in the offer of settlement; (2) 'conventional' costs consequences; and (3) the success fees which are or may become payable.

11. Advising on settlement

When advising on a settlement of the action the barrister should at all times have in mind his/ her obligation under paragraph 303 (a) of the Code to

'promote and protect fearlessly and by all proper and lawful means the lay client's best interests and do so without regard to his own interests or to any consequences to himself or to any other person (including any professional client or other intermediary or another barrister)'.

The barrister's duty must be, when advising the client on a settlement or on a payment in or Part 36 offer, to advise as to the best course of action from the lay client's point of view only.

12. Disagreement over settlement

Difficulties may arise when the lawyers disagree about the wisdom of continuing the case or accepting an offer, whether that disagreement is:

a) between them on the one part and the lay client on the other; or

b) between solicitor and counsel; or

c) between leading and junior counsel.

In such event careful consideration must be given to the lay client's interests. Every effort should be made to avoid unfairly putting the lay client in the position where having begun proceedings s/he is left without representation. However, where, for example, counsel has been misled about the true nature of the evidence or the lay client is refusing to accept firm advice as to the future conduct of the case, the terms of the CFA may permit counsel to withdraw. Before taking this serious step the barrister will have to check carefully whether s/he is entitled to withdraw.

13. Withdrawal from the case

The barrister may withdraw from the case in any of the circumstances set out in the CFA agreement, but only if satisfied that s/he is permitted to withdraw pursuant to part VI of the Code. In the event that the CFA agreement does not contain a term that the barrister may withdraw from the case in particular circumstances, but the Code requires the barrister to withdraw in those circumstances, the Code takes priority over the agreement.

14. Disclosure of existence and terms of CFA

The fact that the action is funded by means of a CFA, and the terms of a CFA, should not be disclosed to the other parties to the action without the express written permission of the lay client, or save insofar as such disclosure is required by the court, the CPR, statute, rule, order, or Practice Direction.

Bar Council CFA Guidance: Part 2 – Practical guidance for barristers (extracts)

Miscellaneous important matters relating to CFAs

14. Particular attention is drawn to the following important matters relating to CFAs.

14.3. The CFA may, or may not, be a binding legal agreement. This is an important decision for counsel. Views differ as to what is appropriate in particular circumstances, however, the APIL/PIBA Agreement Mark 5, approved by the Bar Council for personal injury and clinical negligence cases, is principally designed not to constitute a binding legal agreement, and PIBA advises practitioners in that field not to enter legally binding agreements.

14.4. The solicitor who acts under a CFA may agree with counsel that counsel will be retained on a CFA basis so that counsel's fees are payable only on success. Alternatively counsel can be retained on a conventional non-CFA basis, in which event counsel's fees will be disbursements payable by the solicitor in the ordinary way.

14.5. The client may, under the CFA with the solicitor, be required from time to time to pay disbursements e.g. the fees of counsel not acting under a CFA, experts' fees and the like.

14.11. The solicitor and counsel may wish to consider in appropriate circumstances entering into a mixed fee agreement whereby only part of counsel's fee is treated as a conditional fee. Such an arrangement would set out counsel's hourly rate for work done with the agreement that a proportion of that rate would be paid whether the case was won or lost. The remaining part of the fee would not be payable if the case was lost but if the case was won counsel would be entitled to her/his full hourly rate together with an uplift calculated on the conditional part of her/his hourly rate. This type of arrangement would reduce the risk to the barrister, at the same time reducing the amount of success fee payable by the client in the event of the case being won.

14.12. As a matter of good practice in such a mixed fee agreement the base fee, some of which is to be made conditional on success, must be set at a reasonable and defesible rate as an artificially high rate is likely to be reduced on taxation. The 100% limit by which fees may be increased under the Conditional Fee Agreements Order 2000 must be related to the part of the fee which is conditional to comply with the legislation. It should always be recognised that no 'standard' CFA success fee or part CFA success fee is acceptable. To achieve fairness to the lay client and enable the success fee to be recovered from the other side, such fees must always be calculated having regard to the risk in the individual case.

THE APPROACH TO CFAs IN BARRISTERS' PRACTICES WILL VARY FROM BARRISTER TO BARRISTER AND CHAMBERS TO CHAMBERS

15. There may be some barristers and sets of chambers who will not consider it appropriate to work under CFAs at all, or who will only consider it appropriate to work under them on a one off basis agreed for each particular CFA. Practical considerations may, also, in some cases militate against such arrangements and, indeed, against the use of CFAs at all. Examples of such matters are the difficulty in certain cases of agreeing the terms of the Conditional Fee Agreement (for example the definition of 'success') or the complexity, size and duration of the case or cases concerned.

16. Barristers and chambers intending to continue acting against each other or as judges or arbitrators in cases in which other members of chambers appear should take care not to enter into standing agreements or to establish practices which might prejudice those relationships. [See Ethical Guidance 1–2.]

Forms of CFA

17. As stated in the Ethical Guidance, there is no form of CFA which is as such prescribed by the Bar Council or any other body or specialist association. There is an approved form of CFA for use in personal injury and clinical negligence cases (APIL/PIBA 5) which is strongly recommended by the Bar Council and the Personal Injuries Bar Association and it is planned that further approved forms of CFA will become available. It is for the barrister entering into a CFA to be satisfied that the form of agreement used is appropriate and lawful.

18. Barristers must also consider with great care whether there are any insurance implications involved in a departure from the text of a particular draft. The APIL/PIBA 5 Agreement and the Chancery Bar Association model CFA (which can be downloaded from its website, www.chba.org.uk) have the sanction of the Bar Council and BMIF. Other drafts may also be considered by the BMIF in time. COMBAR and ELBA have produced draft CFAs and supporting documentation and guidance which are currently the subject of consultation. Other Specialist Bar Associations plan to do likewise at the invitation of the Bar Council. Agreements covering part only of the proceedings are being drafted or awaiting approval. It is proposed that such draft agreements and supporting documentation will be sent to all chambers for inclusion in this Guidance, once approved.

19. Some drafts, such as the APIL/PIBA model, are designed for use where counsel is instructed on behalf of a Claimant. It must not be forgotten that such agreements are permitted in the case of Defendants too. In that event, care will need to be taken to ensure that the terms are suitable for such use.

20. Usually counsel should supply the draft agreement for use between solicitor and counsel. If, as is recommended, a model agreement is being used, then any proposed variation from the model agreed, e.g. between APIL and PIBA, should be clearly notified to the solicitor in a side letter accompanying the draft agreement. In the unlikely event that the solicitor supplies the draft agreement then, if it is based on a model agreement, counsel should seek in writing either confirmation that it is the same as the model agreement or details of any variations proposed.

21. It is important that, while oral contact with the solicitor by barrister and clerk must take place, all material points are recorded in correspondence or other writing. If a barrister decides to refuse instructions under a CFA s/he should notify the solicitor of this promptly.

Other documentation

25. Depending on the form of CFA used, other documentation may be required. Examples are in Part 6 to this document. For example, using the APIL/PIBA model, the suggested documentation proceeds on the basis of letters to solicitors. The 'First Letter' enclosing the 'Terms of Engagement' should be sent to the solicitor before any work is done. If it is acknowledged by confirmation of acceptance of the terms, counsel will then proceed to consider whether to act on a CFA in the case. The 'Letter of Acceptance' must then be despatched. The letter in the bundle 'Returned Brief' is designed to cover the returned brief without all the previous letters having to be sent again. It will almost certainly be necessary for chambers to supplement the above documentation, and standard form correspondence may not be appropriate for all situations. However, chambers may wish to consider standard letters for the following options:

25.1. a request for the solicitor/client CFA agreement;

25.2. a request for confirmation of insurance or an explanation for the absence of such insurance;

25.3. requests for further information or instructions (see the 'Ready Reckoner' at Part 7);

25.4. a request for consent to 'screening' if screening could involve the disclosure of confidential information.

26. There is no reason why a copy of this guidance or a written chambers agreement or practice (if that exists) cannot be supplied to a solicitor.

THE DECISION WHETHER TO ENTER INTO A CFA

The barrister's decision

27. The barrister concerned must decide whether or not s/he wishes to enter into a CFA and whether the terms of that CFA are appropriate and lawful. That decision cannot be made by a chambers or a group or a clerk.

28. There are a number of matters which a barrister may think it sensible to consider before deciding whether or not to enter into a CFA. These include the following:

28.1. The procedures or policies agreed or adopted by her/his chambers or any CFA group to which the barrister belongs within chambers. Possible chambers' policies and procedures are set out in paragraph 30 et seq. below.

28.2. Does the barrister wish to enter into a CFA with the solicitor concerned? Some chambers and groups will agree in advance on the solicitors they do and do not wish to enter into CFAs with. Such agreements must be carefully considered in case they give rise to anti-competitive or discrimination problems.

28.3. On what terms has the solicitor agreed to act for the client? The barrister will normally want to see a copy of the CFA between the solicitor and the client and the Law Society's Conditions as they apply to the claim.

28.4. Is there sufficient insurance? Where the lay client is an individual rather than a corporation, the barrister will normally need written confirmation that insurance is in place (unless insurance would be inappropriate e.g. under a CFA covering only the pre-action protocol part of proceedings), or a written explanation why it is not. Where more than one Defendant is sued, copies of correspondence between the solicitor and the insurers clarifying whether and when defendants' costs are to be covered if the plaintiff does not succeed or win against all of the defendants. The barrister must be careful not to advise on these issues, unless s/he is specifically instructed to, and can properly, do so.

28.5. Has the solicitor given the client the information specified in Regulation 4 of the Conditional Fee Agreements Regulations 2000? In particular, has the client given instructions on all other methods of financing costs and, if there any, has s/he reasonably decided to fund the case by CFA?

28.6. Is there sufficient material to judge the prospects of success? The barrister will normally want to see as far as possible relevant papers and e-mails and risk assessment material, including all advice from experts and other solicitors or barristers to the client or any Litigation Friend in respect of the claim, which are currently available to the solicitor.

28.7. What are the prospects of success? How is the uplift to be calculated? Some guidance on this can be obtained from the Protocol in Part 7 to this document which although designed for use in personal injury and clinical negligence cases gives generally applicable assistance in factors common to many different types of case. In addition, there is a full discussion of relevant considerations, including the actuarial basis for the decision, in the Biddle Report and the Watson Wyatt Actuarial Report.

28.8. What is the appropriate 'normal fee' and uplift for this case?

28.9. Is the CFA to be an agreement binding in law?

28.10. Are the terms of the CFA with the barrister appropriate and lawful?

29. It has always been good practice for a barrister to complete in each case a written risk assessment. This remains of significance upon solicitor/client assessment of success fees under old CFAs, when a settlement is considered and when papers are dealt with as a return. A statement of reasons is now prerequisite under new CFAs. The form to be adopted will depend on the case. The Bar Council recommends the protocol which is useful for personal injury and clinical negligence cases and is at Part 7 to this document.

The chambers or group decision (where relevant)

30. Where there is a chambers or group agreement or practice in force, the agreement of any person or group required by the procedures should be obtained before a CFA is agreed.

Chambers' approach to CFAs

31. The approach of different chambers to CFAs will vary. It would be wise for all chambers to discuss the impact of CFAs and whether any chambers' policies may be appropriate regarding CFAs.

One-off involvement in CFAs only

32. As explained in the Ethical Guidance some chambers will consider that there should be no standing agreement or practices within chambers under which work under CFAs can be undertaken. In such chambers any CFAs which are undertaken will be agreed on a one-off basis between those involved. Even if this is the only chambers' policy regarding CFAs, the chambers may wish (subject to other issues such as confidentiality) to establish a committee to monitor CFA work to see how the work done impacts on members of chambers and chambers, and to establish a pool of expertise in chambers on CFA matters. Logs and record-keeping will be appropriate even where work is accepted only on the basis of one-off CFAs.

Chambers or group involvement in CFAs

33. Other chambers will wish to set up agreements and practices regarding the acceptance of work generally under CFAs. For such chambers the following suggestions may be helpful.

34. Chambers should:

34.1. consider whether it should develop standard codes of practice governing the operation of CFAs by their members.

34.2. consider what policy ought to be adopted in respect of returned work. Chambers ought to formulate such policy in the light of the Terms of Agreement which they determine to adopt, but should be aware of the section in the current APIL/PIBA model relating to Return of Work. It will be noted that if counsel is unable to secure an appropriate replacement barrister to act for the client on the same terms as agreed between the original counsel and the solicitor, alternative terms are suggested, one accepting responsibility for additional barristers fees incurred, the other making it plain that no responsibility is accepted. The Bar Council advises strongly against the option of accepting responsibility for additional barristers' fees incurred. Chambers may wish to reach a specific policy on this problem and decide what chambers' response should be to a solicitor who asks for the more onerous clause to be incorporated into the agreement.

34.3. be astute to avoid entering agreements which create partnerships or other prohibited relationships. Reference might helpfully be made to the Biddle Report discussion of these issues but until further guidance is given by the Professional Standards Committee great care should be exercised in the use of the document 'CFA Group Model Constitution' circulated with the Biddle Report.

35. It may be appropriate for chambers as a whole, or in a group within chambers, to agree to accept returns in CFA cases between themselves. If no policy is agreed in advance, then, depending on what term is agreed, costs repercussions and embarrassment may arise where no suitable replacement may be found to cover a return: considerable damage could be done to relations with chambers' solicitors and the reputation of the Bar generally. A lay client may well not understand how such a situation could arise. There is already clear evidence that solicitors are worried about the returns situation.

36. Chambers may well consider it appropriate to publish the pool of counsel who have agreed to do CFA work and to accept CFA returns. It will also be essential to make clear to solicitors what the chambers' policy is about the costs which may arise in the event of an appropriate replacement barrister from the pool not being available to act.

37. Chambers should consider whether they should have a policy on whether or not tenants should seek to charge for considering whether to accept a CFA case. In a complex case, for example, in which a large amount of documentation must be read or where a conference with the client may be necessary in order to assess the prospects of success, it may be possible to agree with the instructing solicitor either to pay privately for such work, or to enter into a separate CFA for that stage of the proceedings with provision (and written reasons) for a percentage increase based on the core documents which counsel has been able to read, in say 2 hours, for the purpose of making a risk assessment. There can, regrettably, be no retrospective annexation of pre-CFA work into a CFA.

Sub-committee/monitoring/advice

38. Chambers might be wise to appoint a permanent sub-committee charged with monitoring chambers' policy and practice on CFAs and keeping abreast of developments in the use and practice of CFA work. The Committee should include the Clerk who has primary responsibility for CFA work. If there is a substantial number of chambers' members who do not belong to the pool of those prepared to do CFA work it should be considered whether the Committee should include one tenant who does a significant amount of non-CFA work. The committee's responsibilities should be to:

38.1. determine whether cases should be accepted only from solicitors who are approved by the CFA team for the purposes of giving CFA briefs and instructions, and, if so, to assess which firms of solicitors are acceptable and therefore 'approved' as providers of CFA instructions for different categories of work;

38.2. monitor chambers' overall CFA exposure;

38.3 monitor individual tenants' CFA exposure;

38.4. advise tenants upon CFA procedures and problems;

38.5. advise chambers on an appropriate protocol to govern the use and practice of CFAs by chambers, and to keep such protocols, the form of agreement, and the form of standard correspondence under review.

Logs and record keeping

39. Chambers should consider establishing a log of all CFA cases. Its purpose would be

39.1 to provide a record from which a picture can be built up to assist in future risk assessment;

39.2. to provide a contemporaneous record for production in the event of any challenge on costs assessment or other complaint by the client, solicitor or insurer;

39.3. to provide a running record of CFA cases to give a picture of chambers' current financial exposure.

39.4. to preserve confidentiality in the monitoring process each case should be given a number. There is no reason why this should not be simply ordinary numbering 1, 2, 3 etc.

40. Each member of chambers doing CFA work should keep a personal log in which to enter the name of the case and its chambers' log number. Such members would then be able to cross-refer to the chambers' log if there was a requirement to check back and obtain essential data in an individual case. In this way others could examine the chambers' log, e.g. to compile a chambers' picture of risk assessment but would not be able to identify the cases in question. The suggested minimum information would be:

40.1. Legal Services Commission Funding (if available) – Was it applied for? If not why not? If it was offered, why was it not taken up? If it was refused was this on the merits, or on means?

40.2. The date of the solicitor's acceptance of counsel's terms.

40.3. As at the date of entering the CFA – the scale of the risk perceived in simple terms, say on a scale of 1 to 5 – and the percentage uplift agreed.

40.4. On each occasion that a value is put on the claim a note of both the full liability valuation and whether any, and if so what, discount for contributory negligence has been made.

41. Proper record keeping is vital.

42. A system should be set up whereby the clerk opens a file for each CFA case and files in it copies of the various letters of engagement and acceptances. It would be wise to date stamp all incoming acknowledgements.

43. Each barrister will be well advised to keep his or her own record in each case in which a note is kept of the list of documents enclosed with each set of instructions, so that if a dispute arises and counsel wishes to withdraw because s/he was not given all relevant available information at the outset, there is no scope for disagreement as to what was sent when.

44. Dated copies of opinions should be kept.

45. Advice on settlement in a CFA case should always be given in writing, if at all possible. If, for practical reasons (for example, a settlement at court door), it is not possible to give the settlement advice in the form of a written opinion, then it will be wise to put the essence of the advice into manuscript and ask the lay client to initial the manuscript note. This should be retained.

46. Counsel's own file should (subject to confidentiality considerations, which should be addressed with clients) be made available to any other counsel who is requested to accept a return or do interlocutory work. It ought, therefore to include:

46.1. copies of all correspondence leading up to and including the CFA;

46.2. a list of the material considered for deciding to enter a CFA;

46.3. a risk assessment;

46.4. if the case has been screened, a note from the 'screener' giving her/his independent assessment.

Screening

47. Chambers should consider whether, in order to control chambers' risk exposure, they should set up some form of screening of individual tenants' decisions on whether to accept or reject a CFA case. Depending on chambers' resources and its risk exposure, and bearing in mind considerations of confidentiality, suggested methods might be:

47.1. a requirement that a tenant may not take a case until her/his decision has been approved by a 'screening' member of the CFA team, being either a silk or a barrister of 7 years' call or more and of comparable or greater seniority or experience;

47.2. a requirement that a tenant may not reject a case before her/his decision has been approved as above;

47.3. a system whereby tenants may ask a 'screening' member to approve her/his decision to take or reject a case where the individual tenant has doubts about the case;

47.4. a system of random audit on a proportion of cases accepted.

47.5. approval of the screening process should require the consent of the solicitor. This might, in some circumstances, be assumed if the process is described in an agreed chambers' protocol which is given to the solicitor with the proposed 'Terms of Engagement' and no objection is received. It should be made explicit in such documentation that the 'screener' assumes no duty of care to tenants, solicitors or clients.

Teams

48. Some chambers will establish a CFA team or teams. Tenants who are prepared to take CFA work from approved solicitors in appropriate cases should so inform the Committee, and thereafter consider themselves part of the chambers' 'CFA Team', and bound by the protocol agreed by chambers. This would imply a long-term commitment to do CFA work. That commitment must include agreement by team members, where available and subject to (1) their pre-existing CFA commitments and (2) client approval:

48.1. to accept returns of CFA work from other team members on a 'for better for worse' basis; and

48.2. to do appropriate interlocutory work on a CFA basis where the tenant generally instructed is reasonably thought by the instructing solicitor to be too senior for such interlocutory work, provided that an agreement approved by the CFA Committee applies to such work.

49. A tenant who wishes to cease to undertake CFA work may, on notice to the CFA Committee cease to take new CFA cases immediately, but should be bound:

49.1. to continue existing cases to conclusion;

49.2. to accept returns, subject to aforesaid, for (say) 18 months after such notice.

Clerks

50. Clerks must understand chambers' policies, agreements and practices regarding CFAs. It is essential that the steps laid down are strictly adhered to. Clerks are advised to consider the 'Practical Guidance for Clerks' at Part 5.

Bar Council CFA Guidance: Part 3 – Statutes, Regulations and Code of Conduct (extracts)

CODE OF CONDUCT, EXTRACTS

104: General purpose of the Code: The general purpose of this Code is to provide the requirements for practice as a barrister and the rules and standards of conduct applicable to barristers which are appropriate in the interests of justice and in particular:(a) in relation to barristers in independent practice to provide common and enforceable rules and standards which require them:(i) to be completely independent in conduct and in professional standing as sole practitioners;

204: Supply of legal services to the public: A practising barrister may supply legal services to the public provided that:(b) he is covered (and in the case of an employed barrister his employer is covered) by insurance against claims for professional negligence arising out of the supply of his services in such amount and upon such terms as are currently required by the Bar Council.

301: Applicable to all barristers: A barrister must have regard to paragraph 104 and must not:(a) engage in conduct whether in pursuit of his profession or otherwise which is:(i) dishonest or otherwise discreditable to a barrister;(ii) prejudicial to the administration of justice; or(iii) likely to diminish public confidence in the legal profession or the administration of justice or otherwise bring the legal profession into disrepute;

302: Applicable to practising barristers: A barrister has an overriding duty to the Court to act with independence in the interests of justice: he must assist the Court in the administration of justice and must not deceive or knowingly or recklessly mislead the Court.

303: A barrister:(a) must promote and protect fearlessly and by all proper and lawful means the lay client's best interests and do so without regard to his own interests or to any consequences to himself or to any other person (including any professional client or other intermediary or another barrister);(b) owes his primary duty as between the lay client and any professional client or other intermediary to the lay client and must not permit the intermediary to limit his discretion as to how the interests of the lay client can best be served;

306: A barrister is individually and personally responsible for his own conduct and for his professional work: he must exercise his own personal judgment in all his professional activities.

307: A barrister must not:

(a) permit his absolute independence integrity and freedom from external pressures to be compromised;

(b) do anything (for example accept a present) in such circumstances as may lead to any inference that his independence may be compromised;

(c) compromise his professional standards in order to please his client the Court or a third party;

(d) give a commission or present or lend any money for any professional purpose to or (save as a remuneration in accordance with the provisions of this Code) accept any money by way of loan or otherwise from any client or any person entitled to instruct him as an intermediary;

(e) make any payment (other than a payment for advertising or publicity permitted by this Code or in the case of a barrister in independent practice remuneration paid to any clerk or other employee or staff of his chambers) to any person for the purpose of procuring professional instructions;

402.1: Insurance: Every barrister in independent practice (other than a pupil who is covered under his pupil-master's insurance) must be entered as a member with BMIF.

405: Fees and remuneration: Subject to paragraph 307 a barrister in independent practice may charge for any work undertaken by him (whether or not it involves an appearance in Court) on any basis or by any method he thinks fit provided that such basis or method:

(a) is permitted by law;

603: A barrister must not accept any instructions if to do so would cause him to be professionally embarrassed and for this purpose a barrister will be professionally embarrassed:.............(e) if there is or appears to be a conflict or risk of conflict either between the interests of the barrister and some other person or between the interests of any one or more clients (unless all relevant persons consent to the barrister accepting the instructions);

604: Subject to paragraph 601 a barrister in independent practice is not obliged to accept instructions: (c) to do any work under a conditional fee agreement.

Bar Council CFA Guidance: Part 5 – Practical guidance for clerks

1. On 30th July 1998 the Government brought into effect the Conditional Fee Agreements Order 1998. It was made under s58 of the Courts and Legal Services Act 1990. The order allowed lawyers to offer conditional fee agreements to clients in all civil cases excluding family cases. On April 1st 2000 the Government brought into effect the Conditional Fee Agreements Order 2000 and the Conditional Fee Agreements Regulations 2000.

1.2 The Order and the Regulations of 2000 have introduced important changes to CFAs. In particular, in respect of all agreements entered into on or after 1 April 2000, the success fee is recoverable from the losing opponent except any proportion of the percentage increase relating to the cost to the legal representative of the postponement of the payment of his fees and expenses.

1.3 Any CFA entered into after the 1st April 2000 must specify the reasons for setting the percentage increase at the level stated in the agreement and, if appropriate, how much of the percentage increase reflects postponement of payment.

2. This type of fee arrangement will impact on the work of the Bar to an increasing extent, particularly now that Legal Aid is no longer available in personal injury cases. We summarize the position of the new fee arrangements as follows:

2.1 Conditional fee agreements: A barrister is entitled to a percentage uplift on his/her normal fee if the case is successful. If the case is lost the barrister agrees to forgo all of his/her fees under the agreement

2.2 It is perfectly proper to enter a part conditional agreement whereby a proportion of the fees is paid on a conventional private basis and the remainder is taken as a conditional fee.

2.3 The Bar Council urge their members not to deviate from any prescribed agreement drafted by the relevant bar association. One of the major implications of this relates to Bar Mutual coverage. If there is to be a deviation, it is essential that all agreements comply with Regulation 2 of the Conditional Fee Agreements Regulations 2000.

3. It should be noted that contingency fee arrangements are not permitted - i.e. counsel takes a percentage of the monies recovered by the client if the case is won. We refer you to Practical Guidance for Barristers paragraphs 2 to 2.3.

4. The keeping of careful records of each conditional fee case is essential. Your Chambers should establish an agreed policy under which CFA cases are dealt with. The Bar Council strongly recommends that sets of chambers appoint a CFA Committee to look at and vet individuals' proposed acceptance of CFA cases. The Bar Council also recommends the appointment of a designated CFA clerk. Our view is that all clerks should be conversant with CFAs.

5. The APIL/PIBA version 5 has been designed for use in the vast majority of personal injury and clinical negligence claims. The Bar Council recommend in the strongest possible terms that version 5 should be used in all such CFA cases unless there are exceptional circumstances justifying a variation of the terms, and regardless of whether the solicitor's agreement was entered into before or after April 1st 2000. The various specialist Bar associations are currently developing their own CFAs and these will be approved in due course. The Chancery Bar Association agreement is now available and can seen on their website www.chba.org.uk. It is important that you become familiar with the paragraphs that need to be completed by Counsel or you. Several of them will include alternative clauses and recommendations.

6. It is worth remembering the following:

    6.1 The cab-rank rule does not apply and it is entirely a matter for counsel whether to do conditional fee work at all, and if so, whether to accept work in a particular case.

    6.2 Fees are not paid until the case is successfully concluded. Payments on account will not be made to Counsel acting on a CFA basis.

7. Meetings have taken place with the two main computer companies regarding the development of new software to assist in the administering of CFAs. We are reasonably confident that Meridan will shortly have available a trial piece of software to assist in the administering of CFA cases. ACE have informed us that they have produced a Conditional Fee Development paper which has been circulated to all members of the user group. The paper is in the process of being finalised and in due course a beta product will be installed in a number of sets of Chambers to beta test.

8. Clear practice guidelines are essential and we recommend that all chambers do the following:

    8.1 When accepting instructions/briefs for new cases you should ascertain and record the method of funding.

    8.2 On receipt, check that papers have all necessary enclosures and send appropriate acknowledgment letter (see appendix letter1.doc).

    8.3 Submit papers to Counsel for risk assessment / screening and statement of reasons / % uplift.

    8.4 Agree % uplift and insert into agreement.

8.5 If case is accepted on CFA basis, send acceptance letter (see appendix letter 2.doc) & Terms of Engagement to solicitors for signature.

8.6 On receipt of signed Terms of Engagement, ensure that instructions are dealt with promptly.

8.7 Record that work has been done. Record the fee.

8.8 Retain copies of Terms of Engagement, all correspondence & Risk Assessment (see 11.4).

It would be prudent to keep records of number of cases accepted, rejected and failed, value of fees charged and value of success fees.

8.9 Monitor exposure of individual barristers to CFAs as well as chambers as a whole.

8.10 Monitor performance of individual firms.

8.11 Render fee note at the successful conclusion of case. The new legislation allows for the uplift and insurance premium to be claimed back from the losing party.

9. The clerk must ensure that he/she inserts the following information into the agreement:

9.1 Counsel's name

9.2 Name of the Solicitor

9.3 Client's name

9.4 Opponent's name

9.5 Date of injury (if appropriate)

9.6 Date of delivery of brief. We consider it to be good practice to establish systems whereby these delivery dates are adhered to. See question 21 of Common Problems.

9.7 Fees

9.8 % uplift/success fee

9.10 Optional clauses have been retained/deleted. Please be aware of paragraph 1 in the Chancery/Combar agreement on the point of enforceability. The Chancery Bar Association agreement can be downloaded from their web-site www.chba.org.uk

9.11 Counsel or clerk's signature.

9.12 It is important that Counsel completes the section dealing with what the agreement relates to (for example see paragraph 3 of APIL/PIBA 5).

10. The following is a guide to assist the clerk in understanding the points the barrister must consider when asked to accept instructions on a conditional fee basis:

10.1 Conditional fee agreements must be in writing and signed by the barrister (or the clerk on the barrister's behalf)

10.2 The barrister, before beginning his/her consideration of whether to accept a Conditional fee case must check that there is: (1) a CFA between the lay client and the solicitor; (2) insurance cover is provided in relation to the costs of the claim.

10.3 The barrister must satisfy him/herself that there is enough material upon which to make a realistic assessment of the risks involved in the case so as to determine an appropriate percentage uplift. This may be the only opportunity the barrister will have in the case to make an assessment affecting the level of uplift, which is appropriate.

10.4 A Risk Assessment and Statement of Reasons form should be completed by the barrister and retained for future use at any assessment hearing. The provisions for the assessment of additional liabilities under funding arrangements are covered in paragraph 6 of the Practical Guidance for Barristers.

10.5 It is counsel's responsibility to communicate his/her unwillingness to undertake a case on a CFA. If requested to give brief reasons in writing. This may simply be done by forwarding a copy of Counsel's risk assessment to the solicitor. As a matter of courtesy you will probably want to make contact with the solicitor as well.

11. Until the new software to deal specifically with CFAs is developed, we further recommend that you ensure the following:

11.1 The fees should not be included in an aged debt until the successful conclusion of the case.

Any interim fee note for all work undertaken within the agreement should be rendered as a draft until the case is successfully concluded.

Bar Council CFA Guidance: Part 6 – Standard letters

(1) Counsel's clerk's acknowledgement letter

[Sols name]

[Sols address]

Your ref: [Sols ref]

Our ref: [Case ref]

Dear [Sir/Madam]

Re: [Case name]

Thank you for your instructions in the above CFA matter.

I will place these before [counsel] for his/her consideration.

Providing [counsel] is prepared to undertake this case upon a conditional fee basis and the relevant documents are enclosed with these instructions I will shortly be forwarding two copies of our agreement to you.

Please do not hesitate to contact me should you have any queries in the meantime.

Yours [faithfully/sincerely]

[Clerk's name]

Clerk to [counsel's name]

(2) Counsel's clerk's letter of acceptance

[Sols name]

[Sols address]

Your ref: [Sols ref]

Our ref: [Case ref]

Dear [Sir/Madam]

Re: [Case name]

Counsel is prepared to undertake this case on a conditional fee basis.

Please find enclosed two copies of our conditional fee agreement, signed by counsel. One copy is for your files. I should be grateful if you would sign the other copy and return it to me as quickly as possible. Counsel cannot commence work on this case until your signed version has been received.

Yours [faithfully/sincerely]

[Clerk's name]

Clerk to [counsel's name]

(3) Returned brief counsel's clerk's letter

[Sols name]

[Sols address]

Your ref: [Sols ref]

Our ref: [Case ref]

Dear [Sir/Madam]

Re: [Case name]

I can confirm that [new counsel] is prepared to accept instructions in the above-mentioned case in which the brief for the hearing [date, etc] has been returned from [original counsel].

[New counsel's] terms of engagement will be the same as those contained in the original conditional fee agreement of which a copy is enclosed herewith.

Upon receipt of this letter, of which two copies are enclosed, please sign and date one copy and return it to me promptly. Once I have received the signed copy [new counsel] will then be engaged on a conditional fee basis.

I look forward to hearing from you shortly but in the meantime if you have any queries please do not hesitate to contact me.

Yours [faithfully/sincerely]

[Clerk's name]

Clerk to [new counsel's name]

Signed (and dated) on behalf of the solicitor ....

Bar Council CFA Guidance: Part 7 – Counsel's risk assessment

To help counsel make a Risk Assessment (1)and give a Statement of Reasons (2) for Conditional Fees in Personal Injury Cases

1. **Parties**: Csl's Ref: .... Sol's Ref ....

Names of Client (*& Litigation Friend) ....

and Defendant(s) (*actual/intended) ....

2. **Proceedings**: Date of injury ....

Nature of claim ....

If the proposed CFA is intended to apply to part only of the proceedings, specify to which part(s):

....

3. **'Success'** is achieving, by final judgment or agreement, the entitlement to damages for the claimant(3). Specify any alternative definition of success that might be intended:

Ready Reckoner	
Prospects of 'Success'	Basic Uplift
100%	0%
95%	5%
90%	11%
80%	25%
75%	33%
70%	43%
67%	50%
60%	66%
50%	100%

....

4. **Information on which assessment based**(4): Instructing solicitor ('Sol') provided Csl with instructions, see copy attached, date stamped .... and the documents listed there

5. The prospects of success(5) are estimated by Csl as ....

6. Csl's Success Fee will be a % increase on his/her normal fees. The % increase in this case will be ....% which comprises the following elements:

    a. An element to reflect the prospects of success (see Ready Reckoner) ....%

    b. An element relating to the cost to Csl of the postponement of the payment of fees & expenses(6)   ....%

Total: ....%

[Sol's uplift: ....%]

7. Statement of Reasons *(7)* Csl's reasons for setting the % increase at the level stated are: (here state the particular risks identified in the risk assessment. N.B. The ordinary risks of litigation are deemed to be incorporated into this statement of reasons and do not need to be repeated here unless a particular risk is heightened on the facts of this case).

[Continue on a separate sheet or attach another document if necessary]

8. Further considerations: Current APIL/PIBA 5 Agreement?   y/n Case requiring screening? Y/n   Csl has reason to believe the client is/may be, a child or patient y/n A leader is likely to be needed y/n This Statement of Reasons is to be attached to the CFA? y/n   [see para.17(3) of A/P5]

Csl's decision: *Accepted at . . . % increase / Rejected &/or advised alternative funding(8) / ADR

Csl's note of the next step due to be taken (if instructed on conditional fees) & any comment:

....

11. Screened by .... on ....

Signed ....Dated ....

[PIBA Risk Assessment, 18/01/2001 Adapted for use with APIL/PIBA 5]

THIS IS NOT AN ADVICE

Read the Notes over [They form part of the Statement of Reasons]

NOTES (These form part of the Statement of Reasons)

(1) This risk assessment ('RA') was made by Csl for his own purposes deciding whether or not to accept instructions upon a conditional fee basis and, if so, upon what percentage increase (i.e. success fee). It is RA material for the purposes of para.5(4) of the APIL/PIBA 5 Model Agreement of .... ('A/P5') for use between solicitors and Csl whether or not a CFA is subsequently entered into. It also constitutes Csl's statement of reasons [referred to in Reg.3(2)(a) of the CFA Regulations 2000/692 ('the CFA Regs')] for the % increase which are to be briefly stated in para.17 of A/P5. It is not an advice to the client or the solicitor. Csl will advise as appropriate in the course of proceedings only after he has accepted instructions. Csl is referred to the Bar Council's 'Conditional Fee Guidance' of February 2001 (available on www.barcouncil.org.uk) and may also contact the CFA Panel Helpline via the Bar Council.

(2) This statement of reasons for setting the % increase will be relied upon by the Costs Judge when deciding whether it is reasonable (see paras. 14.9(3) and 32.5(1)(b) of the Costs PD supplementing CPR Parts 43–48). Keep it, and any attachments, safely.

(3) Under para.19(1) of A/P5 'success' means the same as 'win' in the CFA between Solicitor and Client, which defines 'win' to mean: 'Your claim for damages is finally decided in your favour, whether by a court decision or an agreement to pay you

damages ...' [Law Society Conditions, 3(n)]. Other relevant circumstances are referred to in paras 20, 23 and 26 – see para.19(2) of A/P5.

(4) The reasons for Csl's % increase will be reviewed in light of the information then available (para 11.7 of the Costs PD). It is therefore essential to record what information was before counsel when the risk assessment was undertaken. This is best done by attaching a copy of the instructions and noting thereon any further information or documents subsequently received. Csl should have all the documents listed under para.5 of A/P5. Other documents to ask for include witness statements (name them and state if dated and/or signed), key documents such as police report/accident report / form/ book / photos / sketch plan / GP records / Medical report(s) (give dates), pre-action protocol correspondence with details of any issues raised and offers of settlement already made by either party.

(5) Prospects of success: RA is not a science but the application of knowledge and experience to the facts as known at the time. Try to assess the prospects of success as either: A very good (80%); B Good (60–80%); C Reasonable (50–60%); D Less than evens; or E Impossible to say. These are taken from the Bar Council's guidelines for Csl's advice on the merits for legal aid. In assessing the prospects of success, have regard particularly to the definition of success applicable to this case, any identified risk that the CFA may be terminated without achieving success (e.g. if finely balanced whether reasonable and economic for the action to proceed under para.10(8)(f) of A/P5), and the prospects of beating any Part 36 payment or offer already made. Do not make any allowance in the percentage increase for the extra costs of CFA work in general or for the risk assessment/screening carried out in this case. See further note 7 below.

(6) This element of the percentage increase is permissible but must be specified as a separate element (Reg.3(1)(b) of the CFA Regs 2000 & see para.17(2)(ii) of A/P5). It cannot be recovered from the paying party as an additional liability (CPR 44.3B(1)(a)) and is not one of the factors listed in Costs PD11.8. The Bar Council continues to recommend 3½% p.a. of expected postponement.

(7) The statement of reasons should be short and to the point, concisely recording the main risk factors influencing the risk assessment. State any perceived difficulties with jurisdiction or limitation, establishing a relevant duty, proving breach of duty, causation or quantum. State any perceived risk of adverse findings on contributory negligence, any counterclaim, set off or other likely defence. Specify the reasons why you think the claim may not end in success and otherwise why the circumstances in which Csl's normal or success fees become payable might not arise (see note 5 above). There is no need to state the obvious underlying risks which apply to all claims, some of which are set out below, because these are the ordinary risks of litigation which are relevant and which are deemed to have been included in your RA without specific mention. But state any special factor increasing such risks in this case. Ordinary risks of litigation common to all claims include: (a) the client may not pursue the claim for any reason (e.g. moves abroad, dies, loses interest), is or becomes a person under a disability and the litigation friend and/or the Court does not consent to funding the action under this Agreement; (b) the claim may not be pursued to a successful conclusion if Csl advises it is likely to lose or if it becomes uneconomic or unreasonable for the action to proceed (e.g. the defendant or his insurer may become insolvent

in the course of proceedings, e.g. an adverse order for costs may be made at an inter-locutory hearing, e.g. the cost of obtaining medical evidence to prove the claim may become disproportionately high); (c) the client's or other witnesses' account of the facts may prove to be inaccurate or they may not come up to proof; (d) further evidence may come to light which is adverse to the claim (e) material evidence may be lost; (f) the Court may err in law or fact; (g) the claim may be dismissed or struck out for non-compliance with any rule.

(8) The solicitor may prefer to treat Csl's fees as a disbursement and to use after the event insurers who allow this. There are clear advantages for client, solicitor and Csl.

[Guidance Notes updated 18/01/2001]

Bar Council CFA Guidance: Part 8 – Common problems in conditional fee cases

The following common questions arise from experience in Personal Injuries work but have general application in many other areas.

Chambers' structure

1. Question: I have been dabbling in CFAs for some time but my Chambers has no Conditional Fee Committee, we have no standard form of agreement and no procedure in relation to returned work. What can I do about it?

    Answer: Your position is far from unique and all is not lost. You should lobby fellow members of Chambers and consult your Head of Chambers, Practice Manager and Clerk impressing upon them the need for change. You should consider the contents of this information pack carefully as a group.

2. Question: Why do I need to go to such trouble?

    Answer: The development of Conditional Fee Agreements is a wide-ranging departure from previous methods of payment with considerable risk to individual Members of the Bar. It now covers all civil cases excluding family cases. Indeed, with the withdrawal of Legal Aid in the vast majority of personal injury claims you will need to master CFAs if you are going to compete for work. Your Chambers should establish systems and protocols or else you will expose yourself to unnecessary risk and it will lead to acrimony in Chambers when avoidable difficulties come to light.

Form of agreements

3. Question: What form of Conditional Fee Agreement should I use?

    Answer: A great deal of effort has been expended on your behalf by PIBA negotiating for the Bar Council with APIL on behalf of the Law Society. The APIL/PIBA Agreement (Mark 5) is the current form and its use is strongly recommended in all PI and clinical negligence cases. The Chancery Bar Association (www.chba.org.uk) also has a Bar Council- and BMIF-approved agreement, and other Specialist Bar Associations are preparing model forms of agreement. Many solicitors' 'in house' agreements contain clauses that are disadvantageous for the Bar and sometimes for the lay client. On your own, you are unlikely to be able to negotiate for the best clauses and why waste your time? You may fall into a clause for which the Bar Mutual Indemnity Fund does not offer cover.

If you do not use an approved form of agreement in every case you will waste time, increase the risk you run and you may well find that no one will do your returns.

4.   Question: What about the cap on the amount of uplift payable?

Answer: With the introduction of the new rules, the 'voluntary' cap no longer applies unless the CFA was entered into before 1st April 2000 between the client and the solicitor and included a cap. This will make smaller claims much more attractive for CFA agreements in the future as the uplift will be payable without reference to the amount recovered.

5.   Question: As Conditional Fees were starting up I have given advice and settled papers in cases nominally marked 'Conditional Fee' but I have not always executed an agreement. What should I do?

Answer: Conditional Fee Agreements must be in writing to be enforceable. In practice they should always be signed. You should not enter any more such nominal agreements. In respect of past mistakes you should draw up agreements now in respect of future work. You can enter into a CFA at any point of a case.

6.   Question: I have heard of solicitors entering into second CFA agreements after 1 April 2000 in order to make the uplift payable by the opposing party. They want me to do the same. Can this be done?

Answer: No. Under the Access to Justice Act 1999 (Transitional Provisions) Order 2000 no CFA entered into before 1 April 2000 can be a funding arrangement as defined in CPR 43.2. In addition, any second or subsequent funding arrangement entered into after that date, in respect of an original agreement before that date, cannot give rise to an additional liability which is recoverable from the paying party. See the Practice Direction to Part 48 Transitional provisions concerning the Access to Justice Act 1999 sections 28 to 31 at White Book Volume 1, Autumn 2000 edition, 48PD-008.

Clerking practicalities

7.   Question: How can CFAs best be processed?

Answer: Many aspects are similar to the good clerking of any case.

When accepting instructions/briefs for new cases you should ascertain and record the method of funding.

On receipt, check that papers have all necessary enclosures and send appropriate acknowledgement letter (see appendix letter1.doc).

Submit papers to Counsel for risk assessment / screening and statement of reasons / % uplift.

Agree % uplift and insert into agreement.

If case is accepted on CFA basis, send acceptance letter (see appendix letter 2.doc) & Terms of Engagement to solicitors for signature.

On receipt of signed Terms of Engagement, ensure that instructions are dealt with promptly.

Record that work has been done. Record the fee.

Retain copies of Terms of Engagement, all correspondence & Risk Assessment.

It would be prudent to keep records of number of cases accepted, rejected and failed, value of fees charged and value of success fees.

Monitor exposure of individual barristers to CFAs as well as chambers as a whole.

Monitor performance of individual firms.

Render fee note at the successful conclusion of case. New legislation allows for the uplift and insurance premium to be claimed back from the losing party

8. Question: When opening a set of papers marked CFA, what should a clerk look for?

> Answer: A barrister must have copies of both the agreement between the solicitor and the client and the proposed agreement between the solicitor and the barrister (usually the APIL/PIBA agreement). You should also check to see that insurance cover is in place. If it is not, you can help the barrister concerned by chasing it up to see if there are exceptional circumstances which justify the absence of insurance. Other documents that the barrister will look for are set out on the Risk Assessment Protocol in Part 7 of this file, but they are not all appropriate to every case. If many are missing you can help to save time by speaking informally with the solicitor to see what else can be provided. You can then place a risk assessment form with the papers, a copy of which is included in this information pack.

9. Question: How and when is the uplift identified on the fee note?

> Answer: The fee note should be rendered at the successful conclusion of the case. The fee note should contain the base fees and the % uplift. Suggested wording for fee line is as follows: '—— % uplift of fees as agreed = £ ——'. Any fees incurred outside the agreement being entered into are payable regardless of the outcome of the action without any uplift. Work done prior to the conclusion of the case can be itemised on a draft fee note for the purpose of interim fee information.

10. Question: Are Conditional Fee Agreements subject to assessment?

> Answer: Yes. There are two elements. The first relates to the base fees: the paying party has the right to challenge them in the usual way. If the base fees recovered leaves a shortfall, the solicitor can attempt to recover the balance from the lay client who can in turn challenge the fees under CPR Part 48.9. The assessment of

the base costs is on an indemnity basis (the old solicitor and client taxation) and CPR Part 48.8(2) applies by virtue of Part 48.9(4). The second element is the uplift or 'additional liability':

Old agreements pre-April 2000: Here the lay client has to pay the uplift, which can be challenged under Part 48.9. The Court may reduce the uplift where it considers it 'disproportionate having regard to all relevant factors as they reasonably appeared to the solicitor or counsel when the agreement was entered into'.

New agreements after 1st April 2000 The paying party now has to pay the uplift in the first instance and therefore can challenge it as well as the base fees. He has no liability for any part of the uplift that relates to a charge for delayed payment or preliminary/administrative work associated with the CFA.

The solicitor can then attempt to recover any shortfall from the lay client under CPR Part 48.9, where the test of 'proportionality' is introduced (see above) which is not present when considering the base fees on a solicitor/own client basis.

The practicalities of all this remain to be seen in action. Even though the paying party has no liability to pay any uplift on account of delay/admin., it is permissible to charge within the base fees for the cost of CFA assessment etc., on the basis of time spent. This is preferable to attempting to recover it as part of the additional liability from the lay client. Given the rights to challenge the assessment of the uplift, it is vital to keep a contemporaneous record of the risk assessment for the CFA. It should now be regarded as good practice generally to keep much more detailed records of work done to justify the base fees than has previously been the case. If you don't recover the base fees you can't get an uplift on them!

11. Question: Are we allowed to publicise the membership of our CFA group?

   Answer: Yes. It is a good idea to publicise the names of counsel in your group in directory entries, brochures and web sites of participating members.

12. Question: Is it for the clerk or counsel to notify the solicitor if Counsel is not prepared to undertake the case?

   Answer: No doubt you will want to make contact with the solicitor as a matter of courtesy but it is for counsel to communicate her/his unwillingness directly to the solicitor, and if requested to give brief reasons in writing. Counsel may decide to forward a copy of his risk assessment to the solicitor.

13. Question: Are pupils allowed to undertake Conditional Fee Agreements?

   Answer: Yes, if they are in their second six months of pupillage. Chambers should consider carefully the need for screening and covering returns.

Assessing the risk

14. Question: I have seen the protocol form for counsel's risk assessment in CFAs. It looks unduly onerous and complicated. Do I really need it and why do I need to note the enclosures in my instructions?

Answer: Lawyers have not traditionally assessed chances of success in terms of percentages, although we have become more used to them recently when assessing the chances of success for Legal Aid/Legal Services Commission cases. However, if you continue to rely upon concepts such as 'reasonable chances of success' etc you will not be able to assess the correct uplift and will be running undue risk in relation to Conditional Fee Agreements. If you do not record the documents that you have, should there be a conflict between you and your solicitor and you wish to withdraw at a later date, you may be in a poor evidential position. If you do not assess your risk in a reasonably scientific fashion you will find that other barristers in your Chambers will refuse to do your returns. In fact, a uniform approach across Chambers to the assessment of uplifts is the key, on a swings and roundabout basis, to the problem of returned work. You now have to be ready to justify your uplift when challenged by the paying party. The protocol form enables you to record your reasoning in a standard fashion and improves upon the record of brief reasons that is now required under APIL/PIBA 5 at clause 17.

15. Question: A powerful firm of specialist solicitors has been driving down success fees in order to attract work and insisting on 0% uplift CFAs – effectively Thai Trading agreements – as a condition of sending work. Can they do this to me?

Answer: Given that the paying party now also pays the uplift there should be no reason for such behaviour in the future. 0% CFAs are no longer a marketing tool for solicitors. In any event you should try to forget that Thai Trading was ever decided and read Geraghty & Co. v Awwad [2000] 1 All E.R. 608 C.A.

16. Question: How is it that the uplift necessary to cover me varies so dramatically between 50% and 100% when my assessment of the chances of success varies only slightly between 67% and 50%?

Answer: One answer would be that in a case that you are likely to win 2 times out of 3 (67%) you need to obtain a 50% uplift for each of the 2 victories to cover yourself (50% + 50% = 100% to cover the defeat). In a 50:50 case you need a 100% uplift on the winner to cover the loser.

The above analysis is in fact far too simplistic and the risk run by the Bar is much more formidable. While it would be correct if the CFAs were all entered into immediately before trial and with the same fixed fee, the position in practice is entirely different. The solicitor's costs are 'front-loaded' in terms of preparation and he makes a decent profit to set aside on the settled cases against a defeat. The barrister makes little out of the settled cases and stands to lose much more in a defeat at trial in percentage terms of CFA income. You should consider very carefully your assessment of risk and uplift beyond 67% and approaching 50%.

17. Question: How do I approach a risk assessment?

Answer: In order to work out the basic uplift you need to assess your chance of 'success'. Follow all the steps set out in the guidance on the Protocol form for Risk Assessment. Convert the chances of success into the basic uplift using the Ready Reckoner table in the Protocol form as a starting point only. Consider the point at which you are being asked to enter into the agreement and the possibilities of the case settling or fighting and the length of trial. Try to gain a 'feel', bearing in mind all your experience of the type of case. Where it is one which usually settles without further work from you after settling the papers, but which if it doesn't turns into a messy and prolonged fight, your uplift must be considerably higher than the Ready Reckoner might suggest at first glance. Always record your reasoning on the form. You should also consider causation and quantum. If a payment into court is made at an early stage you are at risk of having to fight the case and even if successful you will not recover any success fee after the date of the payment in. While you will have had the option of advising acceptance of the payment in and withdrawing from the case, that is not always realistic. This is another example of the way in which the odds are stacked against the Bar. The solicitor may not take much additional risk in percentage terms of his overall fees in going on to trial, whereas that is precisely where the Bar makes its living. Consider the effects of CPR Part 44 and the fact that you may not recover your costs on every issue. If you don't recover the base costs it doesn't matter what the uplift is! All in all, if your uplift is the same as the solicitor's, yours is too low or his too high.

18. Question: What do I do if I disagree with my Instructing Solicitor's risk assessment and want to adopt a different percentage uplift to that which the solicitor has agreed with the lay client?

Answer: Remember that the solicitor's perspective, and the solicitor's risk, are different to yours. Remember also that the solicitor may have had less, or different, risk assessment information, than that which you have. Just as counsel's advice should always be independent, it is important that your risk assessment should be entirely independent, and evidenced by your own documented risk assessment criteria.

The conduct of the case

19. Question: Many solicitors that I work for do not abide by the strict terms of the Conditional Fee Agreement in terms of resubmitting the papers for advice. I am overworked and have let things slip. What should I do?

Answer: If you do not monitor the conduct of your CFAs, you increase the risk you run. You should insist upon your strict rights under the Agreement. This is all the more important if you are working for unfamiliar solicitors or the inexperienced. It is easier to be unconcerned with specialist solicitors whom you trust. However, it will be difficult to complain later and withdraw from the CFA if you habitually fail to operate its terms.

20. Question: I assessed the case at a 25% uplift. The papers have come back to me for further advice and following discovery I now assess the risk at 50%. Can I alter the success fee?

Answer: Strictly you could attempt to renegotiate the success fee but you will probably not succeed in anything other than alienating a solicitor and getting a bad name. You should get on with the case at the original uplift. After all, when you assessed it at 25% you did not know whether the case might in fact settle on liability upon receipt of defence so that there would be no risk to you. You must take the rough with the smooth.

21. Question: I have another case where I do not now think it a decent bet at any uplift. Can I withdraw?

> Answer: You can withdraw from Conditional Fee Agreements only if you come within the wording of the clause within your Agreement. If you follow the APIL/PIBA Agreement (Mark 5) you are entitled to withdraw if your advice under Clause 10(8) is rejected or in other defined circumstances under Clause 11. In any case you should look to those Clauses to decide if you are entitled to withdraw. In this particular case, if it is your view that the case is likely to lose and the client rejects that advice then you may terminate the agreement. However, there will be repercussions for your practice if you terminate in borderline cases or regularly. You must also remember that it is the solicitor's duty to report to the CFA insurer if at any time the case is likely to lose and the insurer is then entitled and usually will refuse to continue. Lacking insurance backing the client may be more amenable to your advice; but there will be similar practical repercussions and you should only terminate as a last resort.

22. Question: I have had late delivery of a brief in a Conditional Fee case and my Skeleton Argument was due yesterday. I opened the brief to find that the solicitor, contrary to our agreement that a brief would be delivered 14 days prior to trial, has been trying to settle the case bargaining away my brief. There has been a moderately threatening payment into Court of which I have not been advised. Can I withdraw and return the brief?

> Answer: Whatever your initial reaction and whatever rights you may have under the Conditional Fee Agreement, you must always act in accordance with the Code of Conduct. There are a number of areas in which the Code of Conduct circumscribes your rights under the Conditional Fee Agreement. You are probably in just such a situation. If you were going to act upon the failure to deliver the brief you should have done so promptly in writing over a week ago. It is not your client's fault but your solicitor's. Your overriding duty is to the client. You should do the case and, if you cannot obtain assurances from the solicitor, refuse further CFA work from her/him. You should set up systems within Chambers for the chasing of CFA briefs.

23. Question: How can I best advise a lay client in the face of an offer or payment into Court so that the effects of the CFA can be made clear?

> Answer: In advising on an offer of settlement or payment into Court, the primacy of the lay client's interests remains at all times, whatever the financial pressure on the barrister or coming from the solicitor. This actual or potential conflict of interest should always be made explicit. Thus the client should be told something like: 'They have offered you £200,000. If you accept it you will pay your lawyers' success fee of approximately £x (assuming the success fee is not recoverable from the other side). I do think/do not think it is enough. If you go on, you have y chances of getting more, and z chances of losing completely. If you go on, £a more will be incurred in costs. The result of going on may be that

they end up offering you £225,000. If you were to accept £225,000 when £a costs more have been expended, you would be likely to pay success fees of £b, and thus the net gain to you of going on would be £c.' Unless really clear advice is given along these lines, barristers may be at risk from clients who say they pressurised them into under-settlement. The very same considerations apply when pitching a Part 36 Offer; and in deciding whether to make a Part 36 Offer at all, especially if liability has already been secured and the case is 'safe' while the success fee continues to mount for the lay client.

24. Question: If I lose an interlocutory application with a costs order against the claimant, will I be paid for the application and by whom?

Answer: If you lose the case overall you will not be paid anyway. If you win, the client's insurance backing will not cover your fees on the unsuccessful application. However, on the face of your conditional fee agreement you will have secured a win and can look to the client for payment including uplift, in the same way as a client in a legally aided case would end up paying through a Legal Aid charge. Unfortunately, side agreements between solicitors and clients to the effect that the client will not have deductions from damages on account of costs are common in order for solicitors to attract work. In those circumstances you may be asked to waive your fee but are under no obligation to do so.

APPENDIX 22

APIL/PIBA 5 Conditional fee agreement

CONDITIONAL FEE AGREEMENT
between
SOLICITORS AND COUNSEL

The nature of the agreement

1. In this agreement:

   'Counsel' means: ....

   and any other counsel either from Chambers or recommended by counsel in accordance with clause 25 who signs this agreement at any time at the solicitor's request;

   'the solicitor' means the firm:

   Messrs: ....

   'the client' means: ....

   [acting by his Litigation Friend: ....

   'Chambers' means members of chambers at: ....

2. This agreement forms the basis on which instructions are accepted by counsel from the solicitor to act on a conditional fee basis for the client in his/her claim against: ....

   ('the Opponent(s)') for damages for personal injuries suffered on: ....

   until

   (1)   the claim is won, lost or otherwise concluded or

   (2)   this agreement is terminated.

3. This agreement relates to

(1) issues of jurisdiction;

(2) issues of breach of duty;

(3) issues of causation;

(4) issues of limitation;

(5) issues of damages;

(6) any appeal by the client's opponent(s);

(7) any appeal by the client against an interim order;

(8) any appeal by the client advised by counsel;

(9) any proceedings to enforce a judgment or order.

It does not cover:

(10) any other appeal by the client;

(11) any counterclaim or defence by way of set-off;

(12) any part 20 claim;

(13) part only of the proceedings unless specifically incorporated in this agreement.

[NOTE: delete those parts of the proceedings to which the agreement does NOT relate]

4. This agreement is not a contract enforceable at law. The relationship of counsel and solicitor shall be governed by the Terms of Work under which barristers offer their services to solicitors and the Withdrawal of Credit Scheme as authorised by the General Council of the Bar as from time to time amended and set out in the Code of Conduct of the Bar of England and Wales, save that where such terms of work are inconsistent with the terms of this agreement the latter shall prevail.

5. Counsel has been provided with:

(1) A copy of the conditional fee agreement between the solicitor and the client and the Law Society's Conditions as they apply to the claim;

(2) written confirmation that 'after the event' or other similar insurance is in place, or a written explanation why it is not; and

(3) where more than one defendant is sued, copies of correspondence between the solicitor and the 'after the event' insurers clarifying whether and when defendants costs are to be covered if the claimant does not succeed or win against all of the defendants; and

(4) all relevant papers and risk assessment material, including all advice from experts and other solicitors or barristers to the client or any Litigation Friend in respect of the claim, which is currently available to the solicitor.

(5) Any offers of settlement already made by the client or the defendant.

6. The solicitor confirms that:

(1) he/she has complied with Regulation 4 of the Conditional Fee Agreements Regulations 2000 no 692 and the client has confirmed by signing the solicitor/client agreement that Regulation 4 has been complied with; and

(2) the client or any Litigation Friend has consented to the terms and conditions set out in this agreement insofar as they relate to the client.

(3) Either:

(a) there are no other methods of financing costs available to the client, or

(b) Notwithstanding there are other methods of financing costs available to the client, namely...................., the client has reasonably decided to fund this claim with conditional fees.

7. Counsel is not bound to act on a conditional fee basis until he/she has signed this agreement.

Obligations of counsel

8. Counsel agrees to act diligently on all proper instructions from the solicitor subject to paragraph 9 hereof.

9. Counsel is not bound to accept instructions:

(1) to appear at an interlocutory hearing where it would be reasonable

(a) to assume that counsel's fees would not be allowed on assessment or

(b) to instruct a barrister of less experience and seniority, provided that counsel has first used his/her best endeavours to ensure that an appropriate barrister will act for the client on the same terms as this agreement;

(2) to draft documents or advise if a barrister of similar seniority would not ordinarily be instructed so to do if not instructed on a conditional fee basis;

(3) outside the scope of this agreement.

Obligations of the solicitor

10. The solicitor agrees:

(1) promptly to supply a copy of this agreement to the client or any Litigation Friend;

(2) to comply with all the requirements of the CPR, the practice direction about costs supplementing parts 43 to 48 of the CPR (PD Costs), the relevant pre-action protocol and any court order relating to conditional fee agreements and in particular promptly to notify the Court and the

opponent of the existence and any subsequent variation of the CFA with the client and whether he / she has taken out an insurance policy or made an arrangement with a membership organisation and of the fact that additional liabilites are being claimed from the opponent.

(3)   promptly to apply for relief from sanction pursuant to CPR part 3.8 if any default under part 44.3B(1)(c) or (d) occurs and to notify counsel of any such default.

(4)   to act diligently in all dealings with counsel and the prosecution of the claim;

(5)   to consult counsel on the need for advice and action following:

    (a)   the service of statements of case and if possible before the allocation decision; and

    (b)   the exchange of factual and expert evidence;

(6)   to deliver within a reasonable time papers reasonably requested by counsel for consideration;

(7)   promptly to bring to counsel's attention:

    (a)   any priority or equivalent report to insurers;

    (b)   any Part 36 or other offer to settle;

    (c)   any Part 36 payment into Court;

    (d)   any evidence information or communication which may materially affect the merits of any issue in the case;

    (e)   any other factor coming to the solicitor's attention which may affect counsel's entitlement to success fees whether before or after the termination of this agreement.

(8)   promptly to communicate to the client any advice by counsel:

    (a)   to make, accept or reject any Part 36 or other offer;

    (b)   to accept or reject any Part 36 payment in;

    (c)   to incur, or not incur, expenditure in obtaining evidence or pre-paring the case;

    (d)   to instruct Leading counsel or a more senior or specialised barrister;

    (e)   that the case is likely to be lost;

    (f)   that damages and costs recoverable on success make it unreasonable or uneconomic for the action to proceed;

(9)   promptly to inform counsel's clerk of any listing for trial;

(10)   to deliver the brief for trial not less than ..... weeks/days before the trial;

(11)   if any summary assessment of costs takes place in the absence of counsel, to submit to the court a copy of counsel's risk assessment and make rep-resentations on counsel's behalf in relation to his/her fees;

(12) to inform counsel in writing within 2 days of any reduction of counsel's fees on summary assessment in the absence of counsel and of any directions given under PDCosts 20.3(1) or alternatively to make application for such directions on counsel's behalf;

(13) where points of dispute are served pursuant to CPR part 47.9 seeking a reduction in any percentage increase charged by counsel on his fees, to give the client the written explanation required by PDCosts 20.5 on counsel's behalf;

(14) where more than one defendant is sued, the solicitor will write to the 'after the event' insurers clarifying whether and when defendants costs are to be covered if the claimant does not succeed or win against all of the defendants, and send that correspondence to counsel;

(15) When drawing up a costs bill at any stage of the case to include in it a claim for interest on counsel's fees.

Termination of the agreement by counsel

11. Counsel may terminate the agreement if:

(1) Counsel discovers that the solicitor is in breach of any obligation in paragraph 10 hereof;

(2) the solicitor, client or any Litigation Friend rejects counsel's advice in any respect set out in paragraph 10(8) hereof;

(3) Counsel is informed or discovers the existence of any set-off or counter-claim which materially affects the likelihood of success and/or the amount of financial recovery in the event of success;

(4) Counsel is informed or discovers the existence of information which has been falsified or knowingly withheld by the solicitor, client or any Litigation Friend, of which counsel was not aware and which counsel could not reasonably have anticipated, which materially affects the merits of any substantial issue in the case;

(5) Counsel is required to cease to act by the Code of Conduct of the Bar of England and Wales or counsel's professional conduct is being impugned; provided that counsel may not terminate the agreement if so to do would be a breach of that Code, and notice of any termination must be communicated promptly in writing to the solicitor.

Termination of the agreement by the solicitor

12. The solicitor may terminate the agreement at any time on the instructions of the client or any Litigation Friend.

Automatic termination of the agreement

13. This agreement shall automatically terminate if:

    (1)   Counsel accepts a full-time judicial appointment;

    (2)   Counsel retires from practice;

    (3)   the solicitor's agreement with the client is terminated before the conclusion of the case;

    (4)   Legal Services Commission funding is granted to the client;

    (5)   the client dies;

    (6)   the court makes a Group Litigation Order covering this claim.

Client becoming under a disability

14. If the client at any time becomes under a disability then the solicitor will:

    (1)   consent to a novation of his Conditional Fee Agreement with the client to the Litigation Friend and

    (2)   where appropriate, apply to the Court to obtain its consent to acting under a conditional fee agreement with the Litigation Friend.

Thereafter, the Litigation Friend shall, for the purposes of this agreement, be treated as if he/she was and has always been the client.

Counsel taking Silk

15. If counsel becomes Queen's Counsel during the course of the agreement then either party may terminate it provided he/she does so promptly in writing.

Counsel's normal fees

16. (1)   Counsel's fees upon which a success fee will be calculated (the normal fees) will be as follows:-

    (a) Advisory work and drafting

        In accordance with counsel's hourly rate obtaining for such work in this field currently £................ per hour.

    (b) Court appearances

        (i) **Brief fee**

            (a) **Trial**

            For a trial whose estimated duration is up to 2 days (including ... hours of preparation) £..., 3 to 5 days (including ... hours of preparation) £..., 5 to 8 days (including ... hours of preparation)

£... 8 to 12 days (including ... hours of preparation), £..., and 13 to 20 days (including ... hours of preparation) £...

(b) **Interlocutory hearings**

For an interlocutory hearing whose estimated duration is up to 1 hour (including ... hours of preparation), £..., 1 hour to 1/2 day (including ... hours of preparation) £..., 1/2 day to 1 day (including hrs of preparation) £... over 1 day (including ... hours of preparation) will be charged as if it was a trial.

(ii) **Refreshers**

In accordance with counsel's daily rate obtaining for such work in this field, currently £..., per day.

(iii) **Renegotiating counsel's fees**

(a) To the extent that the hours of preparation set out above are reasonably exceeded then counsel's hourly rate will apply to each additional hour of preparation.

(b) If the case is settled or goes short counsel will consider the solicitor's reasonable requests to reduce his/her brief fees set out above.

(2) The normal fees will be subject to review with effect from each successive anniversary of the date of this agreement but counsel will not increase the normal fees by more than any increase in the rate of inflation measured by the Retail Prices Index.

Counsel's success fee

17. (1) The rate of counsel's success fee will be ... % of counsel's normal fees;

(2) The reasons, briefly stated, for counsel's success fee are that at the time of entry into this agreement:

(i) the prospects of success are estimated by counsel as ...(X)% as more fully set out in counsel's risk assessment, and a percentage increase of ...(Y)% reflects those prospects

(ii) the length of postponement of the payment of counsel's fees and expenses is estimated at ... year, and a further increase of ...(Z)% relates to that postponement

[Note: the success fee at paragraph 17(1) must be the sum of Y% and Z%]

(3) The reasons for counsel's success fee are more fully set out in counsel's risk assessment which is* / is not* (*please delete as appropriate) attached to this agreement.

Counsel's expenses

18. If a hearing, conference or view takes place more than 25 miles from counsel's chambers the solicitor shall pay counsel's reasonable travel and accommodation expenses which shall:

    (1)   appear separately on counsel's fee note;

    (2)   attract no success fee and

    (3)   subject to paragraph 21 be payable on the conclusion of the claim or earlier termination of this agreement.

Counsel's entitlement to fees – winning and losing [if the agreement is not terminated]

19. (1)   'Success' means the same as 'win' in the Conditional Fee Agreement between the solicitor and the client.

    (2)   Subject to paragraphs 20, 23 & 26 hereof, in the event of success the solicitor will pay counsel his/her normal and success fees.

    (3)   If the client is successful at an interim hearing counsel may apply for summary assessment of solicitor's basic costs and counsel's normal fees.

20. If the amount of damages and interest awarded by a court is **less than a Part 36 payment into Court or effective Part 36 offer** then:

    (1)   if counsel advised its rejection he/she is entitled to normal and success fees for work up to receipt of the notice of Part 36 payment into Court or offer but only normal fees for subsequent work;

    (2)   if counsel advised its acceptance he/she is entitled to normal and success fees for all work done.

21. Subject to paragraph 22(1) hereof, if the case is lost or on counsel's advice ends without success then counsel is not entitled to any fees or expenses.

Errors and indemnity for fees

22. (1)   If, because of a breach by the solicitor but not counsel of his/her duty to the client, the client's claim is dismissed or struck out:

       (a) for non compliance with an interlocutory order; or

       (b) for want of prosecution; or

       (c) by rule of court or the Civil Procedure Rules; or

          becomes unenforceable against the MIB for breach of the terms of the Uninsured Drivers Agreement:

       the solicitor shall (subject to sub-paragraphs (3)–(6) hereof) pay counsel such normal fees as would have been recoverable under this agreement.

(2)   If, because of a breach by counsel but not the solicitor of his/her duty to the client, the client's claim is dismissed or struck out:

(a)   for non compliance with an interlocutory order; or

(b)   for want of prosecution, or

(c)   by rule of court or the Civil Procedure Rules

counsel shall (subject to sub paragraphs (3)–(6) hereof) pay the solicitor such basic costs as would have been recoverable from the client under the solicitor's agreement with the client.

(3)   If, because of non-compliance by the solicitor but not by counsel of the obligations under sub-paragraphs (2), (3), (11), (12) or (13) of paragraph 10 above, counsel's success fee is not payable by the Opponent or the client then the solicitor shall (subject to sub-paragraphs (5) to (7) hereof) pay counsel such success fees as would have been recoverable under this agreement.

(4)   No payment shall be made under sub-paragraph (1), (2) or (3) hereof in respect of any breach by the solicitor or counsel which would not give rise to a claim for damages if an action were brought by the client;

Adjudication on disagreement

(5)   In the event of any disagreement as to whether there has been an action-able breach by either the solicitor or counsel, or as to the amount payable under sub-paragraph (1), (2) or (3) hereof, that disagreement shall be referred to adjudication by a panel consisting of a Barrister nominated by PIBA and a solicitor nominated by APIL who shall be requested to resolve the issue on written representations and on the basis of a proc-edure laid down by agreement between PIBA and APIL. The costs of such adjudication shall, unless otherwise ordered by the panel, be met by the unsuccessful party.

(6)   In the event of a panel being appointed pursuant to sub paragraph (5) hereof:

(a)   if that panel considers, after initial consideration of the disagree-ment, that there is a real risk that they may not be able to reach a unanimous decision, then the panel shall request APIL (where it is alleged there has been an actionable breach by the solicitor) or PIBA (where it is alleged that the has been an actionable breach by coun-sel) to nominate a third member of the panel;

(b)   that panel shall be entitled if it considers it reasonably necessary, to appoint a qualified costs draftsman, to be nominated by the President for the time being of the Law Society, to assist the panel;

(c)   the solicitor or counsel alleged to be in breach of duty shall be enti-tled to argue that, on the basis of information reasonably available to both solicitor and barrister, the claim would not have succeeded in any event. The panel shall resolve such issue on the balance of probabilities, and if satisfied that the claim would have been lost in any event shall not make any order for payment of fees or costs.

Cap

(7)   the amount payable in respect of any claim under sub-paragraph (1) or (2) or (3) shall be limited to a maximum of £25,000.

Counsel's entitlement to fees on termination of the agreement

23. (1)   Termination by counsel. If counsel terminates the agreement under paragraph 11 then, subject to sub-paragraphs (b) and (c) hereof, counsel may elect either:

(a)   to receive payment of normal fees without a success fee which the solicitor shall pay not later than three months after termination: ('Option A'), or

(b)   to await the outcome of the case and receive payment of normal and success fees if it ends in success: ('Option B').

(2)   If counsel terminates the agreement because the solicitor, client or Litigation Friend rejects advice under paragraph 10(8)(e) hereof counsel is not entitled to any fee.

(3)   If counsel terminates the agreement because the solicitor, client or Litigation Friend rejects advice under paragraph 10(8)(f) counsel is entitled only to 'Option B'.

(4)   Termination by the solicitor. If the solicitor terminates the agreement under paragraph 12, counsel is entitled to elect between 'Option A' and 'Option B'.

(5)   Automatic Termination and counsel taking silk

(a)   If the agreement terminates under paragraph 13(1) (judicial appointment) or 13(2) (retirement) or 15 (counsel taking silk) counsel is entitled only to 'Option B'.

(b)   If the agreement terminates under paragraph 13(3) (termination of the solicitor/client agreement) then counsel is entitled to elect between 'Option A' and 'Option B' save that:

(i)   if the solicitor has ended the solicitor/client agreement because he considers that the client is likely to lose and at the time of that termination counsel considers that the client is likely to win, and the client goes on to win, the solicitor will pay counsel's normal and success fees;

(ii)   if the solicitor has ended the solicitor/client agreement because the client has rejected the advice of the solicitor or counsel about making a settlement the solicitor will pay counsel's normal fee in any event and, if the client goes on to win the case, will also pay counsel's success fee.

(c) If the agreement terminates under paragraph 13(4) (Legal Services Commission) or paragraph 13(5) (death of client) or paragraph 13 (6) (group litigation order) counsel is entitled only to 'Option B'.

24. If the client or any Litigation Friend wishes to challenge:

(a) the entitlement to fees of counsel or the level of such fees following termination of the agreement

or

(b) any refusal by counsel after signing this agreement to accept instructions the solicitor must make such challenge in accordance with the provisions of paragraphs 14 and 15 of the Terms of Work upon which barristers offer their services to solicitors (Annexe D to the Code of Conduct of the Bar of England and Wales).

Return of work

25. If counsel in accordance with the Bar's Code of Conduct is obliged to return any brief or instructions in this case to another barrister, then:

(1) Counsel will use his/her best endeavours to ensure that an appropriate barrister agrees to act for the client on the same terms as this agreement;

if counsel is unable to secure an appropriate replacement barrister to act for the client on the same terms as this agreement counsel will

*(a) be responsible for any additional barristers' fees reasonably incurred by the solicitor or client and shall pay the additional fees to the solicitor promptly upon request and in any event within 3 months of such a request by the solicitor

*(b) not be responsible for any additional fee incurred by the solicitor or client. (both APIL and PIBA are agreed on the deletions in this para)

(2) Subject to paragraph 25(3) hereof, if the case ends in success counsel's fees for work done shall be due and paid on the conditional fee basis contained in this agreement whether or not the replacement barrister acts on a conditional fee basis; but

(3) if the solicitor or client rejects any advice by the replacement barrister of the type described in paragraph 10(8) hereof, the solicitor shall immediately notify counsel whose fees shall be paid as set out in paragraph 23(1) hereof.

[NOTE: delete 25(1)(a) or 25(1)(b)]

Assessment and payment of costs/fees

26. (1)   If:

     (a) a costs order is anticipated or made in favour of the client at an interlocutory hearing and the costs are summarily assessed at the hearing; or

     (b) the costs of an interlocutory hearing are agreed between the parties in favour of the client; or

     (c) an interlocutory order or agreement for costs to be assessed in detail and paid forthwith is made in favour of the client:

then

     (i) the solicitor will include in the statement of costs a full claim for counsel's normal fees; and

     (ii) the solicitor will promptly conclude by agreement or assessment the question of such costs; and

     (iii) within one month of receipt of such costs the solicitor will pay to counsel the amount recovered in respect of his/her fees, such sum to be set off against counsel's entitlement to normal fees by virtue of this agreement.

27. (1)   The amounts of fees and expenses payable to counsel under this agreement

     (a) are not limited by reference to the damages which may be recovered on behalf of the client and

     (b) are payable whether or not the solicitor is or will be paid by the client or opponent.

  (2)   Upon success the solicitor will promptly conclude by agreement or assessment the question of costs and within one month after receipt of such costs the solicitor will pay to counsel the full sum due under this agreement.

28. The solicitor will use his best endeavours to recover interest on costs from any party ordered to pay costs to the client and shall pay counsel the share of such interest that has accrued on counsel's outstanding fees.

29. (1)   The solicitor will inform counsel's clerk in good time of any challenge made to his success fee and of the date, place and time of any detailed costs assessment the client or opponent has taken out pursuant to the Civil Procedure Rules and unless counsel is present or represented at the assessment hearing will place counsel's risk assessment, relevant details and any written representations before the assessing judge and argue counsel's case for his/her success fee.

  (2)   If counsel's fees are reduced on any assessment then:

     (a) the solicitor will inform counsel's clerk within seven days and confer with counsel whether to apply under Regulation 3(2)(b) of the CFA

Regulations 2000 for an order that the client should pay the success fee and make such application on counsel's behalf;

(b) subject to any appeal, counsel will accept such fees as are allowed on that assessment and will repay forthwith to the solicitor any excess previously paid.

30. **Disclosing the reasons for the success fee**

(1) If:

(a) a success fee becomes payable as a result of the client's claim and

(b) any fees subject to the increase provided for by paragraph 17 (1) hereof are assessed and

(c) Counsel, the solicitor or the client is required by the court to disclose to the court or any other person the reasons for setting such increase as the level stated in this agreement,

he / she may do so.

31. **Counsel's fees in the event of assessment or agreement**

If any fees subject to the said percentage increase are assessed and any amount of that increase is disallowed on assessment on the ground that the level at which the increase was set was unreasonable in view of the facts which were or should have been known to counsel at the time it was set, such amount ceases to be payable under this agreement unless the court is satisfied that it should continue to be so payable.

32. If the Opponent offers to pay the client's legal fees at a lower sum than is due under this agreement then the solicitor:

(a) will calculate the proposed pro-rata reductions of the normal and success fees of both solicitor and counsel, and

(b) inform counsel of the offer and the calculations supporting the proposed pro-rata reductions referred to in paragraph (a) above, and

(c) will not accept the offer without counsel's express consent.

If such an agreement is reached on fees, then counsel's fees shall be limited to the agreed sum unless the court orders otherwise.

Dated: _____

Signed by counsel: _____

or by his/her clerk [with counsel's authority] _____

*[Additional interlocutory counsel _____]

*[Additional interlocutory counsel _____]

*see paragraph 1

Signed by: _____

Solicitor/employee in Messrs: _____

The solicitors firm acting for the client:

By signing and today returning to counsel the last page of this agreement by fax the solicitor agrees to instruct counsel under the terms of this agreement and undertakes to furnish counsel within 14 days of today with hard copies of the signed agreement together with any documents under paragraph 5 of this agreement which are not already in counsel's possession.

Chancery Bar Association terms of engagement for use where Counsel is to be retained on a conditional fee basis

This document is to be completed and used in conjunction with the covering letter to Heads of Chambers from the Vice-Chairman of the Chancery Bar Association dated 21 July 2000.

This document records the terms of engagement ('this agreement') between ... ('Counsel') of [Address] and... ('Solicitor')

1. This agreement contains the terms and conditions upon which Counsel agrees to act in the Action on behalf of the Client. [This agreement is/is not a contract enforceable at law.] The relationship between Counsel and Solicitor shall be governed by the Terms of Work under which barristers offer their services to solicitors and the Withdrawal of Credit Scheme as authorised by the General Council of the Bar as from time to time amended and set out in the Code of Conduct of the Bar of England and Wales, save that where such terms of work are inconsistent with the terms of this agreement the latter shall prevail.

[NOTE: this form of agreement is not intended for use where Counsel is instructed directly by a BarDIRECT client]

DEFINITIONS

2. In this agreement the following expressions have the meanings set out in this paragraph:

(1)   The Action means *the action, the short title and reference to the record of which is .../*the proposed action between the Client and ... for.../*the following part or parts of the action, the short title and reference to the record of which is .../*the following part or parts of the proposed action between the Client and ... for ... *[delete as appropriate and specify in addition whether any counterclaim and/or appeal and/or proceedings to enforce a judgment are included within the definition]*

(2)   The Base Rate means the rates of Counsel's fees described in paragraph 14 below, which are Counsel's normal rates.

(3)   The Client means...[acting by his/her litigation friend]

(4)   The Costs Insurance means the policy or policies of insurance providing cover against the Opposing Party's costs of the Action.

(5)   Counsel means the barrister named above as Counsel who is party to this agreement.

(6)   Failure has the meaning described in paragraph 22 below.

(7)   Normal Litigation Practice means the normal practice adopted in litigation in the [Chancery Division/Commercial Court/Queen's Bench Division] which is not carried out under a conditional fee agreement.

(8)   The Opposing Party means the defendants or proposed defendants to the Action or, where there is an issue between the Client and any other party or parties to proceedings, the determination of which is covered by the definition of Success referred to in paragraph 20 below, that other party or parties.

(9)   Other acceptable counsel means other counsel who the Solicitor has agreed or does agree is acceptable for the purpose of this agreement.

(10) Preliminary Agreement means the agreement date [...] made between Counsel and the Solicitor relating to investigation carried out and advice given by Counsel as a preliminary to entering into this agreement.

(11) The Reduced Rate means the rate of Counsel's fees specified in paragraph 16 below.

(12) The 'Returned Brief, Counsel's Clerk's letter' is the letter a draft of which is at Annex 1 to this agreement.

(13) The Solicitor means the solicitor or firm of solicitors who or which is party to this agreement.

(14) The Solicitor's Conditional Fee Agreement means the Conditional Fee Agreement entered into between the Solicitor and the Client.

(15) Success has the meaning set out in paragraph 20 below.

(16) The Uplift means the difference between Counsel's fees at the Base Rate and Counsel's fees at the Uplifted Rate.

(17) The Uplifted Rate means the rate of Counsel's fees specified in paragraph 15 below.

COUNSEL'S OBLIGATIONS

3. Counsel will (subject to paragraph 5 below) diligently perform in accordance with his/her instructions any tasks in or related to the Action which in Normal Litigation Practice would be performed by a barrister of his/her seniority.

4. In particular, Counsel is not bound:

(1)   to appear at any interlocutory hearing for which s/he reasonably believes that:

(a) counsel of lesser experience and seniority would ordinarily be instructed; or

(b) the court would conclude that the hearing was not fit for the attendance of one or, in a case where two or more counsel are instructed, two or more, counsel;

Provided that in the case set out in paragraph 4(1)(a) above, s/he has first used his/her best endeavours to ensure that other acceptable counsel are willing to represent the client at such hearing [on an agreed conditional fee basis] [who has agreed to act in accordance with the terms of the 'Returned Brief. Counsel's Clerk's letter' (see Annex I hereto)].

(2) to draft documents such as schedules, letters, summonses or witness statements or to advise orally or in writing or perform any other task if such would not be expected of counsel in Normal Litigation Practice;

(3) to accept instructions outside the scope of this agreement;

(4) to accept any brief or instructions where s/he is required or permitted to refuse such brief or instructions.

5. If Counsel is, in accordance with the Bar's Code of Conduct, obliged or permitted to return any brief or instructions in this Action to another barrister or not to accept any brief or instructions in the Action then :

(1) S/he will endeavour to ensure that other acceptable counsel will accept the brief and agree to act [on a conditional fee basis] [in accordance with the terms of the 'Returned Brief, Counsel's Clerk's letter']. However, neither Counsel nor Counsel's Chambers warrants or guarantees that they will be able to arrange for any alternative counsel to accept the brief or instructions or to act [on a conditional fee basis] [in accordance with the terms of the 'Returned Brief, Counsel's Clerk's letter'];

(2) If replacement Counsel cannot be found or does not agree for whatever reason to act [on a conditional fee basis] [in accordance with the terms of the 'Returned Brief, Counsel's Clerk's letter'] that will not be a breach by Counsel of this agreement or retainer.

(3) In the event of Success, Counsel's fees for his/her work, whether or not replacement counsel acted [on a conditional fee basis] [in accordance with the terms of the 'Returned Brief, Counsel's Clerk's letter'], shall be due and paid in accordance with this agreement at the Uplifted Rate.

THE SOLICITOR'S OBLIGATIONS

6. The Solicitor will (subject to paragraph 7(5) below) perform any tasks in or related to the Action which in Normal Litigation Practice would be performed by a solicitor.

7. The Solicitor confirms that s/he has brought the terms of this agreement to the attention of the Client [or any Litigation Friend] and has explained to the Client [or

303

Litigation Friend] the Client's responsibilities and liabilities under this agreement, and that the Client [or any Litigation Friend] has consented to the terms and conditions set out in this agreement insofar as they relate to the Client. The Solicitor will (without limiting the generality of paragraph 6 above)

(1) prosecute and prepare the Action promptly, diligently and carefully and take all necessary procedural steps in time;

(2) provide Counsel with, or make available to Counsel, copies of all documents relevant to the Action as soon as possible after they become available to the Client or the Solicitor;

(3) inform Counsel of all material developments and information relevant to the action as soon as possible after they become known to the Client or the Solicitor;

(4) acquire and provide Counsel with or make available to Counsel any other documents or information relevant to the Action which Counsel reasonably requests and which are available to or known to the Client or Solicitor;

(5) consider with Counsel the need for Counsel to advise on evidence, merits and quantum or to perform any other tasks and the need for any further procedural steps which Counsel may consider necessary at, at least, each of the following stages of the action:

(a) on first instructing Counsel;

(b) upon service of any statement of case or application by the Opposing Party;

(c) upon completion of disclosure and inspection of documents;

(d) upon exchange or service of any witness statement or affidavit;

(e) upon exchange or service of any expert's report;

(f) at any other time when Counsel considers it expedient;

and shall instruct Counsel to advise or to act accordingly, provided that such advice or task would be given or performed by Counsel in Normal Litigation Practice;

(6) communicate Counsel's advice on at least the following matters to the Client forthwith at whatever stage the Action has reached:

(a) advice by Counsel on the merits or quantum of the Action, including in particular that the Action is not likely to end in Success;

(b) advice by Counsel about the appropriate terms, if any, under which the Action ought to be settled, and on whether any Part 36 payment into court or any analogous type of offer should be made or accepted;

(c) advice that the Financial Recovery together with the costs recoverable on Success are such that they are not likely to exceed the Client's legal costs and disbursements likely to be allowed following a conventional (non-conditional fee basis) solicitor and own client taxation;

(d) advice that expenditure should or should not be incurred in instructing Leading Counsel or a more senior or specialised barrister, or instructing experts or otherwise obtaining evidence or preparing the Action.

(7) inform Counsel's clerk in good time of the date, place and time of any hearing fixed in the Action and instruct Counsel and provide all necessary papers for the hearing within a reasonable time before the hearing or, where appropriate, within a reasonable time before the date that Counsel's skeleton argument is due to be lodged and/or or exchanged;

(8) deliver the brief (and, where appropriate, agree stage accrual of brief fees) for any hearing within a reasonable time before the hearing;

(9) forthwith upon receipt of any Part 36 or other offer to settle the Action or any issues in it communicate immediately the terms of the offer to Counsel and seek his/her advice on whether to accept or reject the offer or as to the appropriate terms, if any, under which the Action or issues ought to be settled;

(10) forthwith upon receipt of notice of a Part 36 payment into court, inform Counsel immediately of such payment in and seek his/her advice on whether to accept or reject that Part 36 payment;

(11) give to any other party to the Action information relating to this agreement required by the Civil Procedure Rules and/or any practice direction; and

(12) in any case where the amount of Counsel's fees falls to be assessed by the court, take such steps as may reasonably be necessary to ensure that Counsel is entitled to be paid fees at the Base Rate/Reduced Rate and, where applicable, the Uplifted Rate specified in this agreement, including:

(a) notifying Counsel immediately of any appointment or hearing when Counsel's fees fall to be assessed;

(b) taking reasonable steps to assist Counsel in preparation of argument in support of his/her fees, including obtaining information reasonably required by Counsel for that purpose; and

(c) where Counsel is not present at any hearing or appointment relating to the assessment of his/her fees, acting for Counsel at that hearing or appointment.

TERMINATION OF THE AGREEMENT

Termination by the Solicitor

8. Subject to paragraph 10 below the Solicitor may terminate Counsel's retainer at any time without cause, in which case the provisions of paragraph 26 apply.

9. Subject to paragraph 10 below, the Solicitor may terminate Counsel's retainer with cause in any of the following circumstances:

(1) Counsel becomes unavailable for the trial of the Action, in which case the provisions of paragraph 27 apply; or

(2) the Solicitor has good reason to believe that the relationship of trust between the Solicitor and Counsel has irretrievably broken down, in which case the provisions of paragraph 26 apply; and/or

(3) the Solicitor has good reason to believe that Counsel has in breach of his/her duty to the Client manifested incompetence so as to justify the termination of his/her retainer, in which case the provisions of paragraph 28 apply.

10. The Solicitor shall not have the right to terminate Counsel's retainer on any ground once Counsel has fully performed all his/her obligations under this agreement.

Termination by Counsel

11. Counsel may terminate his/her retainer in any of the following circumstances:

(1) s/he reasonably believes that the relationship of trust between the Solicitor and Counsel [or between Counsel and other Counsel instructed in the Action] has irretrievably broken down;

(2) the Solicitor and/or the Client and/or more senior Counsel instructed in the case rejects Counsel's advice about the appropriate terms under which the Action ought to be settled and/or any Part 36 payment into court should be made, accepted or rejected or on any other material matter;

(3) the Solicitor has failed to comply with any obligation under this agreement;

(4) Counsel is informed of or discovers the existence of an actual or likely set-off or counterclaim or of information which has been falsified or withheld by the Client or the Solicitor which s/he reasonably believes materially affects the likelihood of Success in the Action and/or the amount of Financial Recovery in the event of Success but of which s/he was not aware and which s/he could not reasonably have anticipated from the information before him/her at the date of his/her entry into this agreement;

(5) Counsel is required to cease to act by the Code of Conduct of the Bar of England and Wales or Counsel's professional conduct is being impugned;

(6)　[Counsel becomes Queen's Counsel during the course of this agreement];

　　　[Optional – delete as required]

(7)　the Client dies;

(8)　in the case of an individual client, the Client goes bankrupt or an individual voluntary arrangement is approved in respect of the Client; or

(9)　in the case of a corporate client, a winding up order is made against the Client or a resolution is passed for the voluntary winding up of the Client, or an administration order is made against the Client or administrative receivers are appointed over the property of the Client or a company voluntary arrangement is approved in respect of the Client;

provided that Counsel may not terminate the agreement if to do so would be a breach of the Code of Conduct of the Bar of England and Wales.

12.　Counsel must terminate his/her retainer in the following circumstances:

(1)　Funding is granted to the Client by the Legal Services Commission in respect of the Action;

(2)　the Solicitor's Conditional Fee Agreement is terminated before the conclusion of the case;

(3)　Counsel accepts a full time judicial appointment; or

(4)　Counsel ceases to practise as a barrister.

Provided that Counsel must in the circumstances referred to in sub-paragraph (3) or (4) endeavour to arrange that other acceptable counsel will agree to take over and act on a conditional fee basis. However, neither Counsel nor Counsel's Chambers warrants that it will be able to arrange for alternative counsel to take over. If replacement counsel does not agree for whatever reason to act on a conditional fee basis that will not be a breach of this agreement or retainer by Counsel.

Exercise of termination in writing

13.　Both the Solicitor and Counsel must give notice of termination in writing giving the reason, if any, relied upon.

THE AMOUNT OF COUNSEL'S FEES

The Base Rate

14.　The Base Rate for Counsel's fees to which the Uplift for the Uplifted Rate is to be applied will be as follows:

(1) Advisory work and drafting

In accordance with his/her hourly rate applicable to the type of work involved in the claim, currently £ per hour

(2) Court appearances

(a) Trial

The brief fee will be –

*[based upon the number of days which Counsel reasonably considers are required for the preparation charged at a daily rate of £ to include the first day of trial] or

*[£...for a hearing whose estimated duration is 1 day;

£...for a hearing whose estimated duration is up to 2 days;

£...for a hearing whose estimated duration is 3–4 days;

£...for a full hearing whose estimated duration is 5 days;

£...for a full hearing whose estimated duration is 6–8 days;

£...for a full hearing whose estimated duration is 8–10 days;

£...for a hearing whose estimated duration is 11–15 days;

£...for a hearing whose estimated duration is 16–20 days;

£..., plus £... for each additional week or part of a week, for a hearing whose estimated duration is more than 4 weeks]

(*delete one or other of the above two alternatives as appropriate)

(b) Interlocutory hearings

For an interlocutory hearing the fee will be

*[based upon the number of hours which Counsel considers are required for the preparation charged at an hourly rate of £ plus the hourly rate for the number of hours the hearing is due to last]

*[£...for a hearing whose estimated duration is up to 1 hour;

£...for a hearing whose estimated duration is 1 hour to 1/2 day;

£...for a hearing whose estimated duration is 1/2 day to 1 day; for hearings estimated to last more than 1 day the fee will be the same as for a trial]

(*delete one or other of the above two alternatives as appropriate)

(c) Refreshers

In accordance with his/her daily rate obtaining for the type of work involved in the claim, currently £ per day.

(d) Re-reading fees

In the event of a trial being adjourned for more than one month, a re-reading fee based on the hourly/daily rate specified in paragraph 14(1) above will be charged.

(3) Counsel's rates referred to in (1) and (2) of this paragraph 14 will be subject to review with effect from each successive anniversary of the date of this agreement but s/he will not increase the rates by more than any increase in the rate of inflation measured by the Retail Prices Index, unless s/he has in the meantime become a Queen's Counsel.

The Uplifted Rate and the Reduced Rate

15. The Uplifted Rate which is to apply to Counsel's fees is [...]. The reasons for setting the Uplifted Rate at this level are [...specify briefly the reasons]. [Where any part of the Uplifted Rate relates to the cost to Counsel of the postponement of the payment of his/her fees and expenses state how much of the Uplifted Rate so relates.]

16. The Reduced Rate which is to apply to Counsel's fees is [...]

17. Where the Uplifted Rate becomes payable then if

(1) any fees subject to the Uplifted Rate are assessed, and

(2) Counsel or the solicitor or the Client is required by the court to disclose to the court or any other person the reasons for setting the Uplifted Rate at the level stated in this agreement,

he or she may do so.

PAYMENT OF COUNSEL'S FEES

18. The fees to which Counsel is entitled pursuant to this agreement (whether at the Base Rate, the Uplifted Rate or the Reduced Rate) shall include the fees incurred in respect of the Preliminary Agreement.

[Note: delete this paragraph as appropriate and so as to be consistent with the terms of the Preliminary Agreement]

Fees in the event of Success and Counsel's retainer is not terminated

19. Upon Success the Solicitor will, subject to paragraph 21 below, pay Counsel his/her fees at the Uplifted Rate or, where such fees have already been paid at the Base Rate [or the Reduced Rate], the difference between those fees at the Base Rate [or the Reduced Rate] and at the Uplifted Rate, within [... months of delivery of a final fee note].

20. Success means:

(1)   the Client becomes entitled, whether pursuant to a decision of the court or agreement between the parties, to the relief specified in the Annexe marked [...] to this Agreement; *and*

(2)   where the Client's entitlement to that relief is pursuant to a decision of the court, the Opposing Party or (in the case of multi-party litigation) any Opposing Party is not allowed to appeal against the court decision or has not appealed in time or has entered into a settlement agreement.

21. If the amount of damages and interest awarded by a court is less than a Part 36 payment into Court or effective Part 36 offer then:

(1)   If Counsel advised its rejection s/he is entitled to fees at the Base Rate [or the Reduced Rate] and at the Uplifted Rate for the work done up to the receipt of the notice of Part 36 payment into Court or offer but fees at the Base rate [or the Reduced Rate] only for subsequent work;

(2)   If Counsel advised its acceptance, or did not advise whether it should be accepted or rejected, s/he is entitled to fees at the Base Rate [or the Reduced Rate] and at the Uplifted Rate for all work done.

Fees where the Action ends in Failure and this Agreement is not terminated

22. In the event that the Action ends in Failure (other than in the circumstances referred to in paragraph 23 or paragraph 24 below) and this Agreement has not been terminated then, without prejudice to Counsel's entitlement to be paid in respect of Disbursements in accordance with paragraph 41 below,

no fees will be payable to Counsel.*

Counsel will be entitled to his/her fees only at the Reduced Rate*

[*NOTE: delete as appropriate. The second option is appropriate where Counsel agrees to a reduced rate, which is lower than his/her normal fees, but is payable in any event, with an uplift in the event of success.]

Failure means that the Action is concluded without qualifying under the heading of Success.

23. If the action is dismissed for want of prosecution or because the Client fails to provide security for costs or otherwise ends in Failure as a result of the breach by the Solicitor but not by Counsel of any of the terms of this agreement or a procedural default by the Solicitor and/or the Client but not by Counsel, the Solicitor shall pay

Counsel's fees within three months of the date of dismissal or ending of the Action at the [Base Rate/Reduced Rate/Uplifted Rate].

24. If, because of a breach by Counsel but not the Solicitor of his/her duty to the Client, the action is dismissed for want of prosecution or otherwise ends in Failure Counsel shall, subject to sub-paragraphs (1) to (3) below, pay the Solicitor such basic costs, excluding any element of uplift, as would have been recoverable from the Client under the Solicitor's agreement with the Client.

    (1)   No payment shall be made under this paragraph 24 in respect of any breach by Counsel which would not give rise to a claim for damages if an action were brought by the Client.

    (2)   In the event of a disagreement as to whether there has been an actionable breach by Counsel, or as to causation, or as to the amount payable under this paragraph 24, that disagreement shall be referred to arbitration pursuant to the procedure set out in paragraphs 43 to 46 below.

    (3)   The amount payable in respect of any claim under this paragraph 24 shall be limited to a maximum of [£25,000].

Fees in the event of termination by the Solicitor

25. If Counsel's retainer is terminated by the solicitor and thus before it can be determined whether the Action has ended in Success, the fees (if any) payable to Counsel will depend on the nature of the termination. In all cases the Solicitor has the right to challenge Counsel's fees [although not the agreed rates] in accordance with the Terms of Work referred to in paragraph 1 above.

26. If the Solicitor terminates the retainer under paragraph 8 above without cause, or under paragraph 9(2) above as a result of the Solicitor having good reason to believe that the relationship of trust and confidence between the Solicitor and Counsel has irretrievably broken down,

    (1)   the Solicitor shall immediately upon termination pay to Counsel his/her fees accrued to the date of the termination at the Base Rate [or Reduced Rate]; and

    (2)   in addition, in the event of Success, the Solicitor shall pay to Counsel the difference between his/her fees at the Base Rate [or Reduced Rate] and at the Uplifted Rate.

27. If the Solicitor terminates the retainer under paragraph 9(1) above as a result of Counsel becoming unavailable for the trial of the Action the Solicitor shall:

    (1)   only where Counsel is entitled pursuant to paragraph 22 above to be paid his/her fees at the Base Rate [or Reduced Rate] in the event of Failure, pay his/her fees at the Base Rate [or Reduced Rate] to the date of termination.

    (2)   in the event of Success:

        (a) where (1) above applies, pay to Counsel the difference between his/her fees at the Uplifted Rate and the amount paid pursuant to (1) above; or

        (b) in any other case, pay to Counsel his/her fees at the Uplifted Rate.

28. If the Solicitor terminates the retainer under paragraph 9(3) above as a result of the Solicitor having good reason to believe that Counsel has in breach of his/her duty to the Client manifested incompetence the Solicitor shall:

    (1)   only where Counsel is entitled pursuant to paragraph 22 above to be paid his/her fees at the Base Rate [or Reduced Rate] in the event of Failure, pay his/her fees at the Base Rate [or Reduced Rate] to the date of termination.

    (2)   in the event of Success:

        (a) where (1) above applies, pay to Counsel the difference between his/her fees at the Uplifted Rate and the amount paid pursuant to (1) above; or

        (b) in any other case, pay to Counsel his/her fees at the Uplifted Rate.

Fees in the event of termination by Counsel

29. If Counsel terminates his/her retainer upon any of the grounds specified in paragraph 11 above:

    (1)   the solicitor shall immediately pay to Counsel his/her fees accrued to the date of the termination at the Base Rate [or Reduced Rate]; and

    (2)   in addition, in the event of Success, the Solicitor shall immediately pay to Counsel the difference between his/her fees at the Base Rate [or Reduced Rate] and at the Uplifted Rate.

30. If the termination is by Counsel on the grounds specified in paragraph 12 above, the Solicitor shall pay to Counsel:

    (1)   only where Counsel is entitled pursuant to paragraph 22 above to be paid his/her fees at the Base Rate [or Reduced Rate] in the event of Failure, his/her fees at the Base Rate [or Reduced Rate] to the date of termination.

    (2)   in the event of Success:

        (a) where (1) above applies, the difference between his/her fees at the Uplifted Rate and the amount paid pursuant to (1) above; or

        (b) in any other case, his/her fees at the Uplifted Rate.

Payment of Base Rate [or Reduced Rate] fees in any event

31. The Solicitor will every [3 months] during the Action pay Counsel's fees for work done to that date at the Base Rate [or the Reduced Rate]. In the event of Success, the Solicitor shall pay to Counsel the difference between his/her fees at the Base Rate [or the Reduced Rate] and at the Uplifted Rate.

[NOTE: this is likely to be appropriate only where (1) Counsel is, pursuant to the terms of the CFA Agreement, entitled to be paid his fees at a reduced rate upon Failure, and/or (2) Counsel is requested to act on a conditional fee basis otherwise than by reason of the impecuniosity of the Client.]

32. [In the event of Failure, save where Counsel is in any event entitled pursuant to paragraph 22 above to be paid his/her fees at the Reduced Rate upon Failure, Counsel shall repay to the Solicitor the fees paid pursuant to paragraph 31 above.]

Information and further payment

33. In the event that Counsel may be entitled (including after termination) to [further] payment in the event of Success, the Solicitor must keep Counsel reasonably informed of the progress of the Action, must promptly inform Counsel of Success if it occurs, and must pay Counsel the further payment within [3 months of the delivery of a final fee note].

Payment of fees when the Client is awarded an interim payment

34. In the event that the Client is awarded an interim payment in the Action, whether by Court Order or agreement with the Opposing Party, the Solicitor will pay Counsel's fees for work done to the date of the order for interim payment at the Base Rate [or the Reduced Rate].

35. In the event of Success, the Solicitor shall pay to Counsel the difference between his/her fees at the Base Rate [or the Reduced Rate] and at the Uplifted Rate.

36. In the event of Failure, save where Counsel is in any event entitled to be paid at the Base Rate [or the Reduced Rate] upon Failure, Counsel shall repay to the Solicitor the fees paid pursuant to paragraph 34 above.

Payment of fees in respect of costs awarded or agreed in respect of an interlocutory hearing

37. If:

    (1)   A costs order is made in favour of the Client at any interlocutory hearing and the costs are summarily assessed at the hearing; or

    (2)   The costs of an interlocutory hearing are agreed between the parties in favour of the Client; or

(3) An interlocutory order or agreement for costs to be assessed in detail and paid forthwith is made in favour of the Client;

then the Solicitor will, where sub-paragraphs (2) or (3) above apply, promptly conclude by agreement or assessment the question of such costs and, in each case, within one month after receipt of such costs the Solicitor will pay to Counsel the amount recovered in respect of his/her fees, such sum to be set-off against Counsel's entitlement to normal and success fees by virtue of this agreement.

Counsel's entitlement to fees in the event of assessment

38. If any fees subject to the Uplifted Rate are assessed and any amount in respect of the Uplifted Rate is disallowed on assessment on the ground that the level at which the Uplifted Rate was set was unreasonable in view of the facts which were or should have been known to Counsel at the time it was set, such amount ceases to be payable under this agreement, unless the court is satisfied that it should continue to be so payable.

39. In any case where fees subject to the Uplifted Rate are not assessed, if Counsel agrees with any person liable as a result of the Action to pay fees subject to the Uplifted Rate that a lower amount than the amount payable in accordance with this agreement is to be paid instead, then the amount payable under this agreement in respect of those fees shall be reduced accordingly, unless the court is satisfied that the full amount should continue to be payable under it.

Interest

40. In the event that Counsel's fees are not paid in due time under this agreement, the Solicitor will pay Counsel interest on those fees at the rate of ...

Disbursements

41. The Solicitor will, regardless of whether the Action ends in Success or not, pay Counsel any disbursement costs incurred by Counsel. Such costs are to be paid by the Solicitor to Counsel [within... months of the costs being incurred by Counsel]. Such costs include, but are not limited to the following:

(1) Counsel's reasonable travel costs incurred in connection with the Action;

(2) Counsel's reasonable accommodation and reasonable subsistence costs incurred in connection with the Action;

(3) Counsel's reasonable legal research costs incurred in connection with the Action, including the cost of computer data base research.

Payment of Counsel's fees in any event

42. The Solicitor will pay Counsel's fees in accordance with this agreement whether or not the Solicitor is or will be paid by the Client or the Opposing Party.

RIGHTS TO CHALLENGE AND DISPUTE RESOLUTION

43. Any dispute arising out of or in connection with this agreement shall be referred to arbitration by a panel consisting of a Barrister nominated by the Chairman of the Bar Council and a solicitor nominated by the President of the Law Society, who shall act as arbitrators in accordance with the Arbitration Act 1996. The arbitrators so appointed shall have power to appoint an umpire.

44. The arbitrators so appointed and, where applicable, the umpire, will be entitled to act with or without charge. In the event that any one or more of them choose to charge for their services, the fees and expenses of such arbitrator(s) and/or umpire shall be paid by one or both of the parties as the panel, in their discretion, shall direct. The panel shall not have power to make any order in respect of the costs of the parties.

45. In the event of a reference to arbitration pursuant to paragraph 43 above, Counsel alleged to be in breach of duty shall be entitled to argue that the claim would not have succeeded in any event. The panel shall resolve such issue on the balance of probabilities, and if satisfied that the claim would have been lost in any event shall not make any order for payment of the Solicitor's fees or costs incurred in relation to the Action.

46. The right to refer any dispute to arbitration must be exercised promptly by either Solicitor or Counsel. In the event of termination it must be exercised at the latest within 3 months of (i) receipt of notice of such termination or (ii) receipt of the fee note for the fee being subjected to challenge, failing which the right of challenge will become irrevocably barred.

Chancery Bar Association terms of engagement for preliminary work where retainer on a conditional fee basis is contemplated

This document is to be completed and used in conjunction with the covering letter to Heads of Chambers from the Vice-Chairman of the Chancery Bar Association dated 21 July 2000.

1.   This agreement contains the terms and conditions upon which Counsel agrees to undertake investigation and provide advice prior to deciding whether to accept instructions on a conditional fee basis. [This agreement is/is not a contract enforceable at law.] The relationship between Counsel and Solicitor shall be governed by the Terms of Work under which barristers offer their services to solicitors and the Withdrawal of Credit Scheme as authorised by the General Council of the Bar as from time to time amended and set out in the Code of Conduct of the Bar of England and Wales, save that where such terms of work are inconsistent with the terms of this agreement the latter shall prevail.

2.   In this agreement the following expressions have the meanings set out in this paragraph:

   (1)   The Action means *the action, the short title and reference to the record of which is .../*the proposed action between the Client and ... for.../*the following part or parts of the action, the short title and reference to the record of which is .../*the following part or parts of the proposed action between the Client and ... for ... *[delete as appropriate and specify in addition whether any counterclaim and/or appeal and/or proceedings to enforce a judgment are included within the definition]*

   (2)   CFA means a conditional fee agreement.

   (3)   The Client means.....[acting by his/her litigation friend]

   (4)   The Costs Insurance means the policy or policies of insurance providing cover against the Opposing Party's costs of the Action.

   (5)   Counsel means the barrister named above as Counsel who is party to this agreement.

   (6)   The Opposing Party means the defendants or proposed defendants to the Action or, where there is an issue between the Client and any other party or parties to proceedings, the determination of which is covered by the definition of success referred to in paragraph 20 below, that other party or parties.

(7) Other acceptable counsel means other counsel who the Solicitor has agreed or does agree is acceptable for the purpose of this agreement.

(8) The Solicitor means the solicitor or firm of solicitors who or which is party to this agreement.

(9) The Solicitor's Conditional Fee Agreement means the Conditional Fee Agreement entered into between the Solicitor and the Client.

3. The Solicitor will, as soon as practicable, provide Counsel with, or make available to Counsel, the following material so far as it is available (and which may in accordance with the Code of Conduct of the Bar of England and Wales be reviewed by other counsel):

(1) Copies of all documents relevant to the Action which are reasonably available to the Client and/or to the Solicitor.

(2) Reasonably detailed statements on the subject matter of the Action from witnesses whose evidence is available to the Client and/or the Solicitor.

(3) Any documents containing or recording the advice or opinion of the Solicitor (and any other solicitors or other Counsel who are or have been instructed in the Action, or approached to consider entering into a conditional fee arrangement) on or relevant to the Action.

(4) Any other documents or information relevant to the Action which Counsel reasonably requests and which are available to the Client and/or the Solicitor.

(5) A copy of the Solicitor's Conditional Fee Agreement and the rate of uplift on the Solicitor's normal fees provided for in the Solicitor's Conditional Fee Agreement [(or as a minimum) the rate of uplift on the Solicitor's normal fees provided for in the Solicitor's Conditional Fee Agreement].

(6) A copy of the Costs Insurance (including all relevant schedules, slips or documents containing the terms of the Costs Insurance) or, if none, an explanation as to why there is none and an explanation as to how any interlocutory or final costs orders will be met.

4. Counsel will thereafter advise whether s/he requires to see the Client or any witnesses whose evidence is available to the Client or the Solicitor in conference, and, if s/he does, the Solicitor will arrange such conference or conferences to take place. Such conferences may be attended by other acceptable counsel.

5. After being provided with the material described in paragraph 3 above and after any conference required under paragraph 4 above, Counsel will:

(1) advise either in writing or in conference on the merits of the action;

(2) indicate whether s/he is prepared, subject to agreeing the terms to be included in a CFA, to act in the Action on a conditional fee basis.

6. Counsel's fees in respect of work carried out pursuant to this agreement shall be calculated in accordance with his/her hourly rate for the type of work involved, namely £ per hour.

7. In the event that Counsel and the Solicitor do not enter into a CFA:

    (1) the Solicitor shall pay to Counsel his/her fees for work carried out pursuant to this agreement within [3 months of receiving a fee note] and regardless of whether the Solicitor is paid by the Client; and

    (2) the Solicitor is free to request Counsel to continue to act in the Action other than on a conditional fee basis. If the Solicitor does so request, Counsel will agree to continue to act on a normal fee basis under the Terms of Work referred to in paragraph 1 hereof.

8. In the event that Counsel and the Solicitor do enter into a CFA:

    *Counsel shall not be entitled to any fees in respect of the work done pursuant to this agreement

    *the Solicitor shall pay to Counsel his/her fees in respect of work done pursuant to this agreement in any event at the rate specified in this agreement, such fees to be paid within 3 months of delivery of the fee note.

    *the Solicitor shall pay to Counsel his/her fees in respect of work done pursuant to this agreement in accordance with the terms of the CFA, save that that in the event that Counsel is entitled to be paid fees at the Base Rate or the Reduced Rate in any event during the course of the Action the fees to which Counsel is entitled to be paid pursuant to this agreement shall be paid within 3 months of the delivery of the fee note in respect of those fees.

    *the Solicitor shall, but only in the event that the action ends in success (as that term is defined in the CFA), pay to Counsel his/her fees in respect of work done pursuant to this agreement at the rate specified in this agreement.

[*Delete three of the above as appropriate. The third option is appropriate only if the CFA includes paragraph 18 of the draft CFA.]

319

Chancery Bar Association letter to Heads of Chambers, Senior Clerks and Practice Managers, 21 July 2000

CONDITIONAL FEE AGREEMENTS

Enclosed are copies of:

- a standard form of conditional fee arrangement intended for use in Chancery work;
- a standard form terms of engagement for work preliminary to such an agreement.

Please ensure that the members of your chambers and clerks are informed of the agreements and the terms of this letter by circulating this letter to each member of the Chancery Bar Association within your chambers.

The drafting of a separate agreement in relation to preliminary work was prompted by the concern that a conditional fee agreement could not relate to work done prior to the entry into the agreement. There remain, however, two points of concern in relation to the preliminary agreement.

Firstly, there is a risk, unless the preliminary agreement provides that the fees in relation to the work done under it either are or are not to be paid in any event, that it will itself constitute a conditional fee agreement. If so, it will probably fail to comply with the Conditional Fee Agreements Regulations 2000, and so be unenforceable; and there will also probably be a failure to comply with the notification provisions of the relevant CPR and Practice Direction on Costs.

Secondly, there is a risk that a court would decide that since the fees payable under the preliminary agreement were incurred for the purpose of enabling the barrister to decide whether to accept instructions on a conditional fee basis, the client would be unable to recover those fees from the opposing party to the action on an assessment of costs.

The agreements have been drafted by a small panel on behalf of the Chancery Bar Association in order to assist members of the Association who may wish to undertake work on a conditional fee basis. They have been drafted in the light of statutory provisions and regulations in force as at 3 July 2000. It is, however, up to individual barristers or their chambers, doubtless in conjunction with their clerks, to satisfy themselves as to the appropriateness and legality of the agreements. In this respect we stress:

(a) that the legislative and regulatory framework is the subject of rapid change, and

(b) that unless a CFA complies with the requirements of the Conditional Fee Agreements Regulations 2000 (SI 2000 No. 692) it will be unenforceable.

It is likely that the form of the agreements will need to be changed in the light of further regulations and rules coming into effect and as a result of experience. The Chancery Bar Association would welcome any feedback or comments from barristers and their clerks on the terms of the agreements in the light of their experience and, in particular, in the light of any comments that may be received from solicitors using these or other forms of agreement in practice. It is intended to discuss the agreement with a representative body of solicitors, but this has not yet been done. Feedback from solicitors will accordingly be of particular use.

In order for a barrister to be fully insured by BMIF in respect of work undertaken on a CFA basis, it is necessary for the CFA to have been approved by BMIF. The enclosed form of agreement has been approved by BMIF and cover is available for the obligations under Clause 24. If the agreement is altered in any material respect, therefore, it would be necessary to obtain approval from BMIF for the altered version. Your attention is drawn to the BMIF Chairman's report dated October 1999.

All chambers have already received practical guidance from the Bar Council in relation to the internal documentary processes which chambers should adopt in relation to CFAs. It remains a matter for each chambers to ensure that those processes are in place and adhered to. These agreements assume that such processes will exist and be adhered to.

The agreements will shortly be available on the Chancery Bar Association website (www.chba.org.uk).

Please direct any comments or enquiries relating to the enclosed agreement or CFAs generally to the Administrator: Mary Block – Tel: 020 8883 1700, Fax 020 8444 2368, E-mail: meblock@compuserve.com

Terence Etherton QC
21 July 2000

Chancery Bar Association letter to Heads of Chambers, Senior Clerks and Practice Managers, 21 September 2000

CONDITIONAL FEE AGREEMENTS – REVISED VERSION 2

As a consequence of the recent House of Lords ruling *Hall* v. *Simons* relating to barristers' immunity the standard agreement for work undertaken on a CFA basis requires modification.

Enclosed are the revised versions of:

- a standard form of conditional fee arrangement intended for use in Chancery work;
- standard form terms of engagement for work preliminary to such an agreement

The only change involves the deletion of some wording in clause 24 (1) of the main agreement. There have been no other changes except to the version number in the footer of both documents. The terms of my letter dated 21 July 2000 still apply and you should continue to refer to that letter when using the agreement.

The revised agreement (Version 2) was approved by the Directors of BMIF Limited on Monday 19th September 2000 in respect of work undertaken on a CFA basis and cover is available for the obligations under Clause 24 for both Version 1 and 2 of the agreements. However BMIF have said 'the Board would doubtless expect to see members using Version 2 within reasonably short time of its general circulation.' I would also remind you that if the agreement is altered in any material respect it would be necessary to obtain approval from BMIF for the altered version.

The Version 2 agreements will shortly be available on the Chancery Bar Association website (www.chba.org.uk).

Please ensure that the members of your chambers and clerks are informed of the changes to the main agreement and the terms of this letter by circulating this letter to each member of the Chancery Bar Association within your chambers.

Please direct any comments or enquiries relating to the enclosed agreement or CFAs generally to the Administrator: Mary Block - Tel: 020 8883 1700, Fax 020 8444 2368, E-mail: meblock@compuserve.com

Terence Etherton QC
21 September 2000

After-the-event insurance for use with conditional fees: how the products compare (June 2001)

	Abbey Legal Protection	Amicus Legal Limited	Claims Advance
Name of main conditional fee AEI product(s)	Accident Line Protect (ALP), Cap-it-All, Medical Accident Protect (MAP)	Solus, Solus Plus	Disbursement Funding, Legal Expense Insurance Scheme, Work in Progress Funding
Main areas covered	PI, clin neg (under review), commercial	PI, clin neg, prof neg following personal injury claim, building disrepair only	PI, prof neg, housing disrepair
Disbursements include own counsel's fees	No	Solus Plus: yes Solus: by arrangement	No, but a policy can be endorsed by agreement to do so
Application fee	None	None	None
AEI products available to claimants and defendants	Claimants only	Claimants only	Claimants only
When first AEI CFA launched?	1995	1998	July 2000
Is AEI available which covers both sides' costs?	Yes (Cap-it-All)	No	Yes, but only to panel members and it is individually assessed
Insurers underwriting	Brockbank Syndicate; Lloyd's, London	Lloyd's, London	NIG
Does AEI cover insurance premium if case is lost?	ALP: yes; other: no	Solus: no Solus Plus: yes	Yes

	Collegiate Management Services Limited	Composite Legal Expenses	CFIS (DAS/Lawinsure)
Name of main conditional fee AEI product(s)	Claimants Protection Policy	Conditional Fee Care	Conditional Fee Personal Injury Legal Protection
Main areas covered	All areas considered, with and without CFA	PI only	PI only
Disbursements include own counsel's fees	Optional	No	Yes
Application fee	None	None	None
AEI products available to claimants and defendants	Claimants only	Claimants only	Claimants only
When first AEI CFA launched?	August 2000	July 2000	January 2000
Is AEI available which covers both sides' costs?	Optional	No	No (except by individual request)
Insurers underwriting	Lloyd's, London	NIG	DAS
Does AEI cover insurance premium if case is lost?	No	No	Yes

	Eastgate Assistance	Fastrack Indemnity	First Legal Indemnity
Name of main conditional fee AEI product(s)	Personal Injury Fee Guard	Fastrack Indemnity Scheme	Insured's Costs, Opponent's Costs
Main areas covered	PI	Fastrack PI, housing disrepair & employment	Commercial
Disbursements include own counsel's fees	No	Yes	Yes
Application fee	None	None	£300
AEI products available to claimants and defendants	Claimants only	Claimants only	Yes
When first AEI CFA launched?	1999	June 2000	1998
Is AEI available which covers both sides' costs?	No	No	Yes
Insurers underwriting	Lloyd's, London	Lloyd's, London	QBE
Does AEI cover insurance premium if case is lost?	No	Yes	Yes (if option selected)

	Lawclub Legal Protection	Litco	Litigation Protection
Name of main conditional fee AEI product(s)	Equity	Primus	Conditional Fee Protection Plan, Access to Justice Insurance, Clinical Justice Plan (CJP), Express Clinical Justice Plan
Main areas covered	PI	All main areas of commercial litigation	All main CFA areas. CJP and Express CJP are for Clin neg only
Disbursements include own counsel's fees	No	Yes	Yes
Application fee	None	There is no application or assessment fee. There is a refundable application fee on submission of papers to underwriters	PI (under £50,000 of cover) & schemes: none; PI (over £50,000) & other: from £295
AEI products available to claimants and defendants	Claimants only	Yes	Yes
When first AEI CFA launched?	1998	September 2000	1995
Is AEI available which covers both sides' costs?	No	Yes	Yes
Insurers underwriting	Cornhill	Lloyd's, London	Lloyd's, London
Does AEI cover insurance premium if case is lost?	Yes	In exceptional circumstances only	In exceptional circumstances only

	Mike Young Legal Associates	Oracle Legal Services	Royal & Sun Alliance
Name of main conditional fee AEI product(s)	Legal Care, Accident Care, Claim Care, Legal Care Plus, Action Care Plus, Claim Care Plus	Claim protect	pursuit
Main areas covered	Most areas covered PI and non PI: employment, commercial disputes, occupational disease, accidents at work, clin neg, housing disrepair, wrongful arrests, prof neg, class actions	Housing disrepair	All main CFA areas
Disbursements include own counsel's fees	Yes	Yes	Yes
Application fee	No	None	£200
AEI products available to claimants and defendants	Yes	Yes	Claimants only
When first AEI CFA launched?	1999	November 2000	1999
Is AEI available which covers both sides' costs?	Yes	Yes	Yes. Up to 90% of own costs
Insurers underwriting	NIG	Goshawk	Royal & Sun Alliance
Does AEI cover insurance premium if case is lost?	Depends on type of policy	Yes	Yes

	Saturn Professional Risks	Temple Legal Protection	Wren Insurance Services
Name of main conditional fee AEI product(s)	Conditional Fee Insurance	Temple Litigation Advantage	Nimbus 1, 2, 3, 4
Main areas covered	All main CFA areas,	All main CFA areas excluding defamation	All main CFA areas
Disbursements include own counsel's fees	Yes	No	Yes
Application fee	Yes, if external assessment required	In exceptional circumstances only	Yes, if external assessment required
AEI products available to claimants and defendants	Claimants only	Yes	Claimants only
When first AEI CFA launched?	1998	1999	1996
Is AEI available which covers both sides' costs?	Yes	No	Yes
Insurers underwriting	Lloyd's, London; MMA Insurance	Lloyd's, London	Lloyd's, London
Does AEI cover insurance premium if case is lost?	Yes, if funding option used	Yes	No. Although larger premiums can be insured

APPENDIX 25

Useful addresses

INSURANCE PROVIDERS

Abbey Legal Protection
Ibex House
42–47 Minories
London
EC3N 1DY

Tel: 020 7702 3636

Amicus Legal Limited
2 St Johns Street
Colchester
Essex
CO2 7AA

Tel: 01206 366 500

Claims Advance
Knowsley House
Knowsley Street
Bolton
BL1 2AH

Tel: 01204 393133

Collegiate Insurance Brokers Limited
Roman Wall House
1–2 Crutched Friars
London
EC3N 2NB

Tel: 020 7459 3459

Composite Legal Expenses
Suffolk House
Trade Street
Cardiff
CF1 5DQ

Tel: 02920 222033

C F I S (DAS/Lawinsure)
Available through: LawInsure and CFIS. Address for Lawinsure;
Hexagon House
Cleppa Park
Newport
NP10 8XT

Tel: 01633 654535
(Lawinsure) 0870 241 1345

Eastgate Assistance
Eastgate House
The Business Park
Stephenson Road
Colchester
CO4 4QR

Tel: 08705 234 567

Fastrack Indemnity
Fastrack House
64 Stramongate
Kendall
Cumbria
LA9 4BD

Tel: 01539 732 211

First Assist Group
Marshalls Court
Marshalls Road
Sutton
Surrey
SM5 3LY

Tel: 020 8652 1437

First Legal Indemnity
42 Crutched Friars
London
EC3N 2AP

Tel: 020 7977 1408

Greystoke Legal Services
Greystoke House
80–86 Westow Street
London
SE19 3AQ

Tel: 020 8771 7772

Lawclub Legal Protection
Redwood House Brotherswood Court
Great Park Road
Bradley Stoke
Bristol
BS32 4QW

Tel: 0870 2434340

Litco
Bowcliffe Hall
Bramham
Near Wetherby
West Yorkshire
LS23 6LP

Tel: 08707 322 233

Litigation Protection
Arundel Court
Park Bottom
Arundel
West Sussex
BN18 0AA

Tel: 01903 883811

Mike Young Legal Associates
Barnett House
53 Fountain Street
Manchester
M2 2AN

Tel: 0161 247 8633

Oracle Legal Services
311 Long Lane
Halesowen
West Midlands
B62 9LD

Tel: 0121 561 4144

Saturn Professional Risks
Saturn House
26 High Street
Chesham
Bucks
HP5 1EP

Tel: 01494 774 431

Temple Legal Protection
62 Woodbridge Road
Guildford
GU1 4RF

Tel: 01483 577877

Wren Insurance Services
Wren House Gifford Court
Fox Den Road
Stoke Gifford
Bristol
BS34 8TT

Tel: 0117 906 2100

OTHER ADDRESSES

Academy of Experts
2 South Square
Grays Inn
London WC1R 5HP

www.academy-experts.org

Action for the Victims of Medical Accidents
44 High Street
Croydon
Surrey CR0 1YB

Tel: 020 8688 9555
www.avma.org.uk

Association of Personal Injury Lawyers
11 Castle Quay
Castle Boulevard
Nottingham NG7 1FW

Tel: 0115 9580585
www.apil.com

The Bar Council
3 Bedford Row
London WC1R 4DB

Tel: 020 7242 0082
www.barcouncil.org.uk

British Standards Institution
389 Chiswick High Road
London W4 4AL

Tel: 020 8996 9001
www.bsi-global.com

Centre for Dispute Resolution (CEDR)
Princes House
95 Gresham Street
London EC12 5AL

Tel: 020 7600 0500
www.cedr.co.uk

The Chancery Bar Association

Tel: 020 8883 1700
www.chba.org.uk

Child Poverty Action Group
94 White Lion Street
London EC2V 7NA

Tel: 020 7837 7979
www.cpag.org.uk

Commerce and Industry Group
The Law Society's Hall
113 Chancery Lane
London WC2A 1PL

Tel: 020 7320 5801
www.commerceandindustry.org.uk

The Commercial Bar Association
3 Verulam Buildings
Gray's Inn
London
WC1R 5NT
Tel: 020 7404 2022
www.combar.org.uk

Employment Law Bar Association (ELBA)
www.elba.org.uk

Expert Witness Institute
Africa House
64–78 Kingsway
London WC2B 6BD

Tel: 020 7405 5854
www.ewi.org.uk

Forum of Insurance Lawyers
The Law Society's Hall
113 Chancery Lane
London WC2A 1PL

Tel: 020 7323 4632

Freelance Solicitors Group
5 The Link
West Acton
London W3 0JW

Investors in People UK
4th Floor
7–10 Chandos Street
London W1M 9DE

Tel: 020 7467 1900
www.iipuk.co.uk

Legal Aid Practitioners group
The Law Society's Hall
113 Chancery Lane
London WC2A 1PL

Tel: 020 7336 8565

The Law Society
113 Chancery Lane
London WC2A 1PL

Tel: 020 7242 1222
www.lawsociety.org.uk

Legal Services Commission
85 Gray's Inn Road
London WC1X 8AA

Tel: 020 7759 0000
www.legalservices.go.uk

Local Government Group
113 Chancery Lane
London WC2A 1PL

Tel: 020 7320 5801
www.localgov.com

Pan-European Organisation of Personal Injury Lawyers (PEOPIL)
130 Loyd Road
Northampton NN1 5JA

Tel: 01604 628 213
www.peopil.com

Personal Injuries Bar Association (PIBA)
www.piba.org.uk

Society of Expert Witnesses
PO Box 345
Newmarket
Suffolk CB8 7TU

Tel: 0845 702 3014
www.sew.org.uk

Trainee Solicitors Group
113 Chancery Lane
London WC2A 1PL

Tel: 020 7320 5793

Young Solicitors Group
113 Chancery Lane
London WC2A 1PL

Tel: 020 7320 5793

Index